Chicago and the World

100 Years of the Chicago Council on Global Affairs

To Bob Cordes —
With fond memories of
good years together —

3.10.22

Chicago and the World

100 Years of the Chicago Council on Global Affairs

Richard C. Longworth

A B2 BOOK
AGATE
CHICAGO

Copyright © 2021 Richard C. Longworth

All rights reserved. No part of this book may be reproduced or transmitted in any form or by any means, electronic or mechanical, including photocopying, recording, or by any information storage and retrieval system, without express written permission from the publisher.

Printed in the United States
First printed in August of 2021

10 9 8 7 6 5 4 3 2 1   21 22 23 24 25

ISBN-13: 978-1-57284-300-4
ISBN-10: 1-57284-300-4

B2 Books is an imprint of Agate Publishing.

Agate books are available in bulk at discount prices. For more information, go to agatepublishing.com.

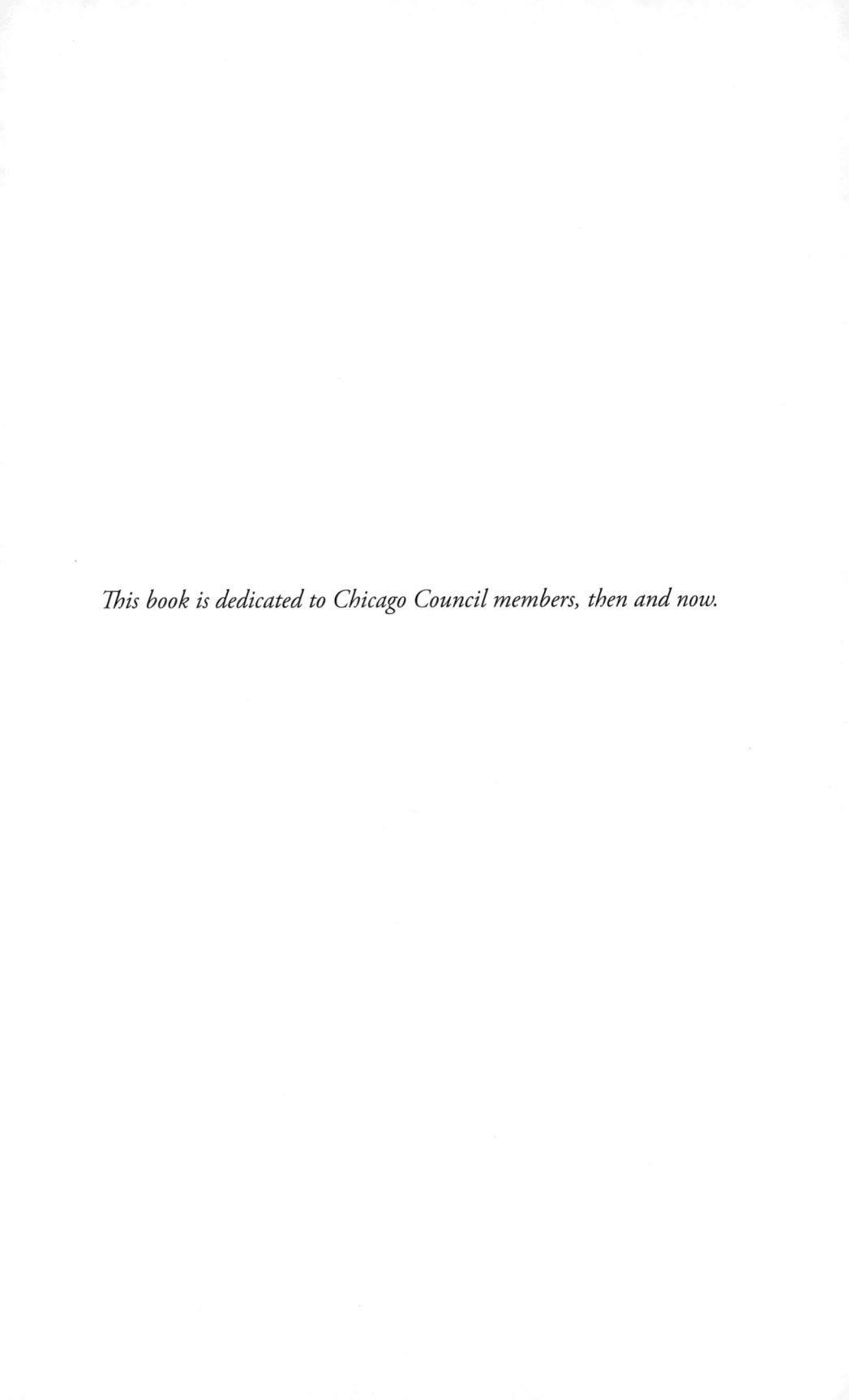

This book is dedicated to Chicago Council members, then and now.

Contents

INTRODUCTION 1

CHAPTER 1
Beginnings 9

CHAPTER 2
The Great Debate 27

CHAPTER 3
War and Post-war 51

CHAPTER 4
Cold War 83

CHAPTER 5
The Travel Club 109

CHAPTER 6
The Rielly Years 139

CHAPTER 7
New World Disorder 175

CHAPTER 8
Millennium 201

CHAPTER 9
All Over Again 233

ACKNOWLEDGMENTS 263
BIBLIOGRAPHY 267
NOTES 271
INDEX 303

Introduction

WALK EAST FROM CHICAGO'S LOOP TO THE SHORE OF Lake Michigan and take a deep breath. What you get is not the briny whiff of a great ocean, with the romantic promise of Europe or Cathay across the waves, but the saltless smell of an inland sea. Chicago is irredeemably midcontinental, far from the trauma and turmoil of foreign lands. If geography was destiny, that would be the end of this story.

But geography is not destiny and never has been. From its birth, Chicago was a crossroads, astride the trading paths and mighty railways that united the nation. It became the industrial heart of that nation, taking in the world's workers and pumping its produce into far markets. With the new millennium it became a true global city, transformed from an industrial powerhouse into one of the cities that run the global economy.

For a century, Chicago has belonged to the world, even if its geography demanded a leap of the intellect and imagination to grasp that reality. During that century, the Chicago Council on Global Affairs has guided and defined the way Chicago thinks about its place in the world. Founded to educate Chicagoans about world affairs, it is now both an educational vehicle that brings the world to Chicago, and a think tank that works to influence that world.

From the start, a major theme has run through the Council's history—the battle against isolationism. The Council was founded after World War I to combat the isolationism that swept Chicago and the Midwest and the Senate's rejection of American membership in the League of Nations. In the next decade, the Council held center stage for the great debate over American participation in the world war to come. After World War II, and again after the Vietnam War, much of America was tempted to pull back from the nation's international obligations; the Council insisted that the nation's well-being depended on an openness to the world. As the Council's centenary neared, a new spasm of America First nationalism, if not isolationism, seized Washington, and turned the Council into an outpost of internationalism committed to the idea that, in the new millennium, a retreat from global engagement was not only unwise but impossible.

This is a history both of the Council as an institution and of the great foreign policy battles and debates as played out on its stage in its first one hundred years. Year by year, the Council's programs reflected the world issues of the day. At the same time, the Council itself changed its structure and adapted its mission to meet the new demands of its members and fill its new role in the world.

The Council's first constitution, written in 1922, announced that it would "give its members opportunity to hear discussions of foreign policies by diplomats, scholars, travelers, and other experts…to meet American and foreign persons who are in touch with international affairs, [and] to provide a forum for the discussion of foreign policies and international relations." In other words, the Council was intended to be purely educational, absorbing the world's wisdom but making no attempt to add to that wisdom.

"We take it to be self-evident that the relations of the United States with all other nations are of vital importance to us and to the world," an early promotional brochure said. "Beyond that we have no theories. We do not propose or oppose any particular policy. We do not advocate any plan for world peace or the cementing of our friendship with any particular nation. We simply provide a forum for discussion and experts to provoke it."

Compare that to the mission statements that evolved over the century. Technically, the Council remains strictly nonpartisan and takes no official stand on policy issues. But it no longer sees itself as a political eunuch. A new statement in 2005 said the Council "provides insight *and influences the public discourse* on critical global issues. We convene leading global voices, conduct independent research, and engage the public to explore ideas that will shape our global future. The Council is committed to bringing clarity *and offering solutions* to issues that transcend borders and transform how people, business, and governments engage the world." As the centenary neared, a new statement imposed another tweak. Now the Council "provides insight, *advances solutions*, and fosters dialogue on what is happening in the world and why it matters to people in Chicago, the United States *and around the globe.*" (Italics added.)

The Council of today has a bias that is not that much different from the Council of 1922—that the only rational response to global complexity is openness. It rejected the isolationism of 1922 and it rejects nationalism now. In 1922, it recognized that the outside world affects Chicago every day. In 2022, it insists that Chicago can and does affect that world. Chicago then was a receptor for outside ideas. Chicago today is a generator of ideas and events. Both the world and Chicago have changed, but this goal—openness, clarity, involvement—remains the same. (If so much has changed, history itself rings with strange echoes. The Council was founded soon after the Spanish flu epidemic of 1918-1920, a truly global pandemic that killed millions around the world and 675,000 Americans. It celebrated its centenary in the wake of another global plague, the Covid-19 pandemic.)

The Council began life as a forum for the simple reason that there was no other. If Chicago wanted serious news about world events, the Council was the only game in town. Even by modern standards, it was a turbulent time, with the struggles between France and Germany over the Rhineland, the inflationary agonies of the Weimar Republic, the rise of Mussolini in Italy, anti-colonial agitation in India, and especially the new Bolshevik regime in Russia. What in the world was going on? The Council tried to answer. An early historian quoted the Council leadership:

> *"It was felt that at the time there existed in the Middle West not only a deplorable ignorance of foreign affairs affecting the United States, but little if any interest in the subject. The treatment of such questions in the press, with a few notable exceptions, was altogether inadequate, and much of the news that reached people from that source was colored by the prejudices of the editors or correspondents. It was therefore believed that there was a real need for a forum for public discussion where both facts and opinion could be freely presented to a large membership…"*

Fast forward one hundred years. The "deplorable ignorance" remains; however, the cause is not too little information but too much, a daily mélange of first-rate journalism and outright lies, available to any American, at the touch of a finger. Indeed, the problem today is worse. In the 1920s, William Browne Hale, one of the Council's co-founders, wrote, "Isolationists differ from others not so much in their interpretation of existing facts as in plans for future action. The facts of commerce, travel, treaties, and war which link American to the rest of the world are the same for all of us."

Today, even the facts are disputed or denied or, for many Americans, simply unavailable. In 1922, two Chicago newspapers had foreign correspondents. Today, none does: in fact, there is scarcely a newspaper between the two coasts with a foreign staff. In too much of America, rational debate on foreign policy has disintegrated. This raises the stakes for the Council and the importance of its activities, both its educational programs and its growing think tank activism. As that early constitution said, the Council "promotes a better understanding of the foreign policies and foreign relations of the United States," because "without such understanding, there can be no world stability, that knowledge is the foundation-stone of international friendliness."

As we shall see, this belief has been tested and strained often over the past century, but it remains the core creed that sustains the Chicago Council to this day.

The Council, founded as the Chicago Council on Foreign Relations, has been the Chicago Council on Global Affairs since 2006. Throughout this book, it will be called simply the Council.

Not only the name has changed. Since 1922, everything—the world, America, Chicago—has changed. Then, the industrial age powered the major nations on the world stage; now, globalization rules. Then, America lay protected behind the twin moats of its two oceans; now, it not only is enmeshed in the global web, but has been the undisputed hegemon for most of the past century. Then, Chicago was a provincial Midwestern factory town, far from the two coasts; now it is among the dozen most powerful global cities.

These changes and what they mean have been the constant concern of the speakers that the Council brought to Chicago. Not that these experts always got things right; far from it. But the richness of the debates chronicled in this history lies in their immediacy. All are reports from the moment, analyses of current crises, delivered by men and women who had no idea how the story of that day would come out. Some were hilariously wrong, others eerily prescient, and some were so wise that we can still profit from their lessons today.

All offer a glimpse into a century as seen by the people who shaped that century and wrote its history. The roster begins with Georges Clemenceau and includes George Marshall, Eleanor Roosevelt, Jan Masaryk, Jawaharlal Nehru, John Maynard Keynes, Reinhold Niebuhr, Edward R. Murrow, Walter Lippmann, Arnold Toynbee, U Thant, Margaret Thatcher, Willy Brandt, Helmut Kohl, Henry Kissinger, Ronald Reagan, Mikhail Gorbachev, Barack Obama, and Joseph Biden. There are Nobel prizewinners and Nazis, one-worlders and America Firsters.

At its founding, Chicago's mayor was a proud isolationist who bragged he would punch the king of England "on the snoot." Ninety-four years later, the Council took another mayor, Richard M. Daley, on his first trip to China.

The Council was founded by a small group of self-consciously international Chicagoans, an alliance of North Shore grandees and University of Chicago intellectuals, coordinated by one secretary working from a tiny office with a borrowed desk and a used typewriter. Today it is not only a lecture forum but a think tank, both absorbing and generating ideas, with a wildly diverse audience and a staff nearing one hundred, plus an equal number of fellows, resident and non-resident, scattered across the globe.

In its early days, the Council was highly social, a gathering place for an elite that could spare two hours over lunch to probe the problems of the world. Seventy-five years later, the *Chicago Tribune* called it "a watering hole for policy wonks" but also "the primary outlet for that influential slice of Chicago with a strong foreign policy itch."

For much of its history, the Council was a lean organization run by a relative handful of employees. After seventy-five years, the staff barely totaled fifteen persons. Since then, that staff has multiplied, especially with the recruitment of young graduates interested in foreign policy, whom it trained and sent on to careers in government, academia, or business.

Mostly, the news—the grist of the Council's mill—has changed. Then, it was the League of Nations, the Naval Treaties, German reparations, the rise of Mussolini in Italy, and communism in Russia. Today, it is globalization, China, terror, global populism, cybersecurity, global cities, pandemics, and immigration—the preoccupations of an interwoven world.

It seems World War II would have ended the argument between isolation and openness. In fact, post-war isolationism remained a political force, especially in the Midwest, championed by powerful voices such as the *Chicago Tribune* and Ohio Senator Robert Taft. Gradually, Cold War realities settled the issue. Pockets of isolationism remained. "US Out of UN" signs still sprouted along Midwestern highways. But real debate was over degrees of openness, of intervention versus restraint—whether the US should be the world's policeman and fireman and defend democracy wherever it was threatened, or pick our fights and intervene only when US national interests were directly threatened. The vigor of the Truman Doctrine and containment, so successful in Europe, led directly to the calamity of Vietnam.

Sometimes the public mood was confident, even triumphant; at other times, chastened, even timid. All this was reflected in the Council's programming. The mood of American foreign policy over the century can be judged by the temper and tone of the speakers who crossed the Council's stage.

Despite the changes, recurring themes—not only the changing place of America in the world, but the proper role of the Council itself—run through its history. Its official nonpartisanship has been stretched but survives. For most of its history, Council leaders debated whether it should be just a forum for outside speakers or plunge into the world of think tanks, challenging the long-established and better-endowed East Coast institutes at their own game. At its centenary, the issue seems settled in favor of a think tank future.

Another debate centers on the Council's relationship to Chicago itself. Is it an elite body serving that "influential slice" of Chicagoans, mostly Council members, with a real interest and knowledge of foreign affairs? Or should it reach out to the rest of the city, including its high schools and immigrant communities, to tap Chicagoans who mostly likely will never become members? The answer varies with the decades and remains unsettled.

As does the Council's leadership role in the broader Midwest. Should it take its message across the region, or is this too ambitious, especially at a time when a globalized Chicago may have left the Midwest behind? In the 1950s, a University of Chicago dean wrote to an early Council president, "The foreign policy problems of the United States are in the Middle West and not in the Middle East." The recent sweep of nativist populism across the Midwest shows this issue has not gone away.

The Council's fiftieth anniversary coincided with the end of the Vietnam War. The keynote speaker was Garrick Utley, a broadcaster and the son of Clifton Utley, an early Council leader and a critical figure in its history. As the nation recovered from Vietnam, he said, it faced a backlash and questioning of its place in the world: "Because we are going to have this restructuring of our national priorities, the work of the Council is by no means at an end." Fifty years after he spoke, and one hundred years after the Council's founding, the work goes on.

Chapter 1

Beginnings

THE YEAR 1922 SAW A SUNBURST OF CIVIC CREATIVITY IN Chicago. Both the Goodman Theater and the Morton Arboretum were born that year. In Washington Park, Lorado Taft dedicated his monumental sculpture, Fountain of Time. The Chicago Civic Opera was founded and WMAQ radio began broadcasting. King Oliver invited Louis Armstrong to Chicago to join his Creole Jazz Band. And George Halas, having brought his Staleys football team up from Decatur the previous year, changed the team's name to the Bears.

On February 20 of that year, a cold and windy Monday, twenty-three men and women met at the Union League Club to found the Chicago Council on Foreign Relations. Unlike their city, they were a worldly group, well-traveled and well-heeled, with the means and time to pay attention to the world beyond the Midwest.

For much of their history, Chicago and the Midwest had stood aloof from international issues, far from the coasts, safe behind the great oceans, and heeded the advice of George Washington and Thomas Jefferson to shun "entangling alliances" beyond those oceans. This remove never was absolute; the Spanish-American War and the doctrine of Manifest Destiny announced America's place in the world, and the Midwest earned part of its living on its trade with that world. But the region had been built by immigrants fleeing the wars, pogroms, and famines of far lands, and remained determined to have as little to do with those lands as possible.

Suddenly, the world had become both nearer and more dangerous. America's participation in World War I had been a shock, almost a loss of innocence. If America had been a world power since the late nineteenth century, this new prominence was slow to register with most of its people, especially in the interior fastness of the Midwest, where isolationism held sway. President Woodrow Wilson grasped this new American leadership at the post-war Versailles Conference, where he helped create the League of Nations. Seven months later, a Senate dominated by isolationists defeated the treaty and vetoed American membership in the League.

"The war introduced international politics to interior America," wrote Adlai E. Stevenson, a future Council president and perhaps its most illustrious member.

> "It revealed problems, names, and places which few people west of the State Department had even suspected. But the war was just a prelude. When the thunder of guns ceased, the rattle of voices commenced. Out of the clamorous meeting of the international creditors in Paris emerged the Versailles Treaty and a host of problems and perplexities. Our comfortable frontier isolation was irrevocably shattered once we began imbibing international politics with our morning coffee.
>
> "The social and intellectual merits of the luncheon lecture soon penetrated Chicago, thanks to the mature conviction of a small group that in the post-war world La-Salle Street, Downing Street, and the Bund were vitally

concerned with one another. We can no longer escape the fact that Europe is only a stone's throw away, nor fail to hear the dawn coming up like thunder out of China. The intelligent thing for us to do is to inform ourselves as accurately as possible. The purpose of the Chicago Council on Foreign Relations is not only to stimulate interest in these questions but to provide reliable information, and the opportunity for unprejudiced discussion of them.

"After all, are not knowledge of our neighbors' problems and the tolerant understanding bred of knowledge the greatest insurance of peace in the world?"

Americans who paid attention, such as the Chicagoans at the Union League Club that day, knew it was no longer possible to raise the drawbridge. French-German territorial disputes were already laying the groundwork for the next great war. Hyperinflation wracked the Weimar Republic. Benito Mussolini and his Black Shirts would soon take power in Italy. V.I. Lenin and his Bolsheviks ruled Russia. In India, Mahatma Gandhi would soon be arrested and tried for sedition. Even by our twenty-first century standards, the world of 1922 was one of turmoil.

But "Chicago was a hotbed of isolation," a later Board president, Edward D. McDougal Jr., recalled. "There was no TV. The Council was the only place there was for discussion of foreign affairs or authentic information on US foreign policy. In the early days the Council was an elite group. It was the fashionable thing to do."

Fashionable maybe, but not widely popular. As historian Thomas Bailey wrote,

"Chicago was long an isolationist citadel, largely by reason of its hives of hyphenates. This huge concentration of isolationism was able to exert disproportionate political

power. The Chicago Tribune *has long enjoyed the rather dubious distinction of being the most influential isolationist newspaper in America, and its prosperity has been insured by a large and sympathetic clientele."*

In Chicago, that clientele started at the top. The mayor of the day, William "Big Bill" Thompson, was wildly pro-German and anti-English: he once proclaimed that he would "crack King George one on the snoot" if the British monarch came to Chicago.

"The Council was a vital place in Chicago during that period of great national debate," George W. Ball, one of Stevenson's law partners and a future under secretary of state, recalled in his memoirs. "It was an oasis of discontent in a complacent society brainwashed each morning by Colonel [Robert R.] McCormick's insistent xenophobia [in the *Tribune*]."

Council lore paints Colonel McCormick and his *Chicago Tribune* as the Council's implacable isolationist foe from the start, and the two institutions did see the world through different lenses. In fact, this ideological combat really heated up only in the late 1930s, over America's participation or non-participation in World War II. The founders' real motivation seems more to have been a desire for deep and scholarly news from abroad.

In truth, Chicago probably got as much day-by-day foreign news from its newspapers as any American city. The *Daily News*' foreign correspondents may have been the best in the nation. McCormick, who proclaimed the *Tribune* to be the World's Greatest Newspaper, set up his own foreign service, with such first-rate reporters as William L. Shirer, Floyd Gibbons, Vincent Sheean, and Sigrid Schultz. Although, as one biographer wrote, the Colonel viewed them more as his ambassadors than journalists, under orders "to communicate the patriotic American viewpoint to European opinion-makers."

The Council founders wanted more than these journalistic accounts. As McDougal said, they turned the Council into "the only place there was for discussion of foreign affairs or authentic information on US foreign policy." Early Council programs had a scholarly length and depth unmatched in the century to follow.

The shock of the war and its aftermath led other internationally minded persons to organize, and not only in Chicago. The Hoover Institution was founded at Stanford University in 1919. In New York, the Council on Foreign Relations followed in 1921; two years later, the League of Free Nations Association, which had been founded in 1918, reframed itself as the Foreign Policy Association. In London, the British Institute of International Affairs came into being in 1920; a year later, it adopted its present name, the Royal Institute of International Affairs, more often known as Chatham House.

—

So, the Chicagoans were part of a trend, responding to the same world events with the same urge to organize. They had been invited to the meeting by a remarkable man and woman, William Browne Hale and Susan Follansbee Hibbard, the Council's co-founders. Hale's father was William Ellery Hale, an early manufacturer and inventor whose hydraulic elevator, an improvement on the original Otis elevator, made skyscrapers possible. His brother, George Ellery Hale, was an astronomer who founded both the Yerkes Observatory in Wisconsin and the Mount Wilson Observatory in California. William Hale was a Chicago lawyer, a graduate of the Northwestern and Harvard law schools, and had worked in the Wilson Administration's war department during the war. Afterward, he attended the Versailles Conference as a part-time correspondent for the *Chicago Evening Post*. He returned to Chicago a fervent admirer of the League of Nations.

Susan Hibbard was Hale's sister-in-law, the sister of his wife Eunice, and their next-door neighbor in Winnetka. Recently widowed and childless, she had the talent and time that, in a later era, may have made her a leader in business and public affairs. She seems to have been at least as much a driving force in the creation of the Council as her brother-in-law. She was a suffragette, and a successful one. In

1913, Illinois became the first state east of the Mississippi River to give women the right to vote for president (but not governor). Hibbard had been a local leader in the campaign for the Nineteenth Amendment, ratified in 1920, which gave women nationwide the right to vote. The League of Women Voters had just been organized, and Hibbard became a member of the national board. During the war, she organized the dispatch of young women to France to serve in troop canteens. Her alma mater, Bryn Mawr College, saluted "her unusual executive ability and her faculty of making people work with her with zeal and devotion."

Women, in fact, played a major role in the Chicago Council from the start. That first February meeting was attended by twelve women and eleven men. Six women sat on the first Executive Committee, as the Board was called. The second speaker was Marguerite E. Harrison, an adventurous foreign correspondent who talked about Russia, where she had been both a spy and a prisoner. Louise Wright was the Council's executive director from 1942 until 1952. At the start, the Council's first and sole employee was Mary Louise "Polly" Root Collier, who organized the meetings and everything else. Before joining the Council, she had spent six years overseas as a volunteer for the American Fund for French Wounded, the Red Cross, and the Near East Relief.

Not that these women enjoyed equal status. If women sat on the Board from the start, it wasn't until 2018, ninety-six years later, before a woman actually served as chair of that Board. Harriet Welling, a long-time Board member and Council vice president, said later that she, like other women officers, "had often been in those old days the token woman at a speaker's table, when they would have one woman, one Jew. I don't think they had one Black in those days."

Despite this, it is worth remembering that the Council on Foreign Relations in New York did not even admit women to membership until 1971.

At that first meeting, the Council set up the Executive Committee and elected as its first president Jacob Dickinson, a Mississippi native who fought for the Confederacy in his teens. Dickinson later became a leading Chicago lawyer, the president of the American Bar Association, and the secretary of war in the Taft Administration. He was described as an "imposing Southern gentleman" who usually wore a frock coat.

At the Council's first public meeting, less than a month after its founding, Dickinson laid out the case for American involvement in the world and for public knowledge about that involvement. The world has changed since Washington's time, he said. The Spanish-American War made America a colonial power. New technology such as steam, the telephone, and the telegraph erased distance. Most important to the Council's audience, foreign trade and investment made the United States and Chicago part of an early version of the global market.

The Council may have been formed to fight isolationism, but at its founding, the problem was as much ignorance of the world as isolationism. From the start, the Council saw itself as a source of information for Chicagoans—admittedly, a minority of Chicagoans—with interest beyond the two coasts.

To some people, this ignorance was proper and the Council a waste of time. William Hale, speaking to the Council's first annual meeting, said the Council was formed "on the theory that the people in general have a direct and permanent interest in the foreign policies of the United States." This, he said, "seemed to us self-evident. But one person of intelligence and considerable distinction declined to join this Council, solely on the ground that the people have... no sufficient information and therefore no direct responsibility for foreign policies," which were best left to the State Department. Hale said President Wilson's advocacy of open diplomacy made this point moot. Foreign affairs had become part of the public debate. The more the public understood them, the better.

For most of its history, the Chicago Council has been officially nonpartisan, presenting many views but advocating none. But that's not how it came to life. The first constitution stressed the Council's educational role was "to promote general public interest in the foreign policy of the United States [and] to give its members opportunity to hear discussions of foreign policies by diplomats, scholars, travelers, and other experts." But the last article in this constitution saw the Council as a force as well as a forum. One purpose, it said, was "to adopt as the policy of this Council and to advocate from time to time such principles and policies for the foreign affairs of the United States as many seem wise."

This advocacy role did not survive the Council's first two meetings. The first meeting, on March 18, featured George Wickersham, a founding member of the New York Council and the attorney general in the Taft Administration. Wickersham spoke on the Washington Naval Conference, an early disarmament effort that produced five treaties intended to limit the fleets of the nine signatories, including the United States.

Wickersham made a powerful case for the treaties. He called them "the most remarkable body of agreements that has ever been reached by any international conference in history." In the audience was a young Northwestern historian named Kenneth Colegrove, who was to play another controversial role in the Council thirty years later. When Wickersham finished, Colegrove moved that the Council ask Illinois' two senators to vote to ratify the treaties. The audience accepted Colegrove's motion unanimously.

That vote could have made the Council a partisan organization, but it was overturned at the next meeting. The advocacy clause remained in the constitution for some time, but the Council never again took such a public stand. As a 1923 promotional pamphlet put it, "we have no theories. We do not propose or oppose any particular policy. We do not advocate any plan for world peace or the cementing of our friendship with any particular nation. We simply provide a forum for discussion and experts to provoke it." A 1928 Council publication spelled out the rationale: "It was concluded that any attempt to battle as an organization for or against the adoption of definite polices would lead to trouble, in that it would encourage propaganda within the membership and alienate those who have become members solely because of their desire to form an intelligent opinion on foreign affairs without becoming involved in a program."

Walter Lichtenstein, a Council president in the 1930s, told a Council audience that the Council "desires to offer a forum to all possible points of view." But he also said,

> "The Council itself assumes no responsibility for the opinions expressed by speakers and it does not necessarily follow that the majority of the members of the Council or even of the Executive Committee are in agreement with the point of view of a particular speaker. But it seems to me...that unless we permit the expression of divergent opinions and policies, this institution would no longer be worthwhile and would in fact soon die of dry rot."

In practice, this meant the Council could seek support without selling its soul. Speakers could be chosen for their expertise, not their politics. It meant the Council was purely educational, not an action group. It meant that the Council could reach an audience that, at least in those days, spanned partisan barriers. It also, in later years, cemented the Council's tax-free status.

Officially then, the Council takes no position on public policy, domestic or foreign. In practice, it has very definite, if broad, beliefs: as its current president Ivo Daalder put it, the Council is "nonpartisan but not neutral." From its start, it opposed isolationism and favored American involvement in the world. For much of its history, this stance was relatively uncontroversial. But the Council's early leaders supported the League of Nations, a minority enthusiasm in Chicago. In the 1930s, Council leaders, if not the Council itself, campaigned for American aid to Britain and other warring allies, a highly controversial position at the time. In the new millennium, as the Council neared its centenary, this insistence on involvement and openness often put it at odds with official policy in Washington.

Keeping a bipartisan balance posed practical problems. A Chicagoan who attended two early programs on Russia complained that it was "a pro-Bolshevik field day." Graham Aldis, a Board member and future Board president, noted, "Our membership is certainly not what is ordinarily described as 'radical' or even 'parlor pink,'" and said it was simply easier to get liberal than conservative speakers. Most speakers, he said, were either critics or defenders of administration policies and, "as things stand now, the Council can practically get only the first class."

Hale, in his report to the Council's first annual meeting, agreed that the only speakers it could find strongly favored US recognition of the new Soviet regime in Russia. He lamented that, shortly after the programs, the editor of the *Tribune*, Robert R. McCormick, wrote that "he opposed in general any participation by America in European affairs." McCormick, later a vivid, if combative, figure in Council history, could have given balance to those Russia programs, he said, but by then it was too late.

This problem of striking a balance between liberal and conservative speakers and, indeed, of getting conservative speakers at all, has varied with administrations and, to some degree, persists today.

—

The Council was only ten months old and operating from a tiny, twenty-dollar-a-month office when, on November 28, 1922, it staged its first extravaganza, a speech by Georges Clemenceau, the former premier of France and a towering figure in world affairs. Le Tigre, who came to America to urge closer relations with France, was to give one speech in Chicago. One week before his arrival, the Council was chosen to organize it.

Nothing the Council sponsored in its subsequent century matched the pomp of that Clemenceau visit. The Council rented the Auditorium Theater for $900 and paid another $1400 for loudspeakers and an amplification system. Local moguls such as Julius Rosenwald, Samuel Insull, and Cyrus McCormick paid fifty dollars for boxes at the Auditorium.

The city pitched in. Civic leaders, accompanied by General John Pershing, greeted Clemenceau when his private railway car, attached to the Manhattan Limited, pulled in. From Union Station, he rode through the city in an open car, accompanied by a troop of cavalry, two platoons of police, and a squad of motorcycles. The French tricolor waved from every building down the LaSalle Street parade route and to the Palmer House Hotel. From the lakefront, booming guns added a military salute.

At the Auditorium, 5,000 persons heard the French leader proclaim, "Let us reason with each other, discuss with each other, even curse each other, if that be necessary, but step by step, through unceasing efforts, let us strive to achieve that which moves the world—truth, justice, liberty, and right."

The real point of Clemenceau's speech was a plea for American support for French reparations from the Germans and an Anglo-American guarantee of the French occupation of Germany's Rhineland. Of Germany's plans for another war, in an alliance with Russia and Turkey, he said, "When there is an alliance between the barbarian and the anarchist and the German militarist, haven't we the right to believe this is not in the interests of peace?" Not that France wanted war. "No indeed. We do not want to crush the man who owes us money."

It was a bellicose speech, more controversial in Paris than in Chicago, still provincial enough to be wowed by the famous visitor. Less than two months later, France occupied the Ruhr Valley of Germany.

No one at the Auditorium knew it then, but both issues—reparations and occupation—fomented the German resentment that led to the rise of Adolf Hitler and, eventually, World War II.

The Clemenceau program left the infant Council with a $300 deficit, but it established the new organization as a Chicago institution. So did the appearance in April of 1923 of Lord Robert Cecil. The British statesman, whose work on the League of Nations later won him the Nobel Peace Prize, spoke on the League and disarmament before 2,500 persons in Orchestra Hall.

Most Council programs were not big, evening lectures but smaller, two-hour lunches, often on Saturdays at hotels such as the Palmer House, the La Salle Hotel, and the Stevens Hotel (later the Hilton Hotel and Towers). Attendance ranged from sixty persons (for a speech on "The Present Crisis in the Philippines") to the 350 people who came to hear Rufus Dawes, a Chicago civic leader, speak on the Dawes Plan to resolve German war reparations. (The Plan was named after his brother, the future US vice president Charles Dawes, but Rufus Dawes served as an expert on the commission that drew it up.)

Catering, then as now, presented problems. Board minutes say that Susan Hibbard complained about the food at a Stevens Hotel luncheon, and "Mr. Stevens" returned the entire check. Mr. Stevens presumably was Ernest Stevens, the hotel's owner and father of the future Supreme Court Justice John Paul Stevens. After debate, the Board sent the check back to Stevens, "minus fifty dollars, this being the approximate difference between fresh peas and new potatoes and canned peas and old potatoes."

In these early years, the Council tried to stage two programs a month, and the topics highlighted the major international issues of the day. Marguerite Harrison said the communist government in Russia was better than the tsarist regime it replaced and urged US recognition of the Soviet Union. Sidney Hillman, president of the Amalgamated Clothing Workers of America, agreed, noting that the Soviets had abandoned their "war communism" policy of crash nationalization, with the result that "the business section of Moscow now is as active as any other big city."

Jane Addams is best remembered in Chicago as the founder of Hull House, but she was widely traveled and an ardent internationalist when she spoke to the Council on "Impressions of Political Movements in the Orient."

In 1926, W.E.B. Du Bois became the first African American speaker to the Council. He saw benefits to increased cooperation with likeminded people in Europe and other countries. "Black folks all over the world are beginning to recognize their common kinship and common problems," he said in a speech at the Palmer House.

Some speakers dealt with issues that remain headlines to this day. Norman Angell, a British member of Parliament, foresaw a European economic union, and argued that trade was already so broadly continental that national borders no longer made sense. Count Richard von Coudenhove-Kalergi, an Austrian-Japanese aristocrat and the founder of the Pan-European Union, urged a United States of Europe (excluding Russia, Turkey, and Britain). The Board debated whether to invite a rabbi to lecture on the situation in Palestine; there is no record whether this program ever took place. But a British diplomat, George Young, said the British government might surrender its mandate, or control, over Palestine, which would bring peace between Arabs and Jews there.

A former Hungarian foreign minister, Gustave Gratz, decried the post-war Treaty of Trianon, which awarded parts of Hungary to Romania, Czechoslovakia, and Yugoslavia and demanded full rights for Hungarians living in those countries—still a battle cry for the Hungarian government ninety years later.

Alexander Kerensky, the president of the short-lived pre-communist government in Russia, spoke on the politics of his country. Quincy Wright, a University of Chicago professor, spoke on "France and the Syrian Mandate."

Mussolini had just taken power in Italy. Torn over keeping a balance on fascism, the Board brought in speakers on both sides. Bruno Roselli, a Vassar professor, said Mussolini had restored economic stability to Italy. A Columbia professor, Arthur Livingston, said Mussolini's government "is injurious to the morals of the middle class and founded upon a theory of gang rule." Gaetano Salvemini, an exiled Italian professor, urged America to open its doors to émigrés like himself.

Walter A. Strong, publisher of the *Chicago Daily News*, met Mussolini and told the Council that he was "the most interesting character I have ever met...There is a worldwide recognition of the economic accomplishments of fascist Italy." According to Strong's descendants, Mussolini offered the Chicago publisher a job as the finance minister of Italy. Strong seems to have been surprised and flattered by the offer and even mentioned it to his wife Josephine, who quickly vetoed the idea. But he probably saw it for what it certainly was, a public relations ploy, and it's doubtful he seriously considered it.

Often the Council staged debates between two opposing points of view. Olivia Rossetti Agresti predicted a great future for Italy under Mussolini; Ferdinand Schevill disagreed. Opposing speakers debated the occupation of the Ruhr and, on two occasions, the merits of the International Court. Bernadotte Schmitt of the University of Chicago blamed World War I on Germany, while Harry Barnes of Smith College said Russia and France were the culprits.

Nobody used the word "globalization," but several speakers talked about the growing economic links between countries. Paul Douglas, a University of Chicago professor and future senator, said that postwar Germany was too poor to buy coffee, so coffee-growing Brazil couldn't buy cotton goods from England, where Midlands factories were shutting down. Again, Germans couldn't buy woolen clothes, so flocks of sheep in Australia and New Zealand were shrinking.

In the post-war years, the craving for permanent peace echoed through many Council programs. William Hale himself saw the

League of Nations as the world's best bet for peace. Everyone saw the specter of another war in the old rivalries of Europe and sought salvation in international—even global—organizations. Irving Fisher, a Yale economist, foresaw the death of one hundred million persons in a new war, with gas bombs that could asphyxiate New York City or Chicago. Only the League could prevent this.

Major General John F. O'Ryan, a wartime commander and later founder of the American Legion, called for a global super-organization to prevent war. The world was interwoven with railroads, the telephone, mass communications, "the Ford car, the motorcycle, and the aeroplane." He continued,

> "All are making impractical the preservation of local habits, dress, and customs, as well as provincial languages. All this makes for better understanding…Obviously, the maintenance of peace and the abolition of war can only be brought about through an organization created and maintained for the purpose, which is in its genesis a world organization and not a national organization."

—

Patterns that would guide the Council for the next century were taking shape. One was the Council's independence. Its name suggested that it was a branch of the Council on Foreign Relations in New York—a confusion that dogged the Council for eighty years until its change of name in 2006. There never was any organic link between the two organizations. Indeed, the Chicago Council turned down an invitation in June of 1922 from the managing director of the New York Council to "join in publishing a quarterly magazine they have just purchased." This may have been a good opportunity missed. The magazine, previously known as the *Journal of International Relations*, became *Foreign Affairs*, and went on to become the preeminent journal on international relations.

Some early notes suggest that the Council was formed to beat an attempt by the Foreign Policy Association to form a Chicago branch. A letter from a close friend of Susan Hibbard quotes her as saying the FPA refused a link to the nascent Council because the Council planned to have Jane Addams on its Executive Committee and the New Yorkers presumably wanted nothing to do with that Chicago radical! Actually, Addams, while an early member of the Council, never served on its Executive Committee.

Debate continued on the issue of nonpartisanship. In 1928, co-founder William Hale suggested that, instead of passing resolutions committing the Council to a position, it might take a milder "sense of the meeting" stand. Other Board members argued that the distinction between the two would be lost to the general public and, especially, to politicians seeking Council support. The Board voted and Hale lost.

The first program, with George Wickersham, began the post-speech Q&A sessions that continue today. The Council president, Jacob Dickinson, borrowing from Quaker terminology, urged "any whom the spirit moveth [to] rise and speak your sentiments," and suggested only "that no speaker exceed the limit of ten minutes"—a garrulous luxury compared to the terse Q&A format that evolved over the years.

In its early years, the Council leadership was dominated by civic leaders, many of them from the North Shore, such as Hale and Hibbard. But the intellectual center of gravity shifted south to the University of Chicago, with professors such as Schmitt, Douglas, and Schevill, plus Harold Lasswell, Samuel Northrup Harper, Quincy Wright, and Jacob Viner. As a result, most programs resembled university lectures. This intellectual quality clashed with box office appeal. Executive Committee minutes from 1925 concluded, "An address that promises to have dramatic rather than scholarly interest brings out the largest number of people. But to act on this conclusion would be to go counter to all the purposes of the Council." Eventually, the Council decided that it was more important to be interesting than academic, and programs increasingly featured as many practitioners, including journalists, as professors.

The Council's first and most successful publication was a Hyde Park project. A monthly newsletter, initially called *News Bulletin* and then *Foreign Notes*, began in 1925, partly to maintain interest among members who couldn't attend meetings and partly to make up for the lack of in-depth foreign news in Chicago newspapers. Despite the work of the *Tribune* and *Daily News* foreign correspondents, Chicagoans who sought a deeper understanding of international issues had to rely on the Council. *Foreign Notes* served the same purpose.

The first issue said that the publication's policy "will be to print the principal international news in compact form, without comment." The first editor was Harold Lasswell, a University of Chicago political scientist. The editorial board was equally distinguished, and its members wrote most of the articles, largely because they brought a deep interest to the task, but also because the publication could not pay for outside contributors.

Foreign Notes contained very long reports and analyses of foreign events, but virtually nothing about Council programs, apart from the occasional announcement of an upcoming speech. This continued to 1960, when it switched to reports and texts of Council speeches.

The Council had been founded strictly as an educational organization, but the success of *Foreign Notes* led Hale, in 1926, to suggest that it sponsor original research. It did not have the funds to hire staff researchers, but it published three books under the heading of "American Policies Abroad"—one on Mexico, one on the Caribbean, and one on US relations with Britain. All sold well, but by the time the third volume appeared, the Depression had begun, and the project ended. Hale financed the final publication. In ensuing years, the Council dipped its toe into research programs, but it wasn't until the twenty-first century that it became a full think tank.

The Council was growing. From its first office at 35 North Dearborn Street, the Council moved, in 1924, to larger quarters at the Marquette Building, now the home of the John D. and Catherine T. MacArthur Foundation. Polly Collier returned to Europe and her assistant, Isabella McLaughlin, became executive secretary. The Council, which began with 176 charter members in 1922, had 759 members by the end of 1923, 967 in 1924, and nearly 1,500 members in 1929. The population of the city was more than three million residents, and the Council made no attempt to reach most of these residents. But it had established itself as a unique organization, a forum where the elite of Chicago could debate international affairs and educate itself on the world beyond the city. As the decade neared its end, the Council—like the city and the nation itself—seemed both strong and confident.

That was soon to change.

On October 29, 1929, several hundred Council members went to the Palmer House to hear Ameen Riahni, a Lebanese American theorist of Arab nationalism, and Alexander Dushkin, director of the Chicago Board of Jewish Education, debate "The Arab and the Jew in Palestine." The mild autumn day quickly became Black Tuesday. By the time Board member Lessing Rosenthal called the meeting to order at one o'clock, twelve million shares had been traded on the New York Stock Exchange. When it ended two hours later, a record sixteen million shares had been traded and the Dow Jones Industrial Average, already down 13 percent the previous day, lost another 12 percent.

The 1930s had begun. The decade began with the Crash and a global depression and ended in war. At first, the Council's membership and funds cratered. But its role in preparing the city and the Midwest for war made the decade one of the most important in its history.

Chapter 2

The Great Debate

THE DECADE, ONE OF THE WORST IN AMERICAN HISTORY, moved the Council into the national debate on foreign policy. In reality, the decade lasted from that Black Tuesday in 1929 until the fateful 1941 Sunday at Pearl Harbor. It witnessed the rise to power of Adolf Hitler, Mussolini's attack on Ethiopia, the Spanish Civil War, new Japanese aggression, and the Second Sino-Japanese War. Then, in dizzying succession, it saw the German Anschluss against Austria, the Munich conference, the Molotov-Ribbentrop Pact between Russia and Germany, Hitler's invasion of Poland and, eight months later, his Blitzkrieg conquest of France and the Low Countries, Dunkirk, Germany's Barbarossa attack on Russia and, on December 7, the Japanese attack at Pearl Harbor.

All these events—the tension that led to war and the war itself—took place thousands of miles from America. But they ignited the great debate over what they meant to the United States and, more important, what this country should do about them.

Should the US stand aloof, leaving the Europeans and Asians to sort out their own problems, which were none of our business? This was the isolationist stand, and many Americans, protected by the two oceans, and with the carnage of World War I still fresh in their memories, agreed. Or should this country come to the aid, with money and arms, if not men, of Britain and the European democracies? This was the interventionist stand, based on the belief that the wars in Europe and Asia were no internecine squabbles, but a fight between democracy and totalitarianism, with the fate of all democracies—including America's—at stake.

It was literally a life-or-death debate. It was only partly about sending aid to the Allies. The real issue was whether the United States, after more than a century of isolationism, and not really having a foreign policy, should become involved with the world.

As the decade wore on, it dominated the Council's activities, both on its stage and behind the scenes. The Council itself, as an institution, remained resolutely neutral and invited speakers on all sides—even professed Nazis. But many of its leaders led the interventionist cause in Chicago and the Midwest. According to one historian, "The Council had turned during the 1930s into a virtual conduit for anti-fascist advocacy."

The line between the Council's proper role as a forum or a force became a thin one indeed. In the end, it was a proud moment. The Council led the battle against isolationism, then a potent force in Chicago. It prepared Chicagoans for the need to help America's allies. More important, it helped prepare the nation—or at least the central part of it—for the challenges and sacrifices of the war to come.

This heartland was the part of the country furthest from the smoke of battle and most inclined to sit out a war. But when that war came, the Midwest sent its leaders to Washington and its sons to fight and turned its industry into the arsenal that won the victory.

For this, the Council can take a bow. During the 1930s, it educated a core of Chicagoans in foreign affairs and trained many of them for leadership roles in the eventual war. It filled a vital educational role: when the decade began, average attendance at Council meetings was 267 persons; when it ended, crowds of 2,000 or 3,000 commonly packed hotel ballrooms to hear Council speakers. Radio broadcasts of its meetings reached another 200,000 people across the Midwest.

—

The Council's fortunes crashed, along with the economy, when the Depression began. Membership plunged and did not return to its pre-Crash level of 1,500 until 1935. Tight budgeting and aggressive membership campaigns offset some of the losses; so did letters to members appealing for funds. The Council held only seventeen meetings in the 1931-32 season. Even so, it had only $71.56 in the bank when 1931 ended.

Council membership cost five dollars. The luncheons that preceded all lectures cost $1.50 for Council members and $2 for non-members. To keep audiences up, members could skip the luncheons and attend the lectures for free.

Through the decade, the Council was led by two of the most important characters in its history, Adlai E. Stevenson II, a future Democratic candidate for president, and its executive secretary, a brilliant and tireless academic and journalist named Clifton Utley.

Clifton Utley was a tall, dynamic, young Hyde Parker, a graduate of everything that scholarly community offered, from the University of Chicago kindergarten to the university itself, where he got his PhD before studying in Munich and Algiers. Back in Chicago, he worked with Quincy Wright, a political scientist and a member of the editorial board for *Foreign Notes*. At Wright's request, Utley took over the editing of *Foreign Notes* in 1929. He doubled the pages from two to four and wrote much of the copy himself.

At the time, Utley later recalled, "There was an abysmal ignorance of what was going on in countries all over the world. We simply tried to fill people in on what was happening. The *Tribune* and McCormick didn't think it was important that people know what was happening in the rest of the world. The Middle West was world enough to them. We'd go to small towns to make a talk, and you know you can get the feeling of an audience in about twenty minutes, and you'd learn that the *Tribune* dominated the town."

This may have been unfair to Colonel McCormick, who gave Utley an early platform. *Foreign Notes* had attracted attention and Utley began to lecture around Chicago on foreign affairs. McCormick, the *Tribune* publisher and later the Council's nemesis, learned of his popularity and offered him a twice-monthly radio broadcast on the *Tribune*'s station, WGN.

—

In 1931, the Council's executive secretary Alice Benning went to Switzerland for a summer vacation. Three weeks later, she sent a resignation letter to the Council president, Graham Aldis, explaining, "Things happen rapidly here in Geneva. Three weeks ago, I was a safe and sane executive secretary, now I am engaged to be married to a Mr. Charles Darlington." Her new fiancé was an American economist at the League of Nations and a future US ambassador. Suddenly, the Council needed new guidance. Utley, only twenty-six but a rising academic and journalistic star in Chicago, got the job.

He later recalled, "My getting the directorship of the Council was a Depression move. They wanted somebody who could edit *Foreign Notes* and serve as executive director. They wanted a guy who could be had for one salary. So, they combined [the two jobs] and called the job 'director.'" Benning had been earning $200 per month and Utley got $70 for editing *Foreign Notes*. Utley asked for $300 to do both jobs, but settled for $250 so, as he said, "they saved money."

The Council got a lot for its money. Utley served as executive director until 1942, became a favorite speaker at Council programs, and turned the Council into a major forum. In addition, he continued his broadcasts, spoke around Chicago and the Midwest on foreign affairs, lectured at local universities, and was a frequent host on the University of Chicago's Round Table broadcasts, which drew fan mail from many states.

In 1972, the Council gave Utley its World Understanding Award. When he accepted the award, Utley recalled that, when he began, "The Middle West was the most negative part of the world, and the most holding back in foreign policy, that the country had seen. I think the Council made a great contribution toward converting that negation into an affirmation." For that, Utley himself deserved much of the credit.

—

Despite the tight budget, the Council continued to bring in good speakers, such as Maurice Hindus on Russia and Dorothy Thompson on European minorities. In mid-1931, the British economist John Maynard Keynes came to speak on the war debts and reparations imposed on Germany at Versailles. He predicted, "It is no longer a question of Germany's capacity to pay. It is a question of her state of mind, of what she will choose to endure."

From the start, the Council tried to tie its programming to the headlines. Meetings seldom were scheduled more than four weeks in advance, to promote timeliness—quite an achievement in an era where most communication was by telegram and most travel was by train. The policy paid off on February 4, 1933, when a former German foreign minister, Richard von Kühlmann, spoke on "Germany Under Hitler," barely five days after Adolf Hitler became chancellor of Germany. Unfortunately, von Kühlmann was more timely than prescient. He called Hitler "a dreamer, an exceptionally gifted speaker, certainly a good patriot," but a leader with little influence whose popularity was already shrinking. Like many members of the German establishment, he indicated that the great threat to Germany was not the Nazi Party but the Communist Party. The Hitler menace "has been somewhat exaggerated," he said, by newspaper correspondents playing to the American taste for "spectacular and emotional things."

Utley sought a geographical balance in programming, but the main focus in the early 1930s was on Asia, especially after the Japanese invasion of Manchuria in 1931. That changed with the rise of Hitler. Later in 1933, twelve hundred persons came to hear the *Chicago Daily News* correspondent Edgar Ansel Mowrer talk on "The Sickness of a Great People." Other journalists, such as Wallace Deuel and Leland Stowe, and academics such as the University of Chicago historian Frederick L. Schuman, added their insights on Hitler and Nazism.

All the speakers viewed Hitler with alarm and, in September of 1933, the Council president, Walter Lichtenstein, a German-born Jew and leading Chicago banker, urged that a "speaker representing the National Socialist point of view" be invited. That speaker was Friedrich Schönemann, a professor at the University of Berlin and a Nazi sympathizer. His speech at the Palmer House stirred "numerous and noisy protests," according to Executive Committee minutes. Over jeers from the audience, Schönemann said many German Jews still "held fine positions and will continue to hold them." In fact, "By a system of cliques, the Jews had monopolized whole fields of public endeavor," especially in law and medicine. Schönemann continued, "Then, too, when Hitler began his drive against the communists and social democrats, it was found that the leaders were nearly always Jewish, so that in throwing one force [the Nazis] against their strength that had terrified the nation, Hitler was unintentionally fighting Jews."

Asked about book-burning in Germany, Schönemann said, "A tremendous flood of books on nudism and of a generally pornographic nature unfit for either juvenile or adult reading had inundated Germany, and these were burned. I am sorry to say that the authors of many—of a majority—were Jews."

"Just tell the truth!" shouted a man in the Palmer House balcony. "Don't lie."

A week later, Schönemann gave the same speech in Boston and incited a riot that involved 5,000 Bostonians and the police; six persons were arrested.

Melchior Palyi, a Hungarian-born Chicago economist, said that Nazi Germany lacked the resources to go to war. "It would be suicide for Germany under present conditions to start a war, and she is not likely to commit suicide." Emil Ludwig, a German author, cautioned against hopes that the German military would overthrow Hitler. "Their history shows that they will take advantage of any form of power. Hitler gave them back their power."

Increasingly, the Council drew on journalists as speakers, especially the celebrated foreign correspondents of the *Chicago Daily News*. Paul Scott Mowrer, Edgar's brother, spoke about France. William Stoneman talked about Soviet Russia. Former *Daily News* correspondent John Gunther spoke on Austria in 1934, and told the Council, "The situation in Germany is serious but not hopeless, and in Austria it is hopeless but not serious."

Jay Allen, a veteran of both the *Tribune* and the *Daily News*, reported on the Spanish Civil War, but stressed "an organized attempt to falsify the news from Spain"—the fake news of another era. He blamed the Catholic church, where "distinguished prelates had written memoranda about foreign correspondents to various papers... We are made out as liars...The Catholic press in this country pins labels on every correspondent who has written the news from loyalist Spain." He was referring to the territory controlled by pro-government and anti-Franco forces.

The Japanese ambassador to Washington, Hiroshi Saito, assured a crowd of 1,000 that Japan had no aggressive aims in the Far East and wanted only peaceful cooperation with China. Burton Crane, a veteran correspondent in Tokyo and part-time crooner known as "the Bing Crosby of Japan," said Japan would not go to war and warned that US aid to China only drove Japan into the fascist camp.

Shingoro Takaishi, the president of the Tokyo newspaper *Mainichi Shimbun*, blamed the Sino-Japanese War on China's "anti-Japanism." Besides, he said, "China is such an abnormal country that her integrity is a fiction…Your ideal is that all men are created equal, but in the face of social realities, you are compelled to forget it."

Demaree Bess, a *Christian Science Monitor* correspondent, just back from the Stalinist show trials in Moscow, said "irrefutable evidence" proved the plots against Stalin were genuine, and justified his moving "with complete implacability and complete thoroughness."

History in this case, as in many others, has shown otherwise. But the Council could not wait for history. Its programs thrived on immediacy, on facts and opinions straight from the front lines of both war and diplomacy, presented as history in real time to Chicagoans who did not know how events would turn out but wanted as many sides of the tumultuous decade as they could get.

Clifton Utley remained one of the Council's most popular speakers. His Council contract allowed him annual summer trips to Europe. When, in September of 1935, he gave an eye-witness report on Germany, the 1,200 listeners so jammed the Union League Club that it banned any more rentals to the Council—a prudent move, because Utley drew 1,500 persons to the Palmer House the next year.

Utley also pioneered the Council's use of radio beyond his twice-weekly, twenty-minute talks on WGN. In 1938, station WAAF offered to broadcast Council meetings as a public service. At first, the Council was wary, fearing the broadcasts would cut into attendance. In fact, they increased attendance, and soon WAAF broadcast all Council meetings, usually at 1 p.m. after a classical concert. The broadcast reached an audience of 200,000 listeners around the Midwest.

—

In the early 1930s, Adlai E. Stevenson II was a young man about Chicago, the grandson of a vice president (the first Adlai Stevenson), and just beginning his legal career. He was a 1922 Princeton graduate, newly married, well connected socially, and anxious to make his way in the world. The Council itself was fashionable and many of Stevenson's friends belonged to it. One friend, Graham Aldis, was the president; another, Harriet Welling, was on the Executive Committee.

Stevenson joined the Executive Committee and, in 1933, was elected president at thirty-three, the youngest in the Council's history. But his presidency had to wait; he left Chicago almost immediately to work for the New Deal in Washington. In 1935, back in Chicago, he was elected president again and served a full two-year term.

Stevenson himself said, "I've always thought of the Council as my introduction to public life." His biographer, John Bartlow Martin, wrote,

> "The Council was young Stevenson's training ground. It was the place where he first made a public reputation in Chicago. It was where he learned to make speeches in public. From its membership came many of the people who helped him during his campaign for governor, during his governorship, and during his two campaigns for the presidency. It represented Adlai Stevenson's first real move upward and outward from the world of Bloomington-Princeton-Lake Forest-LaSalle Street, the schoolboyish, frivolous, moneyed world he had heretofore inhabited all his life. The Council was his launching pad...It was a milestone in his life."

"The Council made him a public figure," another biographer, Porter McKeever, wrote. By working to make Chicago more worldly, he became more worldly himself. As Council president, he reached out to leaders outside Chicago and the US. The foreign correspondents of the *Daily News* returned often to Chicago and spoke to the Council, and Stevenson became friends with many of them. A product of the Northwestern law school, he used the Council to build contacts at the University of Chicago.

"Under Stevenson, the Council changed from a small elitist group of like-minded people to a larger, more public, and more diverse group," Martin wrote. "During his first year, Council membership increased from 1,606 to 2,141."

As Council president, Stevenson is best remembered for his introductions of speakers. These introductions seemed casual, almost ad lib, but they weren't, and they didn't come naturally. As a former Council president, Walter Fisher, recalled, "When Adlai made his first introductory speech, it was so halting that I wondered if he would do."

Stevenson labored on these introductions, "polishing them like a jeweler polishes a diamond," a later Council president, Edward McDougal, said. He gathered information on the speakers four days in advance, spent hours writing and rewriting the brief introductions, and then memorized them. They were informative, full of facts, but witty, eloquent, often self-deprecating—in short, much like the speeches which nearly propelled him to the White House. As his biographer Martin wrote, "The speaking style which during the 1952 presidential campaign came to be thought of as uniquely Stevensonian—not merely the wit and self-deprecation, but the long, complicated sentences, the complex syntax and high level of diction, the seriousness of thought, the use of parallelism and other devices to impart an inner rhythm to the prose—all of this seems to have been developed during the two years he served as Council president from 1935 to 1937."

"He would practice and practice and practice," Utley recalled later. "And the audience thought, 'Aren't you lucky to have such a brilliant president?' He wasn't brilliant, he just worked."

"Adlai had a driving ambition to excel in everything he did," McDougal said. "He burned the midnight oil, and the Council had a lot to do with his ultimate success." George W. Ball, a Stevenson law partner and later under secretary of state, noted the "overflow luncheons" at the Council, and said, "The attraction for many—the more cynical of us suspected—was hardly the wisdom of the speakers so much as Adlai's wise and scintillating introductions."

Even Stevenson's fundraising appeals had style. Speaking to the Council's annual meeting in 1936, he said, "I wish I could squander some more of your precious time telling you not merely that we need money, because your generosity always exceeds what we need, but to tell you how much better we could do our jobs and improve our services if we had a little bit more money than we actually needed. Or, as somebody said, you can work better on a cushion than on a board."

By late 1935, Stevenson could claim, "We have become an institution in this community." A year later, he reported, "Like the armament industry, the Council thrives on trouble and, thanks in some measure to a troubled world, our net paid membership has increased in the last year from 1,606 to 2,050." A year after that, membership was up to 2,371. Stevenson remarked, "Catastrophe, not culture, is still our best ally."

Not everyone approved. A local lawyer named Newton Jenkins refused Stevenson's invitation to the join the Council, "inasmuch as it is my conviction that your organization is a training school for treason to our country." In his response, Stevenson posed three questions: "1. Have you ever attended a meeting of the Council? 2. If so, what did you hear that convinced you that the Council was a training school for treason…? 3. If you have not attended a meeting, on what evidence do your base your quoted conviction?" If Jenkins replied, his letter is lost to history.

One Council speaker, a former under secretary of state named William R. Castle, lambasted the Roosevelt Administration's foreign policy and its recognition of Russia, and attacked Interior Secretary Harold L. Ickes for urging restrictions on oil exports to Italy during the war in Ethiopia. He added, "For the first time in many years, I am afraid we have no foreign policy." Stevenson felt the speech "was grossly partisan and has embarrassed the Council, which has succeeded in preserving a scrupulous nonpartisanship for many years." Ickes and Secretary of State Cordell Hull refused Stevenson's invitations to rebut Castle. Under Secretary of State William Phillips, the first high State Department official to address the Council, came instead. Phillips never mentioned Castle's name, but defended the administration's policies, including its recognition of the Soviet Union, which led to an agreement "which provided for non-interference from Moscow in the internal affairs of the United States."

As the pre-war debate rose in the later 1930s, Chicago's newspapers took sides in their treatment of the Council—the isolationist morning *Tribune* on one side, the interventionist evening *Daily News* on the other. "It was an exciting time," Stevenson recalled later. "The *Tribune* used to send photographers to photograph all empty seats, if any, in halls where we presented programs—and the *News* photographers photographed all the full ones. I'd be a dirty dog in the *Tribune* in the morning and a shining hero in the *News* at night."

At one point, Colonel McCormick became so angry with the Council and Clifton Utley that he banned the name Utley from the *Tribune*. According to Utley family lore, the order stood until 1951, when one of Utley's sons, David, made an all-city high school baseball team and an innocent *Tribune* photographer, unaware of the Colonel's ukase, put the boy's name in the caption of a team photo.

But all the papers, including the *Daily News*, persisted in covering the Council more on the society pages than in the news pages. Council membership was chic and Council events were held in expensive hotels, and women often outnumbered men. A typical article in the *Daily News* read, "After Hitlerism, one of the important subjects of the observation and comment at the luncheon yesterday was millinery. In deference to the subject of the day [Germany], at least fifty new fall bonnets, creased and feathered after the fashion of the Austrian Tyrol, made their first autumn appearance."

The *Chicago Times* wrote about the Council's "flossy" membership. "From Lake Forest and other outposts of seven-figure living are coming the flower of the social register to hear what goes on in Europe, the chances of the strife spreading further, and who's right and who's wrong."

The French ambassador talked of war, but the *Tribune* gave less space to his speech than to the dresses of the women in the audience. It even said the envoy, René Doynel de Saint-Quentin, "has keen dark eyes, white even teeth, and a small black mustache."

When one speaker talked about the persecution of Germany's Jews, the *Daily News* marveled that he could keep some listeners in their seats after the normal end of the luncheon at 2 p.m., when members usually decamped for the 2:15 Saturday afternoon concert of the Chicago Symphony.

Stevenson, long peeved by this treatment, lamented in one of his introductions, "Perhaps in time all of the Chicago newspapers will even realize that the Council is not a club but an important Chicago institution." A *Daily News* society reporter named Mary Welsh responded that her page had given the Council a lot of free publicity. "Why should you or your treasury committee be saddened if your membership grows because we describe hats rather than economic conditions?"

Stevenson scribbled a marginal note—"This is the worst crock yet"—on Welsh's letter. His reply was more diplomatic: "By aspiring to the news pages, I do not mean to disparage the society pages—or bite the hand that feeds us."

There is no record that Welsh replied. Bored with society news, she was already planning her later career as a foreign correspondent. She later became the fourth and final wife of Ernest Hemingway.

—

From 1938 on, speeches to the Council, like the daily headlines, took on a more desperate tone. In 1938, new and shameful words—Anschluss, appeasement, Kristallnacht—entered the vocabulary, shorthand for Hitler's seizure of Austria, the British capitulation to Hitler at Munich, and the violent anti-Jewish pogroms throughout

Germany. In 1939, Hitler seized Czechoslovakia, signed the Molotov-Ribbentrop Pact with the Soviet Union, and invaded Poland. With that, Britain and France declared war: World War II had officially begun. In 1940, the Nazis invaded France, the Benelux nations, Denmark, and Norway. Winston Churchill became prime minister of Britain. France fell. The rout of British forces led to the evacuation at Dunkirk. German U-boats sunk Allied ships in the Atlantic, and German bombers raided British cities. In Asia, Japan attacked China, and, in 1940, French Indochina.

No longer were these just reports from a troubled but distant world. Increasingly, Council speakers talked about what the spread of fascism meant to the US, and what the US should do about it. The great debate had begun.

Edward R. Murrow, not yet famous as a pioneering World War II radio correspondent, had covered the Anschluss for the Columbia Broadcasting System and, in 1938, the Munich conference. Two months after that conference, he told the Council, "There is unanimity on one point at least [in Europe] that the future of Europe will probably be decided by this country. The question most frequently asked is, 'What is the opinion in the United States? What is the foreign policy of the United States going to be?'"

Those questions dominated the Council stage for the next three years. Through its programs, its members and its broadcasts, the Council played a leading role in preparing the Midwest for America's eventual participation in the coming war.

Clifton Utley had been in Germany and Austria that summer and returned with a report on the rapacity of the Nazi regime, the killing in concentration camps, and the German population's willingness to trade its freedom for Hitlerian grandeur. Utley also described the persecution of Austrian Jews, who had "lost mostly everything." So far, the US had admitted 2,000 German and Austrian Jews, he said. The US quota was 27,000. Already, 70,000 Jews had applied for visas.

Asked if the US would be drawn into the war, Utley replied, "In a general European war which would last two years or more, our chances of staying out would be much less than we would like to think." The war began with Germany's attack on Poland in September 1939. The United States entered the war two years and three months later.

Any Americans who claimed ignorance over the plight of German Jews before the war weren't attending Council programs. Besides Utley, Wallace Deuel, the Berlin correspondent for the *Daily News*, said the "Nazis decided that they would like to get rid of all the Jews." Speaking in early 1940, he described the death trains to concentration camps, and said, "The position of the Jews in Germany and Poland and, if Germany wins the war, everywhere else in Europe, and not only in Europe, is… inconceivably horrible."

Upton Close, an author and Far East scholar who later became a fervent isolationist, told the Council that the war in Asia "is already on. It just depends to what extent we propose to defend ourselves, and we cannot defend ourselves and our ideals unless we are willing to get tough."

William E. Dodd, the University of Chicago professor who became a US ambassador to Hitler's Germany (and the subject of the best-selling *In the Garden of the Beasts* by Erik Larson), warned, Hitler "says democracy is a failure, hardly better than communism, and he hates communism worse than anything in the world. If democracy is communism, then it, too, must be destroyed. Can't you see that Western civilization…will gradually decline until the people of Western civilization are too weak to defend themselves?"

Unless the democracies act together, he said, "in the next two or three years…[fascism] will spread, and as it spreads, we probably will be the last great nation standing out."

Douglas Miller, a former American commercial attaché in Berlin, warned, "The final decision in this war is not going to be made in Europe. It is going to be made in America. The Battle of America is the most important battle of this war—the battle for American public opinion."

Miller painted Hitler "as a natural congenital liar. He makes the truth as he goes along, and so with Hitler you cannot argue because he is not conscious of ever telling an untruth."

John Gunther, a former *Daily News* correspondent and author of the *Inside* book series, described Hitler as both "extraordinary" and "detestable," as well as a "mystic and dreamer," with "an extraordinary fixity of aim and fixity of will," a teetotaler, lazy and incompetent, but a master of Germany.

Jan Masaryk, the son of the founder of Czechoslovakia, was a future foreign minister of Czechoslovakia who was murdered by the communists in 1948. His speech drew a record crowd of 3,150 persons to the Palmer House. Speaking four months after the Munich Conference dismembered his country, he said, "If what we did at Munich is permanent peace, I am very glad that my little country paid the supreme price. If it isn't peace, God have mercy on our souls."

He continued, "It is your young and vigorous country which must take the spiritual leadership."

Not all Council speakers, including some of the most eminent, agreed. Lord Bertrand Russell, not yet a Nobel laureate but already one of the world's leading philosophers, defended Munich:

> "It does not matter two pins which side wins the next war. The next war will bring the downfall and destruction of civilization in Europe...and who wins is a question of no importance. The victors will be just as bad as the vanquished. I want to say as emphatically as I can say that I believe the right policy for America is to be isolationist. The best thing America can do for the world is to remain outside these troubles."

Former president Herbert Hoover, a bitter foe of President Roosevelt, scoffed in 1939 at the imminence of war, but said, if it happened, "It is my belief that the Western Democracies of Europe can amply defend themselves against military attack...A war to save liberty would probably destroy liberty. In my view, another great war will make dictatorship universal."

America's best policy, Hoover said, "is to eliminate communist, socialist, and fascist ideas and persons from our own institutions."

With America still officially neutral, the Council went out of its way to provide a platform for both sides, including apologists for militarist Japan, the Franco regime in Spain, and for Nazi Germany. The most provocative was Colin Ross who, despite his Scottish name, was a Vienna-born travel writer and committed Nazi. If the Council wanted the Nazi point of view, it got it. "What is going on in Germany now is a German-Jewish war," he said. "On the point of this German-Jewish question, I think we all stick to Hitler. We Germans do not take Hitler as just the head of state, just the president, or dictator, or even the emperor. For us, Hitler is a genius."

Ross presented Hitler's Germany as Europe's shield against the Asiatic barbarism of Russia. He defended totalitarianism and described Hitler's hold on Germans as a mystical new faith. He defended the sterilization of women who might give birth to "insane people."

The US and Germany are natural friends, he said, "and the only thing we want is, please leave Europe alone. The European people will settle our questions quite all right."

In the Q&A that followed, Ross launched into an anti-Jewish tirade, accusing Jews of being war profiteers who dominated German media and banking. He continued, "But I assure you I personally haven't seen any force or any cruelty against the Jews." Members of the audience shouted, "That's a lie!" A rabbi from St. Louis jumped up and cried, "Why don't you tell the truth?"

Ross and his wife had lived in Chicago for two years in the 1930s. As World War II ended, they committed suicide together.

In the 1930s, Congress passed a series of Neutrality Acts that banned any American trading in arms or giving loans or credits to any parties in a war. With Hitler's attack on Poland in 1939 and his Blitzkrieg against the West in 1940, these acts moved to the center of the Council debates. Stevenson, Utley, and other Council leaders strongly believed they should be repealed.

Two academics debated the acts before the Council. Harry D. Gideonse, the president of Brooklyn College, argued that, while most Americans instinctively favored their European Allies, "If the law stands as it is now read, we will, whether we wish to do so or not, in fact help Germany." Edwin M. Borchard, a Yale law professor, said if the embargo on arms sales was lifted, "It would help one set of belligerents only. This seems to me a clear violation of international law."

William C. Bullitt, Jr., the US ambassador to France, argued, "Isolationism is a prelude to destruction…Our task is to prepare with such speed and to give supplies with such amplitude to those nations which are resisting the aggressors that the aggressors will not be able to destroy them and attack us before we ourselves are prepared to repel aggression."

—

Clifton Utley spoke to the Council while German forces were closing in on the besieged British soldiers at Dunkirk. "A German victory," he said, "would be a considerable disaster for the national interests of the United States." He called for sending both planes and money to the Allies at once and acknowledged this meant "an abandonment of neutrality in any sense that the word is used by international lawyers."

But if America stayed isolationist and the Nazis won in Europe, what should America do? "The answer," Utley said, "is as simple as it is discouraging. It is arm, and arm to the teeth, and prepare for the day when an isolated America may have to reap the bitter fruits of its isolation."

In a debate with Utley, Socialist Party leader Norman Thomas accused leaders of the interventionist camp of being early supporters of Mussolini. America should "keep out of war and things leading to war," he said.

Increasingly, Council programs featured journalists just back from Europe. Despite his isolationism, Colonel McCormick kept a stable of respected foreign correspondents. One of the best, Berlin bureau chief Sigrid Schultz, told the Council that, if Hitler's plan to defeat Britain succeeded, the war could be over in three months. If it failed, the Germans "are ready to dig in for a long war of at least three years." William Stoneman, the London correspondent for the *Daily News*, said Britain could not win the war without massive American aid, and this aid cannot be produced "unless the United States feels strongly enough about this Axis business to be prepared to go the whole hog: that is today to go to war."

—

By 1940, the battle lines were drawn between the interventionists and the isolationists. Both camps were mixed bags that defied easy definitions. The debate split families and friends, with Republicans and Democrats on both sides.

Most polls showed a majority of Americans opposed any involvement in the European war. But they were fired by differing motives. Many believed alliances and other diplomatic agreements compromised American sovereignty. To them, "entangling alliances" handcuffed the nation's ability to act freely in the world. Some, such as Colonel McCormick, recalled the horrors of the First World War, which settled nothing, and were determined to keep American soldiers out of the next catastrophe. Others, again like the Colonel, believed in American exceptionalism, or simply hated Franklin Delano Roosevelt. Many Americans, still scarred by the Depression, felt the first job was to heal the domestic economy. Still others despised the British more than the Germans; one irate listener to Utley's broadcasts wrote him, "Great Britten [sic] is the greatest enemy US ever had." Again, the Colonel, backed by some of the Irish of Chicago and other cities, belonged to this camp. Many Americans saw Bolshevik Russia as a greater threat than Nazi Germany. In all, they were a mixed bag of xenophobes and patriots, and many of them went on to distinguished wartime careers. One such was R. Sargent Shriver, who actually co-founded the America First Committee while a student at Yale but who served with distinction in the war, later helped found the Peace Corps under his brother-in-law, President John F. Kennedy—and who served on the Chicago Council Board for a decade.

The isolationists included an anti-Semitic, pro-Nazi element, personified by the famed aviator, Charles Lindbergh. McCormick held no truck with these views—the *Tribune* denounced Nazi persecution of the Jews, dismissed Hitler as "a passing insanity," and chastised Lindbergh for an anti-Semitic speech he made in Des Moines in 1941. McCormick never joined America First, the Chicago-based isolationist organization, but he gave front-page play to America First rallies, including one featuring Lindbergh.

The interventionists, less complicated, stressed America's new membership in the world community and its self-interest in protecting European democracy from the Nazi threat. But they too were split between those who saw peace in alliances and collective security and those, like Utley, who recognized that America would inevitably be drawn into the European war. Uniting the two factions was the same internationalist attitude that drove the founding of the Council.

To complicate matters, internationalists could be isolationists, too. The debate split the Council, with members on both sides. One leader of America First was Clay Judson, a Chicago lawyer, former Council president, and a close friend of Stevenson.

The isolationist-interventionist debate, like the Vietnam War and the Trump presidency, split friends and families. Harriet Welling, an early Council Board member and a fervent advocate of American support for China against the Japanese, recalled it as "the unhappiest period of my life. Most of my friends were in America First. Most of its leaders were my dear friends. There was great bitterness, with people taking rigid sides."

—

In the spring of 1940, the Kansas publisher William Allen White led the organization of the Committee to Defend America by Aiding the Allies, soon to be known simply as the White Committee. White, a Republican, was a convinced interventionist, and he felt it was vital that a strong chapter be set up in Chicago, the home of the isolationist *Tribune* and a center of isolationism. The Chicago Council became the core of this chapter, if informally. The ties to the White Committee stretched the Council's official nonpartisanship to the breaking point; Utley recalled that Council leaders did discuss its nonpartisan status, "but never with a thought of changing it." But the activities, both in Council programs and in the White Committee, cemented the Council's stature as the key international forum in the Midwest.

White appealed to Paul H. Douglas, Quincy Wright, and Clifton Utley to set up the Chicago chapter. All had close ties to the Council. Utley, of course, was the Council's executive director. Douglas, a University of Chicago professor and future US senator, was a frequent speaker. Wright, another University of Chicago professor whose wife later became the Council's executive director, was a former Executive Committee member. According to official histories, the three men organized a luncheon meeting that recommended Stevenson as president. Stevenson, who had stepped down as the Council president three years earlier, agreed.

Utley, in an interview thirty years later, gave a more colorful version of Stevenson's recruitment. Although he was still Council director, Utley agreed to be the "public relations counsel" in Chicago to the White Committee. "And then I went over to Adlai's office," he recalled, "and I said, 'You've heard of this organization, the White Committee, that's been formed?'

> "'Yeah,' Stevenson said, 'I just read it in the paper.'
>
> "'Believe it or not, I'm the public relations counsel of this organization in Chicago,' I said. 'I would like to have you be president for Illinois.'
>
> "He says, 'Why the hell did you come to me?'
>
> "And I said, 'I came to you because you've got a conscience and most businessmen haven't.'
>
> "And he said, 'Oh, Christ.'"

And then he agreed to serve as the local president.

It was a shrewd choice. Stevenson quickly organized an Executive Committee of local leaders, including many Council members, and no fewer than nine former Executive Committee members, including the Council's co-founder, William Browne Hale.

The White Committee was opposed by the America First Committee, headquartered in Chicago and led by General Robert E. Wood, the chairman of Sears-Roebuck, and, like McCormick, a World War I veteran, and vociferously championed by the *Tribune*. The America Firsters sponsored a mass rally at Chicago's Soldier Field, with Lindbergh as the star speaker. The *Tribune* said 40,000 persons attended. The *New York Times* said the crowd was only 10,000. Whatever the turnout, it was dwarfed by the mammoth stadium. Learning from the isolationists' mistake, Stevenson organized a counter-rally—but at the smaller Chicago Coliseum. The crowd of 16,000 packed the arena; there were no empty seats, and more thousands had to be turned away.

A *Tribune* story quoted unnamed "indignant members of the Chicago Council" who claimed that the Council had been "taken over" by the White Committee. The story said interventionists were using the Council's mailing list, which the Council denied. The two organizations had "an interlocking directorate," which was closer to the truth, and Council programs had become "mere sounding boards for interventionist doctrines."

The Council still insisted on its nonpartisanship. In late 1940, the Council invited General Wood, the America First chairman, to speak to a Council audience on the isolationist cause. It was a rare Council speech that ended up on the *Tribune*'s front page.

"You cannot destroy an ideology [Nazism] by waging war on it," Wood said. "If the war is prolonged in Europe over one or two years, it will result in communism in all Europe and a species of National Socialism in England. If we are involved, it probably spells the end of capitalism all over the world."

Wood defended Lindbergh from "the summit of mud-slinging: you have no right to denounce a courageous, patriotic American citizen as a traitor merely because he disagrees with your views."

Wood said Germany would never invade Britain and he scoffed at the "perfectly fantastic" idea that it would even try to invade the US. The only realistic US policy was to defend North America and let Europe take care of itself.

The debate continued over the next year. In early 1941, the *Christian Science Monitor*, in an article on Chicago's preparation for war, commented, "What are all those people doing around the entrance to that hotel? They're waiting to get into a meeting of the Chicago Council on Foreign Relations. Every week, sometimes oftener, prominent speakers, many of them just over from Europe, tell folks here what's going on and why. Audiences grow larger and larger."

Speakers from both sides crossed the Council stage. In mid-1941, Australian Prime Minister Robert Menzies said the war was no "mere paltry little European conflict…You must face up to this fact, that this war is vital to the United States." Barely two months before Pearl Harbor, a Japanese publisher and University of Chicago graduate named Juiji George Kasai assured a Council audience, "Japan has no territorial ambitions in the Pacific." A month later, John Cudahy, heir to the Milwaukee meatpacking fortune and a former ambassador to Poland, who had interviewed Hitler, was both booed and cheered when he said Hitler had no plans for world conquest.

"I know of no plan for world conquest," he said, "but I suppose even Hitler can be guilty of a bit of campaign oratory."

Paradoxically, as the war neared, interest in Council programs waned. At a committee meeting on December 5, 1941, Utley reported "an increased apathy and feeling of weariness about the entire foreign situation," coupled with "a possible growth of America First sentiment."

Both—the apathy and the growth in America First sentiment—ended two days later, with the Japanese attack on Pearl Harbor. So did the great debate.

On December 12, the Board met to discuss the Council's future. Suggestions that the Council suspend programs for the duration were quickly voted down. Future programs would support the war effort and would even deal with the post-war peace and world organizations.

On December 16, the Council issued a statement recalling that it was founded after World War I, and now devoted itself to helping win the second world war.

"Whatever individual views concerning [American foreign policy] may have been held previously, there can be no discussion or questioning of it now…We are now united in one common purpose: the successful prosecution of the war."

The Council promised to present information on the war, strategy, alliances, and "to promote discussion of post-war policies, and particularly plans for the establishment of peace."

All Americans have a duty to achieve victory, it said, "and the Council on Foreign Relations moves forward into the future, determined to do its full share to win this war."

Chapter 3

War and Post-war

World War II launched the United States on an emotional roller coaster that was reflected in Council programs and activities over the next decade. When the war began, worry and fear dominated the discussion; an American victory seemed not only uncertain but unlikely. Within two years, confidence returned, and speakers spoke less about the war than about shape of the peace to come. Even so, the war's end posed few answers and many questions—about the atom bomb, decolonization, a crushed Europe, a chaotic Asia, the United Nations, and a Russia that was no longer an ally but not yet a foe. Everything seemed possible. By the 1950s, many of these questions had been answered. The Cold War had begun.

Edgar Ansel Mowrer, the *Daily News* correspondent, had just returned from a tour of Asia when the Japanese struck Pearl Harbor. Nine days later, he told the Council, "This is truly the first global or planetary war in human history…It is an ideological war, international in scope. The idea is whether free men can live in certain ways in all portions of the planet, or whether they cannot."

The attack on Pearl Harbor "struck a fearful blow," Mowrer said, but for all that,

> "I seem to see the immense benefits to us of that treacherous and successful Jap attack…It got us into the war at a time when the war could still be won. If we had waited another half year or year, if we had followed the advice of people who in retrospect now seem to have been doped [sic], we could not perhaps have come to the rescue of our friends. They might have gone one by one."

Those friends, he said, included China, the Philippines, Hong Kong, and Singapore. All remained in Allied hands. Singapore, especially, was vital: "The fall of Singapore would be tragic for us. It simply must be avoided."

Mowrer spoke on December 16. Hong Kong fell to Japan on Christmas Day, and the Philippines in April. Singapore fell on February 15, just two days before Adlai Stevenson, by now a special assistant to the secretary of the Navy, returned from Washington to give the Council an extraordinarily gloomy assessment of the war. Like Mowrer, he could not resist a dig at the isolationists, now proven so calamitously wrong. He said,

> "Not only can we lose this war, but at the moment we are losing it; we are on the defensive, fighting desperate rearguard actions, fighting for the time until we can catch up with the thieves whose knives were sharpened long ago… Japan's new order in Asia is all but a reality.
>
> "This is the first really world war in modern history… This is tyranny's—and tyranny is much older than freedom—grandest, mightiest bid for mastery of the world. It is war everywhere for everyone and by everyone. It is

world revolution, a convulsive struggle between ancient and irreconcilable ideas—man or state. We are losing the war for the world which many of us thought America— the richest prize of all—could somehow escape."

Can America win? Stevenson asked. "Not in our present frame of mind. Not until we get mad, fighting mad. Not until all thought, all hope of miraculous escape is banished. Not until we have the will to win, a burning, fierce will to save our great ideal for tomorrow."

By this time, Stevenson had left the Council that had nurtured him and pursued the career that led to a major role in the founding of the United Nations and eventually the Democratic nomination for the presidency. But he remained close to his roots and returned often to speak to the Council. Indeed, he was back in Chicago in mid-1943, to talk less about the war than about that "great ideal for tomorrow," a peaceful post-war world. He recalled his jeremiad of 1941, but said, "that was twenty months ago. The dreadful danger that beset us then has passed. Hitler and Tojo will not dine together in the marble palace at New Delhi and divide the world."

But what now? Stevenson recalled all those campaigns for peace in the interwar years—the nine-power treaty on China, the naval limitations, the League of Nations—"and after twenty years we were in the most dreadful war in history." What we had learned, he said, was that peace fails "unless there is force in the world prepared and determined to crush a peace breaker." He continued,

> *"The first step is to organize the strong men in the community. They dare not compete, hence they must merge their strength for common purposes. When the war is over, the United States and Britain will have unchallenged mastery of the seas and Russia will be the most powerful land force in the world. Together we can do everything. Apart—well, it is unthinkable. The key, of*

> course, is Russia. But what do the Russians want? My guess is that they want friendly relations just as much as we do."

Between these two Stevenson speeches, the Council heard updates on the war from around the world. Princess Juliana of the Netherlands, later Queen Juliana, attended a Council program but left the speaking to a Dutch diplomat who described his nation's contribution to the war. Helen Kirkpatrick, a *Daily News* correspondent, spoke on Irish neutrality. Colonel Hugh Knerr, an aviation expert, stressed the importance of air power, in contrast to Stevenson, who said, "Sea power has saved us from defeat." Major Alexander P. de Seversky also addressed the Council on "Victory Through Air Power," on the same day that American bombers raided Tokyo in America's first offensive blow of the Pacific War.

Archibald MacLeish, the Librarian of Congress, talked about psychological warfare, and Walter S. Lemmon, president of the World Wide Broadcasting Foundation, praised short wave radio as a force for international education and peace.

Joseph C. Grew, a future under secretary of state, was the US ambassador to Japan when the war began and was interned there for eight months. Grew told the Council, "The men now controlling Japan are ruthless, unscrupulous, and dangerous. They are not impeded by the moral scruples which are the basis of good government. They want nothing less than world domination...We cannot treat with such men. We can only defeat them. There is no solution other than complete military victory." He also communicated the need to see that Japan's "feudal military spirit, which has brought death to millions, shall never again rise to do battle in an unrighteous cause."

Lord Halifax, Britain's wartime ambassador to Washington, told the Council of Poland, where nearly two million—including 1.5 million Polish Jews—had died, "by execution or maltreatment...But figures are unrevealing things. They tell us little of the human agony that lies behind every single life or death of each, man, woman, or child, included in that ghastly total."

Leland Stowe, a *Daily News* correspondent just back from the Soviet Union, stressed the strength and determination of that country and its military; Stowe spoke even as the pivotal Battle of Stalingrad raged. But the Russians "are not an aggressive-minded people," he said, so "we have an exceptional opportunity to work out something in a cooperative way with the Soviet Union through the peace." After all, he said, "You can't build a fence around one-sixth of the face of this globe and block it out," although this was, in essence, what America's post-war containment policy did.

Future relations with Russia dominated many Council meetings. Almost all speakers predicted post-war harmony and common interests. As with so many Council programs through the years, these speeches were better guides to the thinking of the day than to the events of the future.

Edmund Stevens, a former communist and longtime Moscow correspondent for the *Christian Science Monitor*, assured the Council "the Russians need peace today. Only a raving maniac at the head of government of such as country as Russia is today could look for any policy but one of peace. Certainly, Stalin and the men around him are not maniacs."

Stevens went on to say that Russia, "in order to have peace, has to have security…and that is why they are so determined that no government with an anti-Soviet orientation shall be installed in any of the capitals of the states along their western border after this war." But he denied that this meant "the Russians are going into the border countries and installing a communist system by force, foisting their system on their neighbors," mostly because the leaders and armies of those countries were not communists.

Oskar Lange, a Polish-born economist at the University of Chicago, agreed with Stevens that the Poles themselves wanted "to be a democratic republic patterned after the Western European democracies than after the political system of the Soviet Union." The American government sent Lange to Moscow as an official emissary, and he reported to the Council that Stalin told him "he wants to respect Poland's independence and not interfere with Poland's internal social, political and economic system." After the war, Lange renounced his American citizenship and returned to Warsaw to work for the communist government there.

If speakers hoped for a post-war harmony with Russia, they often argued for punitive policies toward Germany and Japan.

As early as 1943, Bernadotte E. Schmitt, a history professor at the University of Chicago, urged total Allied occupation of post-war Germany, its complete disarmament, control of its trade to make sure it was not importing arms, and seizure of German art to replace that destroyed in other countries.

"The Germans are not democratically minded," Schmitt said, "and I doubt if we can make them so."

Hans Kohn, a Czech-born historian at Smith College, said both Germans and Japanese are obedient servants of their leaders, giving precedence to the state before the individual, and seized with "as deep faith that they are different from and superior to other peoples, other nations, other races." Because of this, he said, both countries must be invaded and utterly defeated, then disarmed, and finally made to realize "they cannot rearm again."

But there was hope, Kohn said. "If we can convince them that they will not be able...to attack their neighbors and challenge mankind, the Germans and the Japanese will change their dominant political ideals and ideas and become slowly like other nations."

Andre Michalopoulos, a former Greek information minister, argued that Germany should be "dismembered into several states" and its industries "completely dismantled...I am suggesting that the Germans be put in a certain sort of reformatory for twenty years until a new generation can grow up." He continued,

"Place an embargo on Germany. Do not starve them. Let them have food but let them have the minimum of comfort. Deprive them of luxuries and let them see the good work going on outside and prosperity being reborn. Then they will respect the democracies and they will behave and want to become good boys. When you have broken their spirit, then perhaps there is a chance to reform them."

As the war continued, other speakers reflected the odd temper of the times, with victory assured but not yet in hand, with peace visible but its shape unknown. Edgar Ansel Mowrer, who won a Pulitzer Prize for his reporting on the rise of Hitler, spoke to the Council less than two weeks after the Allies' D-Day landing in Normandy. "On the sixth of June," he said, "the bell rang for the last lap of the war." He added, "The last lap is the hardest."

Mowrer reported a cynicism and suspicion of American war motives among the Allies. The French, he said, believed the US wanted to take over French colonies. The British, suddenly "a welterweight among heavyweights," wanted a partnership with America to compensate for their own weakness. The Europeans in general worried that Americans considered Japan, not Germany, the principal enemy—an attitude that he, as a *Daily News* correspondent, partly blamed on "the organs of the McCormick-Patterson Axis press, the Hearst press, and other conscious or unconscious auxiliaries of enemy propaganda." As for the East Europeans, he said,

"It is not that they do not wish to get on with the Russians. They do wish to get on with them. But it is the sort of feeling that a nice dog might have on being caged with a large lion...All this talk about dividing Europe into spheres of influence, or zones of paramountcy, or areas of

particular interest, or flower beds in back gardens frightens these little countries tremendously."

Czechoslovak President Edvard Beneš, whose country was dismembered by the Nazis and later ruled by the Soviets, came to Chicago to plead for these small nations of Europe and their nationhood: "The respect and the maintenance of independence of the small European nations and states is now, and will be in the future, vital to the peace of Europe and the world."

The Council's crystal ball extended to China. T. F. Tsiang, the political affairs director for the nationalist Kuomintang government of China, told the Council, "China in fact has made her own choice, and that choice is the middle way—somewhere between the USA and the USSR."

A more starry-eyed but astute forecast came from a much less official speaker. Agnes Smedley was a controversial and colorful American journalist, part-Cherokee, and a communist. She had a knack for stirring up trouble—by opposing British rule in India, promoting birth control in New York City, protesting oppression in Russia, and fighting Jim Crow laws in the American South. Presumably, the Council did not know that, for twenty years she had also been an enthusiastic spy for the Soviet Union, mostly in China, where she had marched with the Eighth Route Army and interviewed its leader, Mao Tse-tung.

Just back from China, she praised the spirit of the Eighth Route Army and its drive to educate its troops and called it the spearhead of a new democratic China. But she also saw it as the future of China, and democratic or not, it did not include the United States.

"Once the Chinese people get started," she said, "not only the communists but some of the nationalist armies, some of the soldiers of the democratic forces, may stir up a total revolution that will wipe out not only the present government, but wipe us out of China also."

Access to energy resources, especially oil, had been a major factor in the fighting. Harold Ickes, the US secretary of the interior, told the Council that the US not only needed to find and pump more domestic oil, but also needed to make sure it had access to ample resources around the world. At the moment, the US was a net exporter of oil, but this did not last long. Major US and British companies already controlled pumping through their concessions in Middle Eastern countries, and "there is no dispute between the oil industry and the government, either as to our need of access to foreign oil resources, or as to the need of an international agreement on oil." This policy committed the US government to supporting the control of Middle Eastern oil by Western companies, a policy that continued for thirty years, until the rise of OPEC and the oil crises of the 1970s.

—

The League of Nations had failed. On that, no speaker disagreed. But if the nations had bungled peace after World War I, how could peace after World War II be assured? Some form of world government was necessary. On this, all agreed. President Roosevelt had coined the phrase "United Nations" in 1941. The Allies felt they belonged to a United Nations coalition. If another world war was to be prevented, a United Nations had to be brought into being. This imperative, and the shape it would take, dominated many Council programs, both before the end of the war and after it.

The theologian Reinhold Niebuhr set the tone for all that was to come. "Our business in this period of building a world community," he told the Council in 1944, "is the business of continuing responsibility: despite all frustrations and ambiguities, the world community will be built. It is too big a job for any one generation, and our generation is not going to accomplish it."

Jan Masaryk, whose country had been sacrificed at Munich, returned to the Council in 1943 to plead for a UN. "Let us think of the boys who are not coming back," he said. "We owe everything to them. They make this meeting possible, so United Nations now and United Nations after the war, please. It's God's work that we are doing, and the devil must be destroyed."

Beneš, the Czechoslovak president, speaking in 1943, even before D-Day, urged the Allies,

> "Maintain the present war-community of the United Nations, as a basis for the peace organization of the post-war world. This community has the great advantage of having the United States of America and the Soviet Union as original members. With the approaching victory, other nations will certainly join us. I consider it the duty of this great association of powers to prepare the way for an agreement regarding the fundamental issues of the peace to come and for a general system of security as soon as possible—certainly before the war is over."

Journalists agreed. "Let us make no mistake," Edgar Ansel Mowrer said. "The only solution to peace is a measure of international administration and adequate administration." Carroll Binder, Mowrer's former colleague at the *Daily News* and now the editorial page editor at the *Minneapolis Star-Journal*, said post-war America had a choice of three paths to follow: isolationism, empire, or "participation in a system of collective security." He quickly rejected the first two options, because collective security "is the only secure path for our country."

Binder, having done battle with Colonel McCormick's *Tribune* during his career as a journalist in Chicago, could not resist an assault on that isolationist icon:

> "I am not unmindful, whenever I speak in Chicago, that I am addressing a community which, for many years, has been conditioned in cartoon, in editorial, in news

dispatch, and in headline to view the United States as a saintly dupe, who is always losing his shirt in the international poker game, a sap who freely bestows the great riches which are his upon unappreciative, designing foreign peoples, one who 'never lost a war or won a conference.' This America, which is always 'getting into trouble by sticking its nose into other people's troubles,' is portrayed so frequently that I find many of my friends accepting that self-portrait without much question, even when they think they are conditioned against that kind of propaganda."

Midwestern politicians also agreed. Harold Stassen, then still the young governor of Minnesota, told the Council, "The walls of isolation are forever gone." Instead, there should be "a continuing organization of the United Nations of the world as the future way to lasting peace and progress for mankind, preferably one with limited but real military powers."

Senator Joseph H. Ball, who like Stassen was a Minnesota Republican, went further. "The so-called isolationists (they don't like that label, they prefer to be called nationalists nowadays) are beginning to talk out loud again," he said. "You have a great newspaper here in Chicago which I don't need to name. It will be in the forefront of that fight." Ball urged instead an armed UN with "the power to act, instead of forcing the United States to declare war in order to preserve peace. Let's have the world community do a policing job on these international outlaws." He continued,

"One of the arguments which we hear most frequently used against our joining an effective international organization is that we don't want American boys to police the whole world. Ladies and gentlemen, what are American boys doing now? They are stopping aggression all

over the world today, but they're doing it the hard way, the hardest possible way, and it's costing us a thousand lives for every one that it would have cost us if we had been ready and willing to do our share in 1931 and 1936."

By late October of 1944, the groundwork for the UN had been laid by the victorious powers, most recently at the Dumbarton Oaks Conference outside Washington. Soon after, Joseph Grew, by now under secretary of state and a delegate to Dumbarton Oaks, returned to the Council to lay out the new organization's structure, including the General Assembly, the Security Council, an international court of justice, and the Economic and Social Council. The Security Council in particular would have the power to "take action by air, naval, and land forces to restore peace." There was no mention that the major powers on the Security Council would have a veto over its actions. This came later.

Only four nations—the US, the Soviet Union, Britain, and China—attended the Dumbarton Oaks Conference to draw up the outline for the UN. Later, France was admitted to this club and became one of the Big Five, later the permanent members of the Security Council. Lester Pearson, the Canadian ambassador to Washington, and later that country's prime minister, told the Council, "No organization of peace should be based entirely on any small group, even of the mightiest powers. It cannot be shared equally, but in some proportionate way, it must be shared by all free states."

The imbalance could lead to one of three results, Pearson said. "The states other than the Big Five will either try to form power groups themselves and demand a franchise in the 'Major League,' or they will cluster uneasily for security in the shadow of a great power, or they will seek security in isolation and neutrality." As it turned out, the post-war lineup of nations featured variations on all three of those options.

Edward R. Stettinius, Jr., a native Chicagoan, was secretary of state in the spring of 1945 when he came to the Council for his last speech before leading the US delegation to the San Francisco conference, three weeks later, that established the UN. He skipped over the pre-conference diplomatic politicking over major issues, especially the Big Five's demand for a veto in the Security Council, implying that these negotiations were too delicate to discuss. Instead, he focused on the importance of the UN's Economic and Social Council in "the removal of the political, economic, and social causes of war." He urged a post-war order based on "the expansion of private trade and the encouragement of private enterprise." All this, overseen by the Economic and Social Council, was vital. "Without it, the world will be able neither to recover from the effects of this war nor to prevent the next war."

Stettinius spoke to the Council on April 4. Eight days later, President Roosevelt died. Germany surrendered on May 8. The San Francisco Conference opened on April 25 and ended in June with the creation of the United Nations Charter. Six weeks later, the US dropped the atomic bomb on Hiroshima. Eight days after that, Japan surrendered. The war years were over. The early post-war era and all it would bring—the atomic age, the Cold War, the Marshall Plan, NATO, McCarthyism, the victory of communism in China, the Korean War, the Vietnam War, the crippling of the UN by power politics, and America's emergence as a superpower—lay immediately ahead.

As Stettinius said, "Political isolationism and economic nationalism are utterly unrealistic." Perhaps. But they weren't dead, not in the Midwest and not in Chicago. The Council still had work to do.

—

Clifton Utley resigned as executive director in 1942 to become a full-time radio commentator. He was succeeded by Louise Leonard Wright, who guided the Council through the war years until 1951. Wright, probably the first woman to lead a world affairs council anywhere, got a condescending welcome. One newspaper identified her as "the charming wife of Professor Quincy Wright of the University of Chicago's international law department." But she was a formidable figure nationally and in Chicago, a former history professor, long active in the Council, former national chairman of the foreign policy committee of the League of Women Voters, an expert in Latin American affairs, the author of three authoritative handbooks on foreign affairs, and the president of the Woodrow Wilson Foundation. During her tenure, the Council moved locations twice, grew in membership and influence, and adapted gracefully to the changes forced on it by a new and different world.

During the war, the Council's programming shifted from its traditional large programs in hotels to smaller and more frequent meetings, stressing interpretation rather than basic information. Food and gas rationing made the large meetings and luncheons impractical. Radio broadcasts supplied quick, up-to-the-minute news. No longer was the Council the only source in town for foreign information. Hundreds of Council members joined the military, and some, including three former Council presidents—Adlai Stevenson, Laird Bell, and Walter Lichtenstein—took leadership positions in Washington. Both membership and revenue suffered. Wright kept these losses to a minimum. At war's end, Council membership was 2,416, down only 622 after the years of war. Most programs drew 500 or 700 people, although 1,600 came out to hear Grew, Stowe, Halifax, and Beneš.

Wright quickly moved the Council's offices from its quarters in the Marquette Building to the John Crerar Library Building at 84 East Randolph Street. Not only was the rent lower, but the Council led a virtual collective of foreign affairs organizations—the Pan-American Council, the League of Nations Association, the National Film Board of Canada, the International Relations Library, and the American Scandinavian Foundation—into what became known as the International Relations Center. These organizations rented part of the library collectively, and the Council, as the Center's largest member, held the lease for all the groups housed there. One amenity was a large meeting room that became the venue for many Council meetings. It was called the Woodrow Wilson Room, because Wright, who sat on the board of the Woodrow Wilson Foundation, talked that body into giving the Council $2,500 to decorate the room. The Council moved again, in 1948, to 116 South Michigan Avenue, where it stayed for the rest of the century; many of the same organizations, plus the United World Federalists and the Chicago Horticultural Society, moved with it. It also kept the Woodrow Wilson name for its new meeting room, renting out the room often enough, at thirty dollars for an evening, to offset about one-third of the Council's rent.

Wright made the Council busier than ever. In 1942, she and Emily Taft Douglas—a former member of Congress, author, anti-isolationist, daughter of sculptor Lorado Taft, and wife of Senator Paul Douglas—founded the Pamphlet Shop, which sold or distributed thousands of small, paper-bound booklets on foreign affairs, too inexpensive for conventional booksellers to handle. The shop stocked about 450 titles published by 100 or more organizations, including the Foreign Policy Association, the State Department, the UN, and the Carnegie Foundation. About one-third of the pamphlets were sold, and the rest given free to schools and public organizations. Business was brisk; in 1948, the shop sold or distributed 53,430 pamphlets, including 3,850 alone on the Marshall Plan. At first an adjunct of the Council, it became part of the Council in 1945 and lasted until the 1970s.

The Speakers Bureau had been founded by the League of Nations Association in the late 1930s and was run by the International Relations Center through the war. The Council absorbed it in 1945 and broadened it into a major source of information on foreign affairs for the Midwest. With the war, many organizations in Chicago and the Midwest wanted speakers on foreign affairs. The Council reached into its deep stable of speakers to provide experts at moderate fees. Records from 1948-49 report that 419 speakers were booked, about half in Chicago and half around the Midwest.

If membership mostly held up during the war, revenue did not. As deficits mounted, the Board president, Frederick Woodward, warned, "If we continue to operate on a deficit basis, this reserve may evaporate, and so may this Council on Foreign Relations." Wright helped stanch the losses by forming a new membership for persons who gave the Council fifty dollars per year or more. In return, these donors got invitations to informal meetings with speakers such as George F. Kennan, Walter Lippmann, Adlai Stevenson, and Jean-Paul Sartre.

For the first time, the Council sought foundation funding, with mixed success. The Board president, Paul V. Harper, met with the president of the Carnegie Endowment in New York in 1947. Within a year, Carnegie gave $5,000 to the Council's International Relations Center, then abruptly cancelled it. Council records give no reason for the cancellation, but the Carnegie president, whose name was Alger Hiss, was already under suspicion as a Soviet spy, and may have had other things on his mind.

The Council had been formed in 1922 largely to remedy the absence in Chicago of serious news and information on foreign affairs. By the war's end, it faced new and serious competition in this area. Some came from newspapers. The *Tribune*, despite its isolationist foreign policy, kept a strong roster of foreign correspondents, as did the *Daily News*. Radio provided an even greater challenge. By 1947, there was one radio for every two Americans. During the war, broadcasters such as Edward R. Murrow and Eric Sevareid, not to mention the Council's Clifton Utley, had become familiar and trusted voices. Gradually, the tone of Council programming shifted from pure information to analysis and opinion.

In 1947, the Council began a series of cooperative studies with the University of Chicago, which began with seven lectures on France, followed by a series on American foreign policy in 1948, and "Approaches to Peace" in 1949. In 1948, the Council teamed with the State Department to sponsor an "Institute on United States Foreign Policy," a two-day session bringing one hundred public opinion leaders from across the Midwest. State Department officials came from Washington to explain US foreign policy and to hear, for the first time, Midwestern views on the world. This institute continued until the mid-1950s, when the State Department broke it off.

Melvin Brorby, one of Chicago's leading advertising men, joined the Council's Executive Committee in 1945 and later became its president, and a major influence on Council history. Like the Council's co-founder William Browne Hale, Brorby had attended early League of Nations meetings after World War I and lamented the American failure to join the League. In 1946, with membership and revenues still down and its programming facing new competition, Brorby formed the first Public Relations committee, charged with getting the Council's activities off the society pages, through news releases and other methods, and into the view of the city as a whole.

Brorby was a remarkable man and one of the Council's most valuable leaders. Bored by the advertising business, he threw his energies into the Council, especially in its fundraising; more than any other person, he kept the Council afloat during financial crises ahead. He lived to be 101. At a Council party celebrating his ninetieth birthday, Columbia University professor Marshall Shulman said, "Mel is a world citizen. He's made a real difference. I just admire the way that he, as a private citizen, has taken on civic obligations, and made an effort to get people to pay attention to international problems." It was a tribute that could be given to many Chicagoans who served the Council over the years.

Wright also formed the Young Men's Group, composed of young professional and businessmen, each sponsored by an Executive Committee member and invited to special luncheon meetings. Its first chairman was William McCormick Blair, Jr., a young lawyer and friend of Adlai Stevenson, later a US ambassador and, ironically, a worldly leaf on the family tree that also produced Colonel McCormick.

Apparently, it occurred to no one, including Wright, that young women might be equally interested. Only when the Young Men's Group succeeded did the Council form a Young Women's Group. According to contemporary histories, the young women asked to bring escorts, so their group became the Young Adults' Group, with evening suppers and speakers. But the Young Men's Group itself remained resolutely all-male, inviting women only for an annual cocktail party. As a spokesman for the Young Men's Group told the *Sun-Times*, "Our luncheons are educational, and the presence of the fair sex seems to distract from the educational aspect."

A late afternoon World Report series began, along with the usual Evening Forum, giving the Council's varied membership an equally varied choice of programs. The Evening Forums in particular were "so successful it is embarrassing," Wright wrote. "We have sold about 1,100 tickets and have refused about 500 requests. We are arranging at the moment to have a policeman to keep them out!"

Wright continued *Foreign Notes* on a biweekly basis. The publication remained a scholarly compilation of original articles on foreign events. Only later did it begin to report on the Council's activities and reprint its presentations. At the same time, the Council began sessions for high school teachers and brought in high school students for special programs on the UN and other subjects.

Wright was more than an administrator. She traveled abroad often as an official American representative to world meetings, including the Pan-American Conference in Lima; UNESCO conferences in Paris, Mexico City, and Beirut; and a World Health conference in Rome. She was a delegate to the US National Commission for UNESCO. The French government gave her the red ribbon of the Legion of Honor.

Wright had been in Europe when the war ended. She brought back a vivid report on France and its problems. She had gone to observe the first post-war election in France, to talk with French women who had just received the right to vote and, as a veteran leader of the American League of Women Voters, to tell them about the role of American women in politics and governance.

Many of the Frenchwomen she met had been active in the resistance. Now, with the war over and the Nazi foe beaten, she said, the country was suddenly directionless and dispirited. "That beauty which came from a unity of purpose has disappeared. The French people who are weary, undernourished, and consequently discouraged, are facing problems which would stagger a strong, healthy, vigorous nation."

For all her accomplishments, Wright still had a hard time getting Chicago's newspapers to take her seriously. The *Chicago Sun* wrote, "Mrs. Quincy Wright's new Paris hat all but stole the show from her brilliant report on France before the Council on Foreign Relations. The hat, both startling and becoming, topped her severe black frock."

Wright had larger, if unrealized, ambitions for herself—as well as for her husband Quincy, one of the nation's most distinguished political scientists. In a 1948 letter to him, she wrote that she expected George Marshall to resign soon as secretary of state, and that she had just voted for President Harry S. Truman "with the understanding that you would get it. I would like to live in Washington for the next four years." Dean Acheson succeeded Marshall and Wright spent the next four years at the Council.

—

The war's end presented the US and the world with one of history's great blank slates. The atomic era began at Hiroshima, but no one knew whether mankind would survive. Europe's two terrible civil wars had ended, but the continent, where great powers once decided history and colonized the world, lay in ruins. The awful truth of the Holocaust slowly emerged and presented the world with a moral imperative that remains unsettled to this day. Japan, like Germany, lay utterly defeated and occupied. The Maoist Communists and the nationalist Kuomintang fought to rule China. Fascism, a barbarous ideology, had been defeated. A new ideology, communism, loomed in the east, challenging, as Hitler had, the pieties of American democracy and western civilization. In 1945, there was belief, or hope, that Stalin meant well, cooperation was possible, and that the Soviets were still allies. Within a year, that hope faded. The Cold War had not yet begun; rather, there was fear of real war and debate on how to prevent it.

The only solution seemed to be world government—but in what form? And would it work?

World War II is remembered as the "good war" and the soldiers who fought it became the "greatest generation." Both the war crimes of Japan and Germany and the enduring Allied structures created in the post-war world settled the argument—the interventionists were right and the isolationists wrong. But things were by no means so clear at the dawn of peace, especially in the Midwest. The isolationists regrouped. Colonel McCormick's *Tribune*, still the most powerful journalistic voice in the region, trumpeted against the UN, against NATO, against the Truman Doctrine, against America's active world leadership. From Washington, Ohio Senator Robert Taft railed against NATO and the Korean War and came close to winning the 1952 Republican presidential nomination.

But time and politics were changing, in the Midwest and elsewhere. Senator Arthur Vandenberg, a Michigan Republican and pre-war isolationist, joined forces with the Truman Administration after the war to build Senate support for the Marshall Plan, the UN, and

NATO. The two presidential candidates in 1952 were Adlai Stevenson, a product of the Council, and Dwight Eisenhower, a Kansan and former NATO supreme commander.

Mostly, Council speakers took it for granted that a new world had arrived, that isolationism was discredited, and that the peace had to be built and protected. The real debate centered on how to do this.

Oddly, the scientists who had invented the atomic age seem to have played no role in this debate, at least at the Council. The Manhattan Project, which developed the bomb, existed at the University of Chicago, barely six miles south of the Council officers. Immediately after the war, these scientists founded the Atomic Scientists of Chicago and, three months later, launched the Bulletin of the Atomic Scientists, all to educate the public on nuclear issues. But Council records indicate that, for unknown reasons, none of these scientists spoke to Council programs.

The Council did sponsor regular speakers on nuclear issues, but they were political scientists, theologians, even sociologists, some from the University of Chicago itself. For some, the shock of the bomb seems to have provoked radical, even eccentric, proposals.

William F. Ogburn, the chair of the sociology department at the University of Chicago, urged "two major adjustments" to the bomb. The first was "a world government to banish the use of the bomb in war." The second was "the breakup of big cities into towns and villages." Ogburn reasoned that the bomb's destructive power was only efficient when applied to great cities. So, "If we cannot ward off bombs from Chicago, then it could be made into one hundred towns of 40,000 population each. Manhattan Island should be turned back to the Indians…We once lived without cities," he said, "and can do it again." Each town could specialize, he thought, and they could be connected by "helicopter buses driven by tangential jets on the tips of the blades." Of course, people would have to live underground, but "men lived once in caves for about 100,000 years, enough time to become adapted."

Karl Brandt was a German economist who fled the Nazis and taught at Stanford. To the Council, he flatly rejected "the concept of the collective guilt of all Germans" and said it was America's duty not to crush Germany but to rebuild her. Two months earlier, at the Potsdam Conference, the victors—America, Britain, and Russia—had split Germany into four zones and called for the destruction of all German industry with war potential. Potsdam, Brandt said, was "a jerrybuilt architectural monstrosity."

"We did not make the gigantic sacrifices in blood and wealth to replace one sort of totalitarian brutality by another, or to silently consent [to] an orgy of ruthless suppression and slow-motion torture of millions of innocent people," Brandt said. Germany was central to the European economy, he said, so America needed to "rehabilitate Germany before it is too late to salvage thereby the best hope for real peace in Europe. Does it really make sense to demolish in the heart of Europe deliberately the most vital part of the productive capital that has been created by four or five generations?" Potsdam condemned tens of millions of Germans to unemployment and hunger, and "it would be more humane and more logical to reopen the gas chambers of Belsen and Buchenwald, and to blow out the lives of thirty or forty million Germans with lethal gas."

Less emotionally, Helen Kirkpatrick, a foreign correspondent for the *Daily News*, called for an American program for the recovery of Europe. Speaking two years before the Truman Administration proposed the Marshall Plan, Kirkpatrick said, "I do not think we can retire into the comfort and illusory security of the North American continent and say, 'Let the rest of the world get out of the jam as best it can.' All of the elements of revolution will be present in Europe this winter unless there is a little more warmth and a little more food."

Fiorella La Guardia, the colorful former mayor of New York who was the director general of the United Nations Relief and Rehabilitation Administration (UNRRA), told the Council, "We have such a tremendous responsibility. The leadership has come to us."

Samuel H. Cross, head of the Slavonic Department at Harvard, spoke on "Russia as a World Power," and said, "In the interest of world peace hereafter, the two nations (the US and the USSR) have to respect each other, tolerate each other's vagaries and errors, and try to understand each other's interests."

Many speeches over the Council's history dealt with Palestine and the eternal clash there between Jews and Arabs. From 1922, the British ruled Palestine under a League of Nations mandate. In 1948, after fighting between Jews and Arabs, the state of Israel came into being in part of Palestine and the rest—the West Bank—became part of Jordan.

But a true settlement remains as elusive now as it was in 1946, when Robert R. Nathan, an economist who helped lead America's industrial mobilization during the war, studied Palestine and found a "dual economy, a modern economy, and an ancient one," and an equal split politically—"a purposeful avoidance of merger and integration. The differences prevail from top to bottom and are intentional as well as persistent."

Given this, Nathan told the Council, "The only way to solve the conflict is for some clear, positive, consistent decision to be imposed from the outside and to be enforced." This job was up to the US, Britain, Russia, and France, he said. "The kind of policies that have been adopted over the last twenty-five years, moving one way then the other, backward and forward, offsetting each decision with an opportunistic kind of vacillation, can only lead to chaos; it can only lead to confusion; it can only lead to bitterness."

John J. McCloy, the wartime assistant secretary of war, was not yet America's High Commissioner in Germany when he spoke to the Council on the post-war treatment of Germany and Japan. He agreed with Karl Brandt, up to a point: "The idea that one can or should pastoralize the highly articulated industrial area known as Germany is nonsense, and is unworthy of the men who, in a moment of weakness, initially proposed it." This was a reference to the Morgenthau Plan for the partial deindustrialization of Germany. Both the American and British governments toyed with the idea before dropping it. "I think," McCloy said, "we can safely take for granted that Germany is and will be an important part of Europe's economy, or else Europe and the world will suffer."

But having said that, McCloy noted, "The Germans do not seem disposed to clear their own house." Therefore, he concluded, Germany must be occupied by Allied troops, its Nazi leaders must be "rooted out," and it "shall be deprived of that excess or quantum of industry potential without which she would not wage war." If this was done, he said, "We cannot be fairly charged with unenlightened conduct."

More than any other subject, the search for some sort of world government and the building of the UN dominated Council programs as war turned to fearful peace. As usual in Council history, Adlai Stevenson brought a report from the front line—this time from London, where he had presided over the executive committee of fourteen nations charged with filling out the details of the Charter and bringing the UN into being. The first General Assembly had just met. "The baby was tough," Stevenson said, "and somewhat to the surprise of the more cynical midwives, it stood up and trudged off the stage amid a chorus of cheers from a world that has staked everything on its survival."

Stevenson was proud of what he and his country had done. "It is safe to say that each of these successive steps was in large measure due to the initiative and leadership of the United States...When the history of the development and organization of the United Nations is written—whether it ultimately succeeds or fails—we will feel that as a nation. We now have expiated the sins of failure to support and further the effort to organize the world for peace after the last war."

This was a lesson that Stevenson first learned as a young leader of the Council. The Council had also given him a worldview, and the rhetoric to express it. In its depth and foresight, Stevenson's speech was one of the most remarkable in the Council's history.

The failure of the League, he said, had steeled him against "maudlin optimism." Already a "Russian bloc" had emerged. The US was faced with a new ideological rival, isolated and suspicious. "Considering their background, their education, their insecurity, their iron discipline, the limited authority, the mistrust, the secrecy, the conflicts of philosophy and their sense of Slav or Soviet mission on each, it is not so hard to understand why they are so uncompromising, so determined, so tireless, so blunt, and so very difficult."

It was necessary to understand Soviet grievances against the West and respond to them. But the fact remained, he said, that "we are witnessing the twilight of the old imperialism and the dawn of a new imperialism of ideas and propaganda among the miserable masses of the world. Britain and the colonial powers will be the chief targets, but we will not escape."

But this was early 1946, and the Cold War had not yet hardened. "There have always been competing ideologies. There is room for their system and ours to exist side by side."

Clifton Fadiman was the polymathic host of the radio quiz show *Information Please*, and a leader of Americans United for World Organizations. The next war would be fought with atomic weapons, he said, and the UN could not prevent it any more than the League of Nations prevented World War II. Instead, the world must form into a federation, governed by world law, with "a world legislature, a world judiciary, a world executive."

The choice, he said, "is between federation and annihilation. It is in essence a choice between government and chaos."

Edgar Ansel Mowrer, the *Daily News* correspondent and one of the Council's regular speakers, brought the same message: "The United Nations, as now constituted, cannot keep the peace of the world. It cannot keep the peace of the world because it cannot keep the peace between the great powers." The reason, he said, was the decision at the San Francisco conference to give the veto to the permanent members of the Security Council, including Russia, rendering the UN powerless.

"We need a single political management over all the world," he said. "That is to say, limited world government over certain important matters that can no longer be left either to nations or to individuals. Nothing else will do the trick."

In March of 1947, Eleanor Roosevelt, the former First Lady and a key figure in the framing of the United Nations Universal Declaration of Human Rights, said the US had to lead on enforcing human rights: "We, whether we like it or not, and most of us don't like it at all, are today the country that has to lead. Today there is no other nation that can lead the world, and all the other nations look at us."

America's obligation at that moment, Mrs. Roosevelt said, was to take in as many as possible of the million Europeans displaced by the war. "It is our responsibility," she said, "and we have to face whether we will move before another winter comes and people spend another year in futile living." Many—not only Jews but Poles, Ukrainians, and citizens of the Baltic nations—did not want to go back to their countries, which were now ruled by communists. "People, I believe, have the right to determine that they do not wish to return to their country."

Dreams of an untroubled post-war peace and of good relations with the Soviet Union died quickly. Mrs. Roosevelt hinted at it, and Stevenson and Mowrer saw it coming. Some speakers, such as the author Maurice Hindus, assured the Council that Russia's influence in Czechoslovakia was benign. But *Daily News* correspondent Leigh White, speaking on "Russian Expansion in Eastern Europe," told the Council, in mid-1946, that the Soviets had imposed a single-party "progressive democratic front" across Eastern Europe. This was no Scandinavian-style socialism, White said, "but the imposition by force of communist puppet governments which, by abolishing civil liberties and by using terror scientifically, are proceeding to integrate these countries into the economy of the Soviet Union. As far as I know, this process is being carried out against the will of the majority of the inhabitants in all of these countries, except possibly Czechoslovakia."

History moved fast. Only ten days after Mrs. Roosevelt's speech, the US government announced the Truman Doctrine, aimed at aiding Greece and Turkey but, in essence, proclaiming that containment of Soviet Communism had become American policy. That policy, aimed at blocking the expansion of Soviet power globally, guided American foreign policy, for better or for worse, through the Cold War.

Three months later, in June of 1947, Secretary of State George C. Marshall announced the plan of massive aid to Europe that would forever bear his name. In November, Marshall came to the Council and, in a nationally broadcast speech, made it clear that there was a "divergence of purpose" between Russia and America over the future of Europe.

"It seems evident that, as regards European recovery, the enlightened self-interest of the United States coincides with the best interest of Europe itself." Marshall said. He continued,

> *"The proposal for the United States to assist in the recovery of the nations that responded to [his June speech] has no purpose other than to restore Europe as a self-supporting community of states and to terminate as speedily as possible dependence upon us for aid. The opponents of recovery charge the United States with imperialist design, aggressive purposes, and finally with a desire to provoke a third world war. I wish to state emphatically that there is*

no truth whatever in these charges, and I add that those who make them are fully aware of this fact."

The Marshall Plan was controversial and its passage by Congress uncertain. Much of the opposition came from Republicans and isolationists in the Upper Midwest. Marshall's Council speech amounted to a sales job or campaign oration. The broadcast helped. So did the front-page headlines that reported it. In the end, the Plan passed Congress, partly with the help of Senator Arthur Vandenberg.

Marshall's Harvard speech was followed quickly by a Paris meeting of the sixteen European nations to decide for themselves, as Marshall had insisted, how the US money would be spent. "That conference was a turning point in the history of Europe," Sir Oliver Franks, the British ambassador to Washington, told the Council. "It was a turning point…because you had given hope to countries in situations of great difficulty that they were able to respond in terms of confidence and a new resolution to do their own job."

The Soviet takeover in Eastern Europe and the inevitability of the Cold War remained debatable. Some, like General William J. Donovan, the founder of the Office of Strategic Services (OSS), the forerunner of the CIA, told the Council, "There is going on today a war without shooting, a war of subversion, a war that builds upon fear and exploits it upon the psychological, political, and economic front."

Frederick L. Schuman, a professor at Williams College and a frequent and controversial speaker at the Council, said the Soviets had no intention to enslave Eastern Europe. Rather, it was American policy—especially the Marshall Plan, "the exact import of which is very obscure"—that raised Russian fears of an American attack. Such an attack was likely within a year, he said, because of "the bankruptcy of the Truman Doctrine, the failure of the Marshall Plan, and the coming American depression."

In Chicago, isolationism remained vigorous, at least in the pages of the *Chicago Tribune*. Thundering from his gothic skyscraper up Michigan Avenue from the Council, Colonel McCormick said, "Every believer in Americanism, every lover of freedom, must eschew NATO, the United Nations, and all the evils they have in store for us."

Hans Kohn, also a frequent Council speaker and a Czech-born American scholar of nationalism, spoke of his native country on January 30, 1948. Czechoslovakia, he said, was "an integral part of the western world." It was "in the Soviet sphere. That means the Czechs are faithful and loyal allies of Russia, and they will, in their foreign policy, follow the Soviet line." But the Czech communists would not succeed, he said, "thanks to the resistance of the non-communist parties." Most Czechs fought for democracy, he went on. "The struggle is not one between capitalism and socialism. It is one between our form of life, western civilization, democracy…against the most insidious form of a totalitarian police state…On the whole, I must say I came back from Czechoslovakia immensely encouraged."

Four weeks later, the communists seized power in Czechoslovakia in a *coup d'état*. The Czech government was forced to reject the Marshall Plan. In March, Jan Masaryk was found dead, probably murdered. In June, Edvard Beneš resigned as president. Both he and Masaryk had been guests of the Council during the war. Masaryk had praised the role of the Soviet army in defeating Hitler, but foresaw a post-war peace embraced by the UN and a federated Europe. Beneš had said World War II stemmed from events in Europe after World War I—"a revolt against democracy, a revolt against the independence of small nations, a revolt against laissez-faire economics." We can do better the next time, he implied. Too soon, their speeches, like Kohn's predictions, made poignant reading.

John Scott, an American writer who spent nine years working in the Soviet Union, reported on the Soviet takeover of Eastern Europe and its looting of the Soviet sector in Germany, later East Germany:

"By these methods, the Soviet Union has become entrenched as an imperialist power in central and eastern Europe, on the general principle of take as much as you can get and pay as little as you have to. The local reactions are taken care of by local communist parties or local united front parties."

The Soviet blockade of Berlin began in June of 1948 and lasted nearly a year. The Western Allies, led by the US, formed NATO. The communists seized power in China. Lines had been drawn that would last for forty years.

The decade had begun at Pearl Harbor. For the Council, it ended with three important speeches by three very different men.

Arnold Toynbee, the preeminent British historian, talked of a "double revolution"—the eclipse of Western Europe and the rise of Russia and America to world dominance, and the rise of the working class "insisting on having a fair share of the amenities which… have been enjoyed by the middle class in western Europe and North America." Significantly, he said, this meant a great revolution in the demands of impoverished Asians who were realizing that modern technology could lead "to a better human and spiritual existence."

"The masses in China, Japan, India, Indonesia, and Indo-China… will have I think the last word in the world." It was a prediction that seems to be coming true seventy years later.

Toynbee urged a closer transatlantic union and praised NATO as a bulwark against an outside attack. Such a union, he said, could lead in the long run to some form of global government. But this union, he said, had to be based on western Christianity. "I don't think secular democracy, divorced from religion, would be likely to be able to stand up against communism…I think that communism can take the whole of a man's devotion and loyalty, and I don't think a purely secular democracy can."

Abba Eban, who was then known as Aubrey Eban, was only Israel's "representative" to the UN when he made his first of several speeches to the Council in February of 1949. He came to Chicago the day after renewing Israel's application for UN membership. The Security Council accepted that application a month later. The General Assembly followed suit, and Eban became Israel's first ambassador to the UN.

Israel, Eban said, "was not a rational or logical act. It was not the action of practical men; it did not proceed from any cool calculation between advantage and danger. Practical men have their place in this world, I suppose, but their place is not among the liberator of peoples. The liberation of nations is always an act of faith, rising up in defiance of logic."

Israel, he said, had risen from the "monstrous episode of organized inhumanity," the Holocaust, and had repulsed the attack by its Arab neighbors. Now its main task was a peaceful settlement with those neighbors. "Surely there is an international interest in diverting the attention of all the states of the Middle East away from the sterile courses of national rivalry toward the great task of development and rehabilitation in which the welfare of the entire region summons their effort." If Toynbee's vision of a rising Asia took shape seven decades later, Eban's call for Middle East unity still remained a work in progress.

The decade had nearly ended when Jawaharlal Nehru, the first prime minister of India, came to the Council for a speech at the Hotel Sherman. The speech sold out its 1,200 tickets within two days, forcing the Council to issue an apology to members who were turned away. Nehru spoke on the balance between internationalism, which was a necessity for world order, and nationalism, which was a necessity for new states like India.

"I have little doubt," Nehru said, "that some time or other some such world state is likely to evolve…The alternative is a world disaster of unparalleled magnitude." But for now,

> *"The fundamental problem, so far as Asia is concerned, is nationalism. That is the dominant urge. I know that nationalism in its extremist form is a dangerous thing. Nevertheless, until political freedom is won, nationalism remains the strongest urge for a county. Whatever may have been done in the past, it is not possible today to suppress nationalism for long by force, and the sooner that national freedom is established in every part of Asia, the better it will be for world peace."*

It took the US a quarter century to absorb Nehru's lesson. Within a year of his speech, American military advisors began to arrive in French Indochina to help France fight what Washington saw as a communist insurgency but was in fact an uprising propelled by the nationalism that Nehru described. It was the Vietnam War and, increasingly, it came to dominate American politics.

Chapter 4

Cold War

THE 1940S ENDED WITH A PROPHECY ABOUT THE 1950S and, indeed, the decades to follow. When he spoke to the Council, Arnold Toynbee predicted, "The Russians mean to fight us with a cold war. I think we should accept a cold war and fight it over many, many years, and I feel confident that we can win it."

As an historian, Toynbee saw current events as pit stops in the marathon of history. He said,

> "You have to be very patient, to live with the problem, to expect that during all your life and all your children's lives, and perhaps their children's lives, too, this problem will be with you.
>
> "What I believe we need, above all, now, is patience. For Americans, that, I know, is a distasteful thing. But in America, as the most powerful country in the western world, with its great responsibilities, I think it is probably up to you more than any of us to live with our common troubles, and to be patient about them."

Speaking four years later, Frederick L. Schuman, a frequent Council speaker, was equally prescient but less gloomy.

"We are in fact on the way, not toward World War III, but toward a world settlement of great stability and long duration... The two grand alliances which have been waging cold war against one another have reached a global deadlock or stalemate, reflecting a rough parity, equipoise, or balance of power between them which may reasonably be expected to persist for many decades."

When World War II ended, all was chaos. Uncertainty ruled about how America and the world would cope with the atom bomb, with the Soviet threat and the promise of the UN, and with post-war devastation, especially with America's new status as the one global superpower. By 1950, as Toynbee and Schuman said, this vast menu of perils and opportunities had solidified into the slog of the Cold War. Russia had the atom bomb and meant to challenge the US for superpower supremacy. NATO existed and European recovery had begun. The communists had triumphed in China. Two months later, Senator Joseph McCarthy accused the Truman Administration of harboring a communist spy ring. After six months, the Korean War began. A pattern was set that lasted forty years and dominated the foreign policy discussion, globally and at the Council.

But if the future was set, it was not always clear. No less an oracle than Walter Lippmann, the dean of the Washington columnists, looked into his crystal ball with mixed results. Lippmann cited six transformative events of the past year: the Russian A-bomb test, the Maoist triumph in China, the collapse of the British and Dutch empires in Asia, civil wars in Southeast Asia, Yugoslavia's break with the Kremlin, and the revival of Germany as a European power.

All this, Lippmann told the Council in early 1950, marked "the beginning of the end of the idea that the world must, and that the world will, align itself in two camps." From the Balkans to Asia, he said, Russia and the US had lost "control of an important region." This meant further splintering, with Moscow losing control in Eastern Europe and Washington losing its influence in Germany, especially since it could not promise to defend West Germany from a Russian attack.

Many of the former colonies did migrate into the non-aligned camp, but the two great coalitions held together longer than Lippmann expected. On one point, however, he was more farsighted than most. The communist victory in China, he said, does not mean "that Russia has won control of China or has achieved an enduring alliance with China."

—

The United Nations had already been hobbled by the Security Council veto, but its advocates held out hope. Ernest Cross, the American deputy representative to the UN, told the Council that many problems were too big to be handled on a bilateral or regional basis. "We seek to advance the best interests of the American people by cooperating with others through the United Nations to solve problems which are worldwide in scope, whether we like it or not."

Trygve Lie, the UN secretary general, said the response to North Korea's invasion of South Korea showed that the precedent of Korea will not be forgotten. "The world will find it more difficult than ever before to permit any future cases of armed aggression to pass unchallenged. The United Nations' aim in Korea is victory followed by a united and independent Korea under a freely elected government."

When he spoke, the war had been on for three months. It had three more years to run. Forty thousand Americans ultimately died fighting in Korea. It was the first test of America's post-war containment policy, and of Americans' tolerance for limited but costly wars. It was never popular, in Chicago or the nation. The goal—a "united and independent Korea under a freely elected government"—remains unmet seventy years later.

Six months after Jawaharlal Nehru spoke to the Council, the prime minister of Pakistan, Liaquat Ali Khan, took the same platform and agreed with Nehru on two points: "the fact of resurgent nationalism everywhere" and "the extreme poverty and backwardness of the Asiatic peoples and their dissatisfaction with their plight." Pakistan could meet these challenges, he said, because "the Muslims who form the majority of its eighty million people have an ideology of their own which we call the Islamic way of life."

Nehru did not mention Kashmir, but Ali Khan said the disputed status of the region, then as now divided between India, Pakistan and China, had "sorely tried our patience." He called for a plebiscite to settle the matter. Many decades later, it remains unsettled, with one of the longest-serving UN military missions still overseeing a fragile peace.

In early 1950, Senator McCarthy launched "McCarthyism" with an attack on the State Department and especially on the "old China hands," veteran diplomats and scholars with long and deep knowledge of that country. One such scholar was Owen Lattimore, an author and Asia expert, whom McCarthy called "the top Russian espionage agent in the United States."

Six months later, Lattimore came to the Council to deplore the "panic and hysteria" infecting American public life and to plead for an enlightened US policy toward Asia. He said, "Our nerves are shaken by the fear that something big has gone wrong," and continued,

> "In an atmosphere of lies, wild accusations, dark suggestions of conspiracy, and baseless rumors deliberately stirred up, both the conduct of foreign policy by the government and discussion of foreign policy by the public have been made difficult and hazardous...A weird crew of ex-isolationists, ex-communists, pro-Nazi propagandists, fanatics, and cranks working inside and outside of Congress, and resorting to methods intended to intim-

idate both government personnel and private citizens, have laid paralyzing hands on the control of foreign policy, especially in Asia."

But America's problems in Asia ran even deeper, to the nation's attitude toward Asian countries, Lattimore said. These countries "want America's help and friendship, not her domination." Americans believe that "a common fear of Russian aggression and communist subversion is enough to cement together a democratic alliance." Not everyone wants "the system of private enterprise as it exists in the United States." Other countries want welfare states, or socialism, while US policy is being captured by "would-be builders of an American coolie empire who have no vision of Asia except an Asia with American garrisons dispersed all over the map."

The *Tribune* lacerated "the effete members of the Chicago Council" for inviting Lattimore to speak and said his presentation "was a self-serving speech before an audience distinguished for gullibility." Lattimore was later indicted for perjury before a congressional committee run by McCarthy's allies. It took him six years to clear his name and his academic career never recovered.

His views on US policy toward Asia and on American attitudes towards Asians, however, were echoed by other Council speakers.

Even before the Korean War broke out, Lieutenant General John R. Hodge, the former military governor of South Korea when it was under US military occupation, insisted on a unique Korean character. The average Korean, he said, "is the greatest individualist I have ever seen. I call him the Irishman of the Orient. He has many common characteristics with the Irish, believing in fairies, loving a good fight, being gregarious and loving pomp, power, and authority." Despite this condescending caricature, Hodge judged Koreans "fit for self-government…Our ideas of democracy are different, our thinking is different from those people. We must keep that in mind." But in writing their own constitution, he said, they displayed "democracy in action."

Pearl Buck, the American novelist who won the Nobel Prize for Literature for her novels about China, spoke to the Council on "What the Peoples of Asia Want." What they didn't want, she said, was white people in general and Americans in particular.

"It is very important," she said, "for us as Americans, before we approach the peoples of Asia, to realize and to accept the fact that we are, for a moment, I hope and trust, only, the most hated people in the world." Not that we were totally to blame. "Past history in Asia has been against us. Today we almost alone bear the burden of being the white man in a world most of whose people fear and distrust the white men." The "White Man from Europe" came in as a colonizer and dominator. "We came in like the tail after the dog. We took advantage of what others had won." Now the Europeans were out, but the Asians "are still afraid of white people and they are afraid of us. We are young, strong, [and] greedy, they fear, for power, as other white peoples have been. They cannot believe that any white people are not empire builders. It is our task to convince them that we are not."

Instead, the American post-war occupation of some Asian countries was military, not civilian. "We have not convinced the man of Asia of our superior civilization. He has seen our soldiers, and he has seen them under trying circumstances."

In the US, Asians were given rights, "but they divine in us, with that extraordinary third sense which old peoples have, that we do not truly consider Asians our equals, as human beings. They are right." Added to this was the condition of African Americans in the South, including Washington, DC. "I suppose Washington has done us more damage than can be repaired. There's nothing that we do there that is not known in Asia."

Now, Buck said, "we have done nothing to lighten the burden, since the end of the war." The Asians wanted independence and united countries, but the West obstructed this. After the fighting in Korea, "we have to realize that Korea can never belong to what we call 'our side.' Never!" Further south, in Indo-china, the West was "fighting a certain man because he was communist. Indo-Chinese did not care that their leader, Ho Chi Minh, was communist. They only cared that he said he wanted to free his people." It was probably the first time that Ho's name was spoken from the Council stage. The lesson, that he was a nationalist first and a communist second, did not sink in then or later.

Eleanor Roosevelt returned to the Council with much the same message as Pearl Buck, that freedom and democracy mean different things to different people. If we asked many people in the world "what would be to them the most important freedom, it would be to have enough to eat. And that's really something very difficult for us to understand…The fact that while we talked people were dying didn't really mean anything to us, so we couldn't understand why there was a good deal of feeling against the United States."

Because of this, Soviet agents had infiltrated people who wanted freedom and food, and "the very things that we believe in and should support are made almost impossible for us to support, in many cases, because the Soviets have seized upon conditions of misery."

Like Buck, Roosevelt said American treatment of Blacks in the United States was known around the world. "When we fight this battle for freedom in Asia, curiously enough we fight it here at home. Every time there is a failure of democracy here, it makes communism stronger everywhere in the world."

With few exceptions, the Council saw Asia through the eyes of American speakers, not Asians themselves. The main exceptions were south Asians—Indians and Pakistanis. English language facility had something to do with this. So, probably, did Pearl Buck's insight that Americans did not consider East Asians "our equals."

Binay Ranjan Sen, the Indian ambassador to Washington and later director of the UN Food and Agricultural Organization, insisted that India aimed for both political and economic democracy "such as it is understood in the West." But sometimes India would disagree with the US in foreign policy, "because she wants to find her own way in the light of her own ideals. Is not independent thinking the essence of democracy?"

Significantly, nationalism in Europe had been replaced (or so it seemed) by multinational organizations such as NATO. But "in Asia, nationalism is taking the shape of a great humanitarian urge to bring a better life to the masses…That is why support to subject peoples to throw off foreign domination and find full play for their spirit of nationalism forms one of the basic principles of India's foreign policy. This will explain India's attitude on several international questions which has not been the same as of this country."

—

Over the years, the rivalry between the Council and the *Tribune* had been fought mostly on an elevated plane, over different world views; when the attacks got personal, the Council gave as good as it got. But in late 1950, Colonel McCormick let loose with an astonishing editorial titled "Blood on Their Hands." The subject was the Korean War, then six months old, and the *Tribune*'s antipathy to that war, to World War II, to the UN, and to interventionism in general. All were the Council's fault. Council members, it said, "oughtn't to be looking for somebody else to blame for the disaster in Korea when they themselves did what they could to bring it about." It continued,

> *"What has happened in Korea is the direct consequence of a line of policy which has had the support over many years of the great majority of the members of the Chicago Council on Foreign Relations. They whooped up the*

Roosevelt policy that landed us in the second World War, and they are great believers in the United Nations.

"Thanks to these policies, 300,000 American boys lost their lives in the 1941-45 war, and 5,600 more have been listed as killed thus far in Korea. All that the members of the Council can show in Europe in return for the sacrifices is the substitution of Russian for German tyranny and menace; and all that has happened in Asia is the substitution of Russian domination of all of China for Japanese domination of a part of it...

"Men and women who favored the policies that produced these results should dress in sackcloth and strew their heads with ashes. Instead, these self-satisfied asses look everywhere but at themselves and their opinions for the source of the trouble... The UN, the darling of the Council, authorized the war in Korea and was created precisely for the purpose of authorizing just such wars.

"The members of the Council are persons of much more than average influence in their community. They have used the prestige that their wealth, their social position, and their education have given them to lead their country toward bankruptcy and a military debacle. They should look at their hands. There is blood on them—the dried blood of the last war and the fresh blood of the present one."

Decades of resentment burst forth in those few hundred words. The Council's reply held its fire. In a letter which the *Tribune* printed five days later, Council president Daggett Harvey said the nonpartisan Council favored no policy or cause, but only presented both sides of issues. On the UN, Harvey noted, the Council had recently heard both the US representative to the UN and Chesly Manly, who was UN correspondent for the *Tribune*.

Asia continued to be a focus of Council programming in the 1950s, Africa and Latin America much less so. But as the decade advanced, the recurring theme was the Cold War and the challenge of communism. As Charles Malik, a Lebanese statesman and academic, told the Council, communism and the threat of it dominated world affairs. "Communism controls the life of about one-third of the globe, formally and directly. At least another one-third of the world determines its ultimate policies in terms of communism, albeit negatively and by the way of reaction." The two camps, communist and non-communist, constituted "the totality of the effective agents of today's world."

The Soviet Union, Malik said, was totalitarian, "a total state," and totally hostile to the ideals of the West. For that reason, he said, "Peaceful coexistence is a pious hope," because "I cannot get along with one whose whole being not only contradicts mine but is meant on destroying mine." The only hope was for the West to "create those stubborn and irreducible facts which will force communism to change itself and to live at peace with the rest of the world."

Like Toynbee, Malik, a devout Catholic, felt the West had to return to a religious faith strong enough to match the revolutionary zeal of the communists. Eventually, he said, our leaders "will bless the names of Marx and Lenin, not indeed for what they did and meant, but for having roused the rest of us from our slumber and forced us to inquire after our good and return to our God."

Admiral Alan G. Kirk, who was the US ambassador to Moscow from 1949 to 1951, called the Soviet Union "a dictatorship of the highest degree, probably one of the most autocratic, cruel, despotic, and ruthless that has existed on the fact of the earth." But the result was that "some 97 percent of the population is uneasy and unhappy." He felt this presented a potential restraint on the leadership.

John Foster Dulles came to the Council October of 1952 to denounce the Truman Administration's policy of containment—a policy that he had to implement when he became secretary of state three months later. Like Kirk, Dulles focused on the misery and resentment of people living under communism, more in the satellite states than in the Soviet Union itself. It should be US policy to play on this resentment to enable these states to "liberate" themselves.

"We should activate the strains and stresses within the Soviet communist empire so as to disintegrate it," Dulles said. Like Lippmann, he saw Yugoslavia's break with Moscow as more of an omen than it turned out to be. He continued,

> "I'm absolutely convinced that a policy of containment will make war almost a certainty, and a certainty under conditions which would very likely spell our defeat. Today, one-third of the human race is subject to the despotic terrorism of a new Dark Age, and I say that it is morally impossible for us to reconcile us to that condition, or to try to buy security for ourselves by some deal that would confirm that servitude. We cannot settle for a containment which contains 800 million captive souls, and we would not be safe, nor solvent, nor happy in the face of such a menace."

Walter Lippmann returned to the Council in late 1952 to proclaim "that the debate between the isolationists, so-called, and the internationalists, so-called, is now, I think it is fair to say—even in Chicago—completed. Our new basic commitments abroad have received the overwhelming ratification of the Congress and they have the support of the people."

Lippmann spoke just after Dwight D. Eisenhower, recently elected, announced he would make a pre-inauguration trip to Korea to see the war for himself. Lippmann described the trip as a "public and dramatic recognition that the fundamentals of that war need to be reexamined." He said it was "superficial" to expect Eisenhower "to perform any kind of miracle which will suddenly end the war," but predicted the new president-elect would decide whether the war could be won by arms or settled by diplomacy. Eisenhower opted for diplomacy, and the war ended seven months later.

Barbara Ward, the British economist, told the Council that the only real way to fight communism in underdeveloped countries was through generous aid and investment. "Any nation that is fortunate enough in this world of desperate poverty to have a national income of more than $500 per capita a year should contribute something from their own wealth and well-being to raise the standards of those who live across the world's 'tracks,' in those areas of no hope where communism could spread like wildfire because, to some extent, it offers hope."

—

If the Council had to consider communism abroad, it had to deal with McCarthyism within its own Executive Committee. Kenneth Colegrove had been a junior historian at Northwestern in 1922 when, at its first meeting, he moved that the Council endorse a ratification of the Washington naval treaties, the subject of that meeting. His motion passed but was later reversed, which established nonpartisanship as a Council mantra. Thirty years later, Colegrove was a senior historian at Northwestern, an expert on Japan, and a member of the Council's Executive Committee. He also was a fervent supporter of Senator Joseph McCarthy and the John Birch Society, which considered communism "soft liberalism," alleged communist cells operated in all American universities, and demanded the US expel the Soviet Union from the UN.

At the Council, Colegrove's main target was Frederick Schuman, a liberal professor at Williams College, accused of pro-Soviet sympathies but a frequent Council speaker. That the Council scheduled Schuman shortly after Owen Lattimore's speech was "doubly unwise," Colegrove said. He moved that the Council stop asking Schuman to speak. Then he went on to propose a wholesale purge of speakers, both to the Council and on its Speakers Bureau circuit. The purpose, he said, was to let the Board "ascertain for itself how extensively speeches sympathetic towards communism and Soviet Russia had been booked by the Chicago Council."

"In a time of great international crisis," Colegrove wrote, "there is need for caution in the matter of public addresses. And, as usual, someone with a conscience has to take up the unpleasant task of demanding caution…But the attitude of Louise Wright and the Speakers committee compels the submission of such evidence."

There is no indication that the Council gave in to Colegrove. In a reply to one of his letters, Melvin Brorby, the Council president, wrote mildly that "as far as Schuman is concerned, I suppose his remarks will always be somewhat controversial." That seemed to settle the matter. Colegrove left the Executive Committee the next year. Schuman spoke to the Council at least once after that.

Colegrove wasn't the only one looking for Reds under the Council's bed. The Red Squad was a notorious but secretive branch of the Chicago Police Department that spied on suspected communists and other dissidents and subversives. When it was closed down and its files opened, hundreds of organizations learned they had their own dossiers. According to two books on the Red Squad, the Council was among them. The dossier is missing from the Red Squad files, now archived at the Chicago History Museum, but Rick Gutman, a lawyer who fought the Red Squad in court, said he saw it, among similar dossiers for other subversive organizations such as the League of Women Voters, the Planned Parenthood Association, and the United Methodist Church.

Through the years, the Council worked hard, but not always successfully, to avoid the taint of ideological partisanship. Its programs were carefully balanced. Its focus, of course, was international, and hence suspect in the eyes of the *Tribune* and other critics. Surveys of its membership showed a rough balance between Republicans and Democrats. Public perception, however, was another matter.

In 1970, one Board member, himself a liberal, noted the Council was seen as "ultra-liberal, 99 percent Democratic." The same year, the then executive director, William Graham Cole, reported, almost with relief, that he had spoken to Women for Peace on the North Shore, "where I was received very coldly as a virtual fascist." So much, he said, for those who saw the Council "as a communist front organization."

When the Council sought a new executive director in 1971, the Board fretted that the leading candidate, John E. Rielly, had worked for the Democratic Vice President Hubert Humphrey, and this "would lend a partisan appearance to his appointment." Rielly's supporters pointed out that he had also been a consultant to a Republican congressional study group, and he was hired.

—

The publisher William Randolph Hearst, Jr. was just back from a series of interviews with the post-Stalin leadership in Moscow that won him and the reporters who went with him the Pulitzer Prize for foreign reporting. Hearst's speech to the Council was both timely and prophetic. He had met Nikolai Bulganin, Vyacheslav Molotov, General Georgy Zhukov, and Nikita Khrushchev. "Of the four," he said, "Khrushchev was in many ways the most impressive. If any of the four were to grab power to build himself up into a Stalin-like dictator, my guess is it would be this boss of Russia's seven million communist party members." Hearst's prediction came true within the year.

The Council itself began courting Russian visitors. A delegation of Russian farmers, led by the Soviet first deputy agriculture minister Vladimir V. Matskevich, visited the Council for a reception and a press conference. Matskevich claimed his country wanted to buy more American farm equipment. Outside, about one hundred émigré picketers protested peacefully.

The picketers were not so peaceful when Soviet ambassador Mikhail Menshikov spoke to the Council in 1958. The protesters, mostly from Baltic and East European nations, called the ambassador a "pig" and a "murderer," and chased his car down the street as he left. To the Council, Menshikov said his country only wanted peace but was not getting the proper response from Washington.

The European Coal and Steel Community had been formed and events were moving toward the creation of the European Common Market. Arnold Toynbee, back before the Council, had his doubts: "I see no hope of a federated Europe, at least not by itself. It is not strong enough to stand and would not be an effective power despite an aggregation of population and industrial power."

The Eisenhower Administration was more positive. Speaking two months after the signing, in 1968, of the Treaty of Rome that created the Common Market, Frederick W. Jandrey, the deputy assistant secretary for European affairs, assured the Council, "We have no fear of political risks from an integrated Europe."

Jandrey said the US favored German reunification and opposed any policies that "would prohibit the German people for the indefinite future from the exercise of their free will in the orientation of their foreign policy"—definitely not an argument that would have been made a decade earlier.

Jandrey acknowledged fears that a united and strong Europe might become a "third force," no longer a reliable American ally against communism. But he said a wealthier Europe would lead to more trade and to more "opportunities for American capital and experience to assist Europe in building its economic future." In addition, the US needed strong allies, and "Europe and the United States will go forward together."

John Foster Dulles, by now the secretary of state, returned to the Council for a dinner meeting speech. Dulles at first insisted that his speech be off the record, with the press excluded. Chicago newspapers protested that any speech by a secretary of state should be reported to the American people. The newspapers won and reporters attended, but Dulles, possibly in revenge, gave a relatively bland speech.

Ironically, Dulles made news in a press conference before his speech when he said that any Soviet attack on NATO forces in Europe would almost inevitably hit US troops. Any retaliation would depend "on the nature of an attack upon NATO forces in the world," he said. "If it were like Pearl Harbor, the decision would be made on the spot whether to retaliate"—an implication that the decision to start World War III could be taken by commanders on the scene, not by the White House or Congress.

Israel, England, and France attacked Egypt in 1956 and were forced by the Eisenhower Administration to withdraw. Abba Eban, by now the Israeli ambassador in Washington, told the Council that Israel had been right to attack Egypt.

Henry Cabot Lodge, the US ambassador to the UN, pledged that the US would not recognize Communist China and would keep Beijing out of the UN.

Archbishop Makarios, the Greek Cypriot leader, scolded the US for not backing an independent and Greek-dominated Cyprus. Makarios promised that, once Cyprus became independent, "My political functions will cease." Three years later, Cyprus became independent and Makarios became its first president.

At a Council program in the Palmer House, Kwame Nkrumah, the prime minister of newly independent Ghana, made headlines by accusing Dulles of causing the Suez crisis two years earlier. "The State Department was terribly upset," Richard Templeton, Nkrumah's official host, recalled. "I didn't know what the hell was going on, only knowing that there was a great big stink about it. Well, here I was man to man with Nkrumah, knowing that he'd pulled a boo-boo." Templeton said he talked Nkrumah into issuing a retraction, which calmed the waters.

Turkish President Mahmut Celâl Bayar called NATO "the most nearly perfect international organization ever set up for the attainment of peace," and urged its enlargement to "other peace-loving countries of the world."

Tom Mboya, the twenty-eight-year-old Kenyan labor leader and chairman of the All-African Peoples' Conference, told the Council that whites in the African colonies were trying to hold on to power through rigged elections and "false liberty." Kenya became independent three years later, and Mboya became a political leader. Before his assassination in 1969, he helped organize programs for African students to study in the US. One young Kenyan who came to America under this program was Barack Obama, Sr., the future president's father.

One big fish got away. In 1959, the Council invited Fidel Castro to speak. Four months earlier, the Cuban guerilla leader had marched his troops into Havana and seized power. If he came, the Council promised to rent a major venue, such as Orchestra Hall. Council archives give no hint that Castro even answered, and he never came.

—

After ten years as the Council's executive director, Louise Wright left in 1952 to join the Institute of International Education. In its search for her successor, the Executive Committee bumped up against its perennial conundrum—how to balance its mandate for fresh, and even controversial, ideas with its commitment to nonpartisanship. Several Chicago academics and journalists were considered and found to be "too identified with certain political convictions." Kenneth Colegrove, still on the Executive Committee, wrote, "The country is swinging away from an over-tolerant liberal view, especially toward communism, to a more firm attitude toward Soviet Russia and subversive agencies in this country. Accordingly, the Chicago Council should take care to avoid being saddled with an over-tolerant director in the next year or two."

Executive Committee minutes recorded, "It was agreed that there is no objection to a new director having positive ideas, rather it is an asset, but in view of the diversified membership of the Council, it would be undesirable to have a person who is closely associated in the public mind with any particular political beliefs." The problem, then and later, was that any person qualified to lead the Council had to come from public life and its political battles. The Council wanted someone who was not an ideologue but was more than an ideological eunuch. It never was an easy balance.

Wright's immediate successor was Porter McKeever, a former campaign aide for Adlai Stevenson and the director of information for the US delegation to the UN; he later wrote a biography of Stevenson and founded the United Nations Association of the United States. McKeever came to the Council after quitting the UN job with accusations that support for the UN, once the cornerstone of US policy, was shrinking to "the size of a pebble." McKeever wanted all US aid programs brought under the UN, stronger collective security mechanism for the world body, and a campaign of psychological warfare against the Chinese communists.

McKeever moved his family to Hyde Park but when Stevenson ran for the presidency in 1952, he resigned to be publicity director for Volunteers for Stevenson. When Stevenson lost, McKeever returned, then left within a year. He moved to New York for a better paying job with the Ford Foundation.

His successor, Carter Davidson, who served for seven years, was a charismatic journalist, a dashing and much-admired former foreign correspondent with the *Associated Press*, then marooned on a police beat at the *Chicago Sun-Times*. Davidson, an excellent broadcaster, made television a key activity of the Council. But as Harriet Welling, a long-time Council Board member, recalled, "He was more interested in his own career than in the Council." A former Council president, Melvin Brorby, agreed that Davidson "was good in some things and wasn't good in others." One of his short suits was management, but it took several years to show.

The Council faced increasing competition, and for a change, it wasn't from the isolationists. More and more local newspapers and national news magazines covered foreign affairs. Local clubs and professional organizations, such as the Executives Club and the Association of Commerce and Industry, became interested in foreign affairs and competed for speakers who once spoke only to the Council. Television in particular presented hour-long specials and on-the-spot coverage, with a depth and immediacy that had been the Council's trademark.

The Council, alarmed, sought in-house and outside advice, including a study by A.T. Kearney and Company in 1954. As an earlier Council history reported,

> *"The common conclusion of these self-studies was that, although the Council had lost much of its unique character as other groups adopted an interest in international affairs, the Council remained in a position to do many things better than any other organization in the Midwest. There was a greater urgency than ever before that citizens be aware of foreign affairs. The Council decided to continue the expansion of its programming to cover broader areas, while at the same time tailoring its meetings to conform to specialized requirements of particular groups."*

Melvin Brorby, who had pioneered the Council's public relations program, had become the president. In 1953, the Council began holding programs in the suburbs, cooperating with the University of Chicago for "World Politics" programs in eight North Shore suburbs. The Young Men's Group continued and grew. Radio broadcasting, which ended when Clifton Utley left, was revived by Davidson's weekly analysis of foreign news on Sunday afternoons. The Council began giving World Understanding Awards, with the first going to Utley and to Edward R. Murrow.

The Council stayed in the Lake View Building at 116 South Michigan Avenue, but moved from its cramped quarters on the thirteenth floor to the second floor, which offered a kitchen and a larger meeting room, also named the Woodrow Wilson Room. Of all the changes, the move downstairs was the most important. Council members coming to a speech in the Wilson Room complained that they could wait up to an hour to take the elevator up to the thirteenth floor. The new, second floor space solved that problem.

The traditional luncheon programs and large hotel gatherings gave way to smaller and shorter meetings in the Woodrow Wilson Room. This saved money and catered to younger members who had less time for longer and more formal lectures.

The Council began to broaden its financial base. The staff was growing and the move from the Crerar Building had raised the rent. The Council began new membership categories like "Share the Expense" and "Community Service" to bring in funds. A special Helen Morris Memorial Fund was set up to honor the acting executive secretary between the Wright and McKeever leaderships.

Most important, the Council began looking to the corporate community for financial support, a policy that grew over the years and magnified the corporate voice in Council activities. Drives led by Brorby brought in thirty-six corporate sponsorships. A Corporate Sponsor Committee, led by a young Thomas Miner, later one of the Council's fiercest competitors, brought in more.

By 1951, Council membership stood at 2,200 persons, down slightly from 1945, but basically stagnant. Two years later, a membership campaign added 605 members—better, but not enough, and the Council announced a drive to sign up 5,000 members. It eventually reached that goal, but it wasn't the membership drive that did it. Instead, it was a novel travel program, designed a decade later and by different leaders; that story will be told in the next chapter.

To burnish its image, the Council experimented with galas, special evenings, even flower shows. In 1954, it sponsored an International Holiday Ball in the Aragon Ballroom, with an all-nations orchestra and an international floor show. In 1955, it built a benefit around a Chicago visit by the New York Philharmonic, with a party in the new Prudential Building, then Chicago's tallest building. In 1957, it sponsored a speech by the actor Douglas Fairbanks, who brought the Council publicity if not much enlightenment on foreign affairs. In 1958, it co-sponsored the Chicago World Flower and Garden Show at the International Amphitheater, an arena best remembered in Chicago as the venue of the calamitous 1968 Democratic National Convention.

In 1959, the Council made its biggest social splash with a black-tie benefit preview of a Broadway show *The Girls in 509*, starring Imogene Coca. The event marked the re-opening of the Civic Theater, with a dinner party at the Tower Club atop the Lyric Opera building next door, and a post-theater party in the foyer of the Lyric itself. Unfortunately, as one society reporter wrote at the time, "the foyer was so chilly that most of those attending kept their coats on."

For a decade, a new-fangled broadcasting medium called television had been eating into the Council's traditional monopoly on foreign news. In 1955, the Council joined the television age with a weekly half-hour show called *World Spotlight,* hosted by Carter Davidson, the executive director and a veteran correspondent and broadcaster. The program appeared on WTTW, the Chicago educational television channel, and continued for four and a half years; it eventually produced 250 programs and reached 110,000 viewers each week. At the same time, the Council produced a series of radio programs on the Chicago stations WMAQ and WLS, reaching an estimated audience of 200,000.

All this—the benefits, television, and flower shows—brought the Council both visibility and deficits. Some members felt the organization had lost its way. A contemporary history judged that "benefits were not the Council's best means of fundraising." The Civic Theater extravaganza netted the Council only $504.55. Recruiting new members and corporate sponsors worked better. But Davidson spent so much of his time and energy on broadcasting that he neglected his other Council duties, including fundraising. This growing financial strain was visible as early as 1955, when the Council treasurer, Richard H. Templeton, reported a $2,000 deficit on a $63,000 income. "Financing the Council is no different than building a house," Templeton said. "The bigger the building, the greater the budget that has to be met."

Melvin Brorby, in a later interview, blamed the growing financial squeeze on both Davidson and on Brorby's successor as president, Charles Bane. Foundation grants enabled Davidson to hire extra staff to help produce his weekly *World Spotlight* program on WTTW. After four years, the grants stopped. "Carter should have let a couple of people go right away, but didn't do it," Brorby said.

Davidson could have offset this expense with fundraising, as later executive directors would have done. But in those relatively early days, the Council, tightly staffed, had no development arm. Instead, the major fundraising was left to the Executive Committee. Brorby recalled that he and some other dedicated members spent evenings and weekends scrounging for donations, because that's what directors did in those days.

"My successor [Bane] almost put us out of business," Brorby said, referring to how Bane had not used the members and sub-committees of the Executive Committee to fundraise to cover Davidson's spending. In later days, as the Council grew, its staff took on these duties.

Bane's successor as president, Richard Templeton, recalled the Bane era as "a nightmare period." He continued,

> "[Bane] would not even call a meeting with the Executive Committee. We were spending money like drunken sailors, and we were going right down the drain, and you couldn't even get the chief executive officer to call a meeting of the Executive Committee, never had a Board meeting where they discussed finances.
>
> "I called a meeting and got Charles in and recited the fact that something had to be done. We were going right down the tubes. God, I'll never forget that day. Charles looked at me. He said, 'Dick, are you asking for my resignation?'
>
> "And I said, 'No, Charles, I'm asking from you one thing—to call a meeting of the Executive Committee to discuss our financial situation openly.' And I said, 'If you are unwilling to call such a meeting, then I think I will work with the Board to have you thrown out.' And he called the meeting."

(Bane himself was an interesting and controversial Chicagoan. A coal miner's son, he was a Rhodes Scholar, a leading civil rights lawyer, and the founder of the United Way of Illinois. President Richard Nixon later nominated him for a seat on the US Court of Appeals, but the nomination foundered on accusations of tax-dodging and anti-Semitism. With Bane out, Nixon nominated John Paul Stevens, the scion of Chicago's Stevens Hotel (later the Hilton Hotel), a stepping-stone to his later seat on the Supreme Court.)

In 1959, the Council, facing more deficits and a negative net worth of $3,942, "undertook a substantial retrenchment, effecting economies in payroll, in operating expenses, and in some activities," according to a Council report. Payroll was slashed by one-third and total spending by 20 percent. The intention was to "establish a surplus, instead of continuing the deficit net worth which existed when the year began."

This surgery worked, the report said, but left the patient on life support. The cuts eliminated the deficit. But the report also concluded, "It has therefore become clear that unless additional support can be obtained, the Council cannot continue to operate on the restricted basis which is making this surplus possible without reducing its effectiveness and jeopardizing the worthwhile educational role the Council has played in the Chicago community for nearly four decades."

As Templeton hinted, Davidson had been thinking big. But when he left in 1960, the Council was almost broke. Two Board members, Templeton himself and Stanley Freehling, personally endorsed a $8,000 bank loan that kept the Council in business.

In truth, the problems were not only financial but existential and, for all the studies by Kearney and others, are still debated. Nearly forty years after its founding, did the Council still have a role? If so, what was it? Did the old format of mostly speakers talking to an elite audience still work?

In 1957, the Council's program committee reached a dour and radical conclusion. "The Council is a membership rather than a service organization," it said. "This is a mistake. Headliner luncheons are attended by old, uninfluential Council members…The Council ought not to have speakers for the sake of meetings." It continued,

> *"The Council is not now successfully competing with other organizations for speakers of national prominence and should not. The Council's aim has been to get people to talking about foreign affairs. Now that other organizations are finally doing what the Council has done for so long, it is foolish for the Council to waste its energies in competing for the privilege. It should either disband or move on to new fields where it is needed."*

The program committee identified two of those "new fields"—high school and college students and, especially, "the busy businessman. More programs should be business-oriented, of value and interest to businessmen because they can see 'a dollar working.'" Suggested topics included air travel, shipping, exports, imports, private international law, and trade.

Sixty years later, these questions remain only partly settled. Over the years, the Council did not reduce its programs but expanded them. Attempts to reach high school students flared fitfully, then mostly died. Audiences remain elite but younger, and more diverse. Corporate and business programming has increased but has never dominated Council activities as the program committee of 1957 would have wished. The deeper question of the Council's proper audience—academics? businesspeople? all of Chicago, or only its elite?—echoes still.

An early history of the Council noted that the organization actually had little room to maneuver. "The Council was forced from the very beginning to depend upon the wealthier segments of Chicago's populations, and could never move too far from this supporting base. The Council was forced to maintain a tax-exempt status in the eyes of the law, and a socially acceptable status in the eyes of the group most able to support it." Again, sixty years on, those imperatives remain.

Chapter 5

The Travel Club

PERHAPS NO LEADER IN THE COUNCIL'S HISTORY WAS LESS qualified for the job than Edmond I. Eger. The Council's new executive director came from neither academia nor government, but from advertising. He had an interest in foreign affairs, but no experience at all. He had run his own ad agency and worked for the Admiral Corporation, a now-defunct appliance maker best known for its radios and refrigerators. He retired at age fifty-eight to work on a master's degree in political science at the University of Chicago. He lived not in Hyde Park or the North Shore, the habitual roosts of Council leaders and members, but in Flossmoor, a prosperous but not chic southern suburb. He got the job because his wife Rebecca, a member of the Council's Executive Committee, attended a meeting during which Council leaders, faced with a financial crisis, decided they needed a new leader with business experience.

"I looked across the table at Mrs. Eger and she looked at me," recalled Richard Templeton, the president at the time. "I said, 'Becky, is Ed going to be home tonight?' And she said yes, and I said, 'Will you find out whether he can have lunch with me tomorrow?' And it happened like that."

Carter Davidson returned to broadcasting and the Council hired Eger, but only as acting executive director, and only for one year.

Ed Eger may have saved the Chicago Council. He swiftly shed the "acting" part of his title and became executive director, a job he held for nine years. Within four years he tripled the Council's membership and quadrupled its net worth. By the time he left in 1969, total membership was 20,000, or eight times what it was when he took over. And he did it not with a scholarly focus on foreign affairs, but with a keen eye for the small print in the rules of the Civil Aeronautics Board (CAB), at that time the regulator of civil aviation in the United States.

The CAB forbade commercial airlines to run charter flights, but membership organizations, such as the Council, could. Moreover, they could charge about $250 for a round-trip to Europe, well below the commercial fare. These organizations could not make a profit on the charters but were allowed liberal deductions on expenses. More important, these charter flights were limited to members: to join a Council charter flight, travelers had to join the Council and pay its ten-dollar membership fee. Those fees added up fast. The Council's annual income quickly passed $100,000 for the first time and kept climbing.

The first charter was a BOAC turboprop that left Chicago for Paris on September 18, 1961, and returned from London a month later. That first fare was $279, but included "first-class catering, a complimentary bar, and luggage allowance of sixty pounds." Seats sold out immediately. Within two years, the Council offered six charters, then eight or nine. By the end of the decade, there were twelve or more flights, and round-trip fares ranged from $215 to London to $290 to Athens.

The Council also arranged more elaborate round-the-world charter flights, starting in 1963, with a trip that embraced Tokyo, Hong Kong, Bangkok, Delhi, Bombay, Cairo, Athens, and London, included briefings, high-level meetings, and an evening with Indian

Prime Minister Jawaharlal Nehru at his home. The total price, for air fare and all land travel and hotels, was $1,875; the air fare alone was $1,075, about $200 lower than the cheapest around-the-world commercial air fare. By 1969, there were seven of these tours; two to Asia, an around-the-world trip, plus tours of Africa, the South Pacific, South America, and Eastern Europe, which lasted more than a month and cost up to $2,260.

These cheap charter flights created a lucrative embarrassment for the high-minded Council. Its planners tried to put an educational gloss on these flights, with diplomatic briefings and other perks, but they were essentially a cheap European vacation for rookie Council members.

"There has been some question concerning the motivation of new members joining the Council," the minutes of a 1964 Executive Committee meeting reported primly. "There has been some feeling that the trips have been seized upon as the main reason for membership participation." A year later, the Executive Committee fretted that the flights "are geared to appeal largely to the most common aspects of tourism and that to this extent planned tours may tend to damage the image of the Council." One member, Mrs. Harold Strauss, urged that the flights "be more selective, stressing experiences that contribute to a more profound understanding of the culture visited rather than emphasizing mere sight-seeing." Eger replied that most persons going to Europe for the first time "prefer to make a general survey of an area," that is, to go sight-seeing.

Embarrassment or not, the charter flights kept the Council in the black for fifteen years, until the CAB closed the loophole. Eger's successor, John Rielly, recalled that the flights lasted four and a half years after he arrived in 1970, and gave him funds to expand programs. During those years, Rielly said, "charter flights took over the Council. Sometimes, the Council would arrange briefings. Otherwise, it was just cheap airport-to-airport."

Rielly recalled that Thomas Coulter, a Chicago civic leader, "once asked me, 'John, what do you do?' I said, 'I run a foreign policy organization.' He said, 'That's no foreign policy organization. That's a travel club.' And he was not entirely wrong."

—

The 1960s began with a new mood of confidence that communist power had peaked and the US was winning the Cold War. The decade's early years were not a quiet time, by any means: they embraced the U2 incident, when the Soviet Union shot down an American spy plane and captured its pilot; the disastrous CIA-sponsored invasion of Cuba at the Bay of Pigs; the building of the Berlin Wall; and the Cuban missile crisis, the most dangerous single moment of the Cold War. But Council speakers conveyed a sense of growing Soviet isolation and weakness, and a feeling that America had matured into its new superpower status and its role as a world leader.

And then came Vietnam. The last half of the decade was dominated—in world diplomacy, in politics, in the streets of America, and in the speeches from the Council stage—by the war in Vietnam and what it was doing to America. In the summer of 1968, the debate over the war exploded into the violence of the Democratic National Convention, played out in Chicago's Grant Park, right at the Council's front door.

Suddenly, America was rethinking, not for the first time, its nature as a nation and its place in the world. When the Council was founded in 1922, the US had retreated into isolationist safety behind its two oceans. In the 1930s, the Council helped prepare the nation to intervene in the war beyond those oceans. In the post-war years, some isolationism remained, but the tone of Council meetings, like the tone across the nation, reflected the reality that America, by default or design, had become the dominant power, with a mission to defend freedom everywhere.

Vietnam called that messianic self-image into question. Council speakers began to ask whether even the mighty and confident US, like lesser nations, had limits that must be obeyed.

Appropriately, Garrick Utley began the questioning. His father, Clifton Utley, the former Council executive director, had insisted in the 1930s that America had an obligation to come to the rescue of the European democracies. In 1965, his son, the Saigon bureau chief for NBC, asked, "How did we ever get into the position of laying our national prestige on the line in a country and for a cause we are not sure is viable?"

By decade's end, Eric Sevareid, the CBS correspondent and commentator, told the Council that the problem lay with the American belief "that freedom is indivisible." He continued,

> "This seemed to be obviously and overwhelmingly true in the 1930s and in Stalin's period of post-war expansion. But if this is an immutable condition of mankind, then our prospects are poor indeed. It would not take very many rents in that common vessel to drown us all. But both peace and freedom have been divisible, coexisting with war and tyranny, most of the time through human history. The world ship of state is designed with many protective bulkheads.
>
> "Our power is vast. But power associated with the Messiah complex and justified by a faith that becomes a dogma, uniformly applied to a world that is, in fact, infinitely varied, this is a danger… We had better think most humbly about this vast power of ours and the ease with which it permits us to intervene almost anywhere, which makes action easier than hard thought."

"I am not an isolationist," Sevareid insisted. But with Vietnam, we had become "badly overextended"—in money, in people, in wisdom. America, an immodest nation, needed modesty and restraint.

None of this was in view when the decade began. If the last half of the decade focused on Vietnam and China, the first half continued to deal mostly with Europe—mostly updates on a relatively static situation. The building of the Berlin Wall in 1960 symbolized the division of Europe, and the Soviet invasion of Czechoslovakia in 1968 cemented it. As Robert F. Byrnes, an East European expert from Indiana University, told the Council, "One of the main consequences [of the Czech crisis] is that the Cold War has been renewed, probably indefinitely as far as you and I can foresee…We don't really have very much hope in the years ahead."

Ten days before John F. Kennedy's inauguration as president in 1961, the Council brought eight CBS foreign correspondents to Chicago for a tour of global problems and trouble spots. As journalistic panels go, it was a galaxy of stars, led by Edward R. Murrow and the team—"Murrow's Boys," as they were known—that he had built over the years.

Peter Kalischer, the Far East correspondent, reported a reservoir of good will toward Americans, leading "people to look forward to us for leadership." David Schoenbrun saw the Algerian struggle for independence from France as a template for nationalistic liberation movements everywhere, which "is going to be one of the great issues facing Mr. Kennedy." Daniel Schorr, in Germany, said, "Russia no longer exerts completely unparalleled and unrivaled leadership" over its allies, and the US, "instead of leading, now leans on our allies," financially and otherwise. Schorr concluded, "There's been a shake-up on both sides."

Alexander Kendrick, in London, noted that Russia and America no longer had a monopoly on nuclear arms. Richard Hottelet, at the

UN, predicted "open civil war in Cuba by the end of the year"—a misreading, shared by the Kennedy Administration, that led to the ill-fated Bay of Pigs attack. Murrow himself enthused prematurely over the incoming Kennedy cabinet; he deemed it "remarkable for its youth" and noted it included more technicians than crusaders—a positive assessment of the presidential advisers who were later known derisively as "the best and the brightest," the men who plunged the nation into Vietnam.

Harlan Cleveland, the assistant secretary of state for international organization affairs and future US ambassador to NATO, told the Council that the West was winning the Cold War and that the US, thrust into world prominence, had matured into steady leadership. Soviet actions "produced a moral revulsion in Europe. By about 1950 the bloom was off the rose. The tide of communism in Western Europe began to ebb. It has been ebbing ever since." Islam and nationalism were blocking Soviet advances in the Middle East and "the sordid story of Dr. Castro and his sell-out to Moscow" had undermined communism prospects in Latin America.

The Soviet Union, Cleveland said, "is half modern and half rural slum." By contrast, the post-war decades "add up to evidence of a maturity which is becoming a dominant motif in American public reaction to each successive crisis."

Cleveland didn't predict the collapse of Soviet communism, but his warning that the erosion of the communist faith in Russia did not mean an end to trouble with that country was prophetic.

"A Soviet Union in a more nationalistic frame of mind could conceivably be as troublesome as a Soviet Union promoting an illusory world revolution of the proletariat," he said. "It would still cling to totalitarian principles; it would still be fearful of the open society… Living at peace with its neighbors will not come easy to a state with so many phobias and neuroses."

Adlai Stevenson, who had chronicled the birth of the UN for the Council over the years, was the US ambassador to the world body when he headlined a lunch in early 1963 to mark, belatedly, the Council's fortieth anniversary. Early euphoria over the UN had subsided into an assessment that it was useful but worked no miracles. Stevenson said,

> *"The UN is not the whole answer to world peace and never was from the day the world divided after the war. It is not a world government. It is admittedly unable to impose any settlement on the great powers against their will, though it can on occasion exercise a potent persuasive force. It is a reflection of the divided world in which we live, but the consensus of its members represents a moral force that cannot be lightly ignored.*
>
> *"The United States has an aim in this world, an aim to build a community of nations, diverse, tolerant, and genuinely independent—but bound together by a sense of common humanity and by a common interest in peace and progress. To build this community, one of the instruments is the UN. It is not a magic lamp. Perhaps it is only a candle in the window. But its spirit is that of community, tolerance, give and take—without which there can be no peace."*

The psychologist Erich Fromm told the Council the Soviet Union was "about the most conservative country anywhere in the world, perhaps with the exception of Spain." He continued,

> *"By 'conservative,' I mean a country in which submission to authority, emphasis on duty, on morality, on family, are the most important values preached and acted upon... The important thing is that we get over the idea that the Russians are still out to conquer the world for communism, when what they really want is exactly what*

the Czarist government wanted, what the British government wanted, namely, to keep their power and, if possible, to enlarge it a little if the price isn't too much."

Fromm's speech excited angry protests from American conservatives who resented being lumped in with the Kremlin. So did a partisan speech by Gilbert Harrison, the liberal editor of the *New Republic*. Harrison had been scheduled to speak on "US Foreign Policy—If Goldwater Becomes President," at a noon luncheon on November 22, 1963. At the same moment, President Kennedy was assassinated in Dallas and the meeting was cancelled.

Harrison came back eleven months later, when Senator Barry Goldwater was running for the presidency. Harrison's views on the Arizona Republican hadn't softened, and several members complained. The Council had to issue a statement confirming its mandate to present "partisan points of view by qualified persons holding these views," such as Harrison. The statement said the Council tried hard to get a conservative speaker to balance him. It invited Clare Boothe Luce, Richard Nixon, William Buckley, Senator William Knowland, and Raymond Moley, a *Newsweek* columnist, but struck out. It asked Goldwater's presidential campaign to name a speaker, but its only suggestion was a Bradley University political scientist too obscure to draw a good audience.

The Council recognized the need to keep its programs balanced but, not for the first or last time, came away "frustrated and disappointed."

In an oral history for the Council, Harriet Welling, a longtime Board member, recalled the Harrison luncheon at the Palmer House when the news of the Kennedy assassination arrived. She was sitting with Bill Mauldin, a Pulitzer Prize-winning cartoonist for the *Sun-Times*, when Kay Field, the former wife of the *Sun-Times* publisher, Marshall Field IV, came over "and spoke to Mauldin, and Bill said to me, 'The president has been shot.'" Edward McDougal, the Council president, adjourned the meeting.

On the way back to Kay Field's apartment, the group dropped Mauldin off at the newspaper, where he drew his classic cartoon, published the next day, of the statue of a mourning Abraham Lincoln at the Lincoln Memorial, slumped over with his head in his hands.

"I said to Bill, 'Mrs. Kennedy is going to want that,'" Welling recalled, and indeed she did.

—

George Ball was an Evanstonian who got his first taste of foreign affairs at Council luncheons in the 1930s. He later became under secretary of state in the Kennedy and Johnson administrations and the leading internal opponent of the two presidents' Vietnam policy. In a thoughtful speech to the Council in 1964, Ball talked about the "responsibilities of a great power," as the US had become.

"The United States today is carrying a large part of the responsibilities of the free world because it must," he said. "If it did not play its present role, many essential responsibilities would not be met at all." It has unique power, he said, but "this power remains effective only because the world knows that we are prepared to use it—and will try to use it wisely."

The burden-sharing debate had begun even then, and Ball said other nations "must be willing to commit [their] share of resources to the solution of common world problems." But for the US, "responsibility in the conduct of foreign affairs is essential to our leadership of the free world…The leader must share with others the task of deciding what to do, or else he finds he is not a leader but a loner. The exercise of power is no different in international affairs: the strong must consult the weak if the strong presume to act on behalf of the weak."

Philip Hauser, a University of Chicago sociologist, looked at the population explosion in 1964 and its impact on world politics. The world population then was 3.2 billion and growing by a billion every twelve or thirteen years. Moreover, most of these new billions would jam into cities, creating "mass frustration, misery, despair, acute poverty, social unrest, [and] political instability." Two of the fastest-growing nations were China and India, one communist and the other relatively free and socialist. The nation that best solves its population problem will have a great effect on the future political and economic course of much of the Third World, Hauser said.

The race between population growth and poverty is especially acute in China, he said. "I wish that some of our statesmen in Congress would learn that…the quickest way to peace with China is to get her an increase in per capita income, so that she, like the USSR, has enough to lose not to fight."

Another frequent Council speaker, D. Gale Johnson, a University of Chicago agriculture economist, looked at the population explosion and saw potential famine. The only solution, he said, was a doubling of land under cultivation or finding new crops to grow. The latter is better, he said, and might be possible, but this "doesn't necessarily mean that it can or will happen." Three years later, the Green Revolution—the dramatic explosion in crop yields in Third World countries through new technologies and new methods of cultivation—emerged in India.

During the Cold War, the Middle East ranked low on most Chicagoans' list of priorities. But William Polk, a policy planner at the State Department, described a time bomb that went off forty years later.

The problem, he said, was the "new men." "The young men who have either gone abroad to study, or who have been stimulated by such subversive propaganda as the American movies, can no longer find their satisfactions within the society in which they were born. They must acquire a great deal more."

He warned if they did "not [find] any possible way into a modern industrial society," they would crowd into the cities and "become an extremely dangerous and violent element in the societies that we are dealing with. This will convert the politics of the Middle East, most of Africa, and South Asia, into something very different from what we have seen to date. This is an extremely widespread problem."

Some Council speakers saw the future clearly, others less so. John Kenneth Galbraith, the Harvard economist, said that poverty could be eliminated only by a guaranteed annual wage—an idea still alive fifty years later, but no closer to realization.

Constantinos Doxiadis, the Greek architect and city planner, had studied Detroit and predicted, by the end of the century, Detroit would "converge with Chicago at Battle Creek. These two cities are going to merge into one big city connected by a corridor which will start in northern Milwaukee, Chicago, Battle Creek, Ann Arbor, Detroit, Toledo, and then Cleveland and Pittsburgh. When it reaches the Appalachian Mountains, it will stop." One year later, the Detroit riots doomed both that city and Doxiadis' dream.

—

Perhaps the first speech the Council heard on Vietnam came in 1962 from its former executive director, Carter Davidson, who had just been there and said the US was winning the fight. He acknowledged, "This is a dirty war, and we are fighting in a dirty way so that we can be sure of winning it."

Neighboring Laos would be collateral damage, Davidson said. "Laos is just about the end of the world. There are people there who have not even seen the wheel, and they are not politically aware enough to care what kind of government they have. Frankly, they are not worth saving." Davidson's disdain foreshadowed America's Laos policy, such as it was, in the coming decade. From 1964 to 1973, American planes dropped more than two million tons of ordnance on Laos, mostly to disrupt the Ho Chi Minh Trail, making that country the most heavily bombed in history. Some of the bombs detonated on impact, but others continue to explode to this day, killing and maiming thousands of persons, half of them children.

General Maxwell D. Taylor, an architect of the early US intervention strategy in Vietnam and later an ambassador to Saigon, was equally optimistic, if less blunt, when he spoke to the Council in 1964.

Like many supporters of the war, Taylor linked Vietnamese nationalism to international communism. America's goal there, he said, was to "give an emerging country the right of choice of independence or communist enslavement." To achieve this, "We reluctantly introduced American ground forces to supplement the Vietnamese." As a result, "We clearly have the initiative on the ground for the first time in several months…We are moving in a direction which promises success."

Garrick Utley, who made his name as a Saigon correspondent, had a similar, if more tentative, take. "The most important development in Vietnam in the past ten years was, of course, the American decision to escalate the American commitment." This has "blunted or neutralized the Viet Cong army…We are getting the first tentative signs of a military stalemate. We are not winning in Vietnam, we are not winning militarily, but are not losing as we were very rapidly just a few months ago."

The Viet Cong are nationalists first and communists second, Utley said. "They think they can keep fighting, and this is what they are doing, without negotiation—that sooner or later our patience will become exhausted, and we will give up. They may be right. We don't know now."

In 1965, French President Charles de Gaulle, chafing against American leadership, began to pull France out of NATO activities. William Stoneman, the London correspondent for the *Daily News*, told the Council that NATO was a bulwark against World War III. "NATO is the kind of thing that people dreamed about," he said. "Its very existence is enough to bring tears to the eyes of anybody like myself who saw how horrible the effects were of our non-participation in such an alliance either before 1914 or before 1939. And yet this great, unprecedented deterrent to world war General de Gaulle today is setting out to destroy or to undermine."

Stoneman's colleague, the Paris correspondent Paul Ghali, described de Gaulle as driven only by "his fundamental urge to keep France independent." The Cold War between Russia and America gave the French president a chance to establish France, and a Western Europe led by France, as an independent third power. De Gaulle opposed US policy in Vietnam, Ghali said, not because it was bad policy in itself, but because "it handicaps all his efforts to expand France's economic and politics influence in the Far East."

Barbara Ward, the British economist, returned to the Council to argue that the US was in Vietnam to fight for a principle—that the fate of nations should not be decided by outside force—but that, "in the light of Asian history, the least suitable power to uphold this principle in Asia is a large, white, capitalist, Western power." American forces can do this, she said, but at the cost of "the endless proliferation of violence." A better solution would be negotiations that transferred the American role to an international force.

Senator John Tower, the Republican senator from Texas, said world leadership required the US to "maintain our defense perimeter as far from our own shores as possible and as close to the enemy's shores as possible. Essentially this is why we are in Vietnam today." American soldiers have "turned the tide of battle in that unhappy land," he said, but "we're going to have to commit still more American ground troops."

Any fear of Chinese retaliation was groundless, Tower said. China did not have the ability to intervene and besides, if it did, "we could with virtual impunity bomb China's industry out of existence."

To Tower, it was all about the domino theory. "Should Southeast Asia fall to China, she would then be free to work her evil will on Burma, India, Pakistan, and ultimately the African countries."

—

All these issues—American power, nationalism, the communist threat, Vietnam—came to a head at a debate between two of the nation's leading political scientists, Hans Morgenthau of the University of Chicago and Zbigniew Brzezinski of Columbia University. Brzezinski, later the national security adviser in the Carter Administration, argued, "Without our engagement, without our involvement, the world, particularly the Third World, will quickly degenerate into international chaos. The United States, in relationship to that world, being the only global power, is today a stabilizing force, and that is precisely its historical role."

Morgenthau responded, "It is a complete distortion of the actual situation to say that because the United States is the most powerful nation on the earth, it has a kind of global hold inevitably, imposed upon it by some kind of unknown and invisible Providence, in truth of course imposed upon ourselves by our own government, by ourselves, and therefore we can do what we want, throughout the world." In fact, he said, the US had vital interests somewhere and secondary or trivial interests elsewhere. It was "a lack of discrimination, of judgment, that the United States puts…a major portion of its resources in a situation in Vietnam, which is at best of secondary interest to the United States." Because of this policy, Morgenthau claimed, "we are forced to oppose revolutions throughout the world."

Brzezinski retorted that Vietnam was important because "The fact that we have made a commitment in itself somewhat transforms its importance…If we now ignore it, of course no other nation will take very seriously our commitment."

Morgenthau got in the last word: "If West Germany should become communist, it would be a major defeat for the United States. But if South Vietnam should go communist, it would be deplorable, but it would not be a major defeat."

—

A steady run of speakers, from Washington and from Vietnam, continued the debate. *Time* magazine still supported the war. John Steele, one of its Washington correspondents, told the Council in 1966, "Not even the harshest critics of our policy suggest, as they did a year ago, that we are over-extended in Vietnam, that we are likely to be driven out, and that we are embarked on a war we can't possibly win." Vu Van Thai, South Vietnam's ambassador to Washington, blamed the war on China, but said, "The present crisis paves the way toward real stability." U. Alexis Johnson, the deputy under secretary of state, said that North Vietnam was the aggressor and the war had "nothing to do with liberation." The US had to fight, he said, because "Aggression is no less aggression if it is taking place in what seems a distant Vietnam."

Wayne Morse, the Democratic senator from Oregon and an early opponent of America's Vietnam policy, told the Council the war had "demonstrated the limitations of force in general as a means of furthering and maintaining political objectives." American bombing of the north had done nothing to stop infiltration into the south or to destroy the will of the North Vietnamese. "In fact, many evidences come out of North Vietnam that our bombing has served to enhance the determination of North Vietnam to fight back."

Basically, Morse said, "We have adopted the rationalizations of the white man's burden and all the justifications for military domination that those rationalizations conceal."

With revolt growing on American campuses, the Council co-sponsored a panel on the draft that brought together Milton Friedman, the conservative University of Chicago economist, Senator Edward Kennedy, the liberal senator from Massachusetts, a young Illinois Republican congressman named Donald Rumsfeld, and General Lewis Hershey, the head of the Selective Service Administration, the nation's draft board. Friedman and Kennedy, coming from opposite ideologies, agreed that the draft should be scrapped. Kennedy urged a lottery to replace the draft while Friedman called for an all-volunteer army. "The use of compulsion is repugnant in our society," Friedman said, and violated the concept of freedom.

The Chicago debate was a milestone in the death of the draft. Participants took the arguments back to Washington. President Lyndon Johnson favored the draft but his successor, Richard Nixon, wanted to end it. By 1971, it was gone.

Arthur Goldberg, the Chicago lawyer who went from the Supreme Court to become President Johnson's ambassador to the UN, defended the administration's policy in Vietnam. At the same time, he defended the university students who picketed his speech, arguing, "We will emerge from the current debate about Vietnam stronger, so long as we do not equate dissent with disloyalty."

Roger Hilsman, a former assistant secretary of state and a critic of the war, said that communism in Vietnam could not be defeated with an American invasion of North Vietnam. "It will not get us out of the quagmire but only into a bigger quagmire with a great risk of confrontation with China," he said.

Robert W. Barnett, a deputy assistant secretary of state, claimed that American strength in Vietnam had led to the bloody purge—more than a million persons died—of communists in Indonesia, created greater confidence throughout Asia, and even led to the passion of the Cultural Revolution in China. In the same month, George McTurnan Kahin, a Southeast Asian expert from Cornell University, told the Council that American power in Vietnam was killing civilians, destroying villages, and alienating the people the US needed as allies. "Our pacification program has failed in the past," Kahin said, "and is certainly continuing to fail."

Dean Rusk, the former secretary of state and an architect of the Vietnam war, spoke on the eve of the Vietnam Moratorium, a massive world-wide demonstration against the war. Rusk gave a nod to free speech but said, "There is a price to be paid." The protests would only stiffen Hanoi's refusal to negotiate a settlement, he said.

Senator Frank Church disagreed. The Idaho Democrat, a future chairman of the Senate Committee on Foreign Relations, said that American policy in Vietnam "is a showcase of bankruptcy, a hopeless war fought for insubstantial stakes." In fact, he said, the US policy in Vietnam and the Soviet invasion of Czechoslovakia revealed a mutual "neurotic sense of insecurity…In their foreign policies, the two superpowers have taken on a remarkable resemblance. Concerned primarily with the preservation of their own hegemonies, they have become, in their respective spheres, defenders of the status quo against the pressures of revolutionary upheaval in which each perceives the secret hand of the other." Church called for a different policy, "that we abstain hereafter from military intervention in the internal affairs of other countries under any circumstances short of a clear and certain danger to our national security."

William Bundy, another architect of the war who had just stepped down as assistant secretary of state, defended the war in a speech to the Council. But on the same trip, he met privately with the Committee on Foreign and Domestic Affairs, a Council group for young leaders who held off-the-record meetings with visiting speakers. What he heard that night was the unanimous opposition to the war of the young Chicagoans, all budding members of the city's establishment. David Rosso, one of the Committee's leaders, talked with Bundy later, when he was editor of *Foreign Affairs*. "I never imagined a meeting of young leaders who were unanimous against the war," Bundy told Rosso. According to Bundy, the meeting led him to begin to reevaluate his stance on the war.

Some Council speakers spoke in measured tones. Others let it rip. David Schoenbrun, the CBS correspondent, was one of the latter. He began by declaring the Vietnam War "illegal, immoral, un-American, un-winnable...In Vietnam we are pursuing very narrow, very selfish, very stupid purposes which are in fact damaging the United States itself more than they are damaging even Vietnam, which is being destroyed."

Echoing Sevareid and Morgenthau, Schoenbrun declared, "Interventionism is the most extreme form of isolationism." An isolationist, he said, "is a man who prefers his own village, who doesn't want to mix with other people. What happens when that kind of man discovers that the world is too much with him, and he cannot keep the world out, he decides the only thing he can do is to make the world over in the image of his village. Then he'll be at home everywhere. That's the meaning of interventionism."

Schoenbrun, speaking shortly after the 1968 Soviet invasion of Czechoslovakia, had no more regard for Moscow. "That rape of Czechoslovakia was a signal of the doom of the Soviet empire. It was a sign of Russian weakness, not of Russian strength." He continued,

> "I have seen beginning in the '30s a great push to bring America into the world, to make America accept a role as a world power, as it should have, as it must, today and tomorrow. But I have seen us overdo it, as we have so many times, watching us go from total isolationism to total interventionism, and that must stop! We must become truly internationalist, not interventionist, and there is a very different thing."

At the time, the US refused to recognize Communist China, recognizing instead the nationalist regime on Formosa, or Taiwan.

"Totally incoherent. Maybe I ought to whisper it," he said, and then did whisper, "There is a China. And since the Chinese are notoriously and devilishly cunning, they've located it—in China. To the despair of the Department of State. Yes! There is a China. It's in China. Not in Formosa."

In fact, China, and what America should do about it, remained a constant topic. Max Freedman, a Washington correspondent for the *Manchester Guardian* (as *The Guardian* newspaper was then known), called for an "unfettered review of Chinese-American relations [to] break the bondage of dogma that has so grievously fettered American policy since 1949."

Mark Gayn, a China-born analyst for the *Toronto Star*, told the Council, "There is both progress and weakness in China." Gayn, speaking in 1965, said the progress extended to agriculture: "In all my recent travels in China, I never saw starving people." This was just after the "Great Leap Forward" years, in which some thirty-six million persons starved. He also portrayed a China living in ignorance of the outside world and feverishly industrializing—but with outmoded equipment that was immediately obsolete.

Many speakers agreed Communist China was basically a nationalist and defensive power, with no interest in expanding abroad. Charles Taylor, a columnist for the Toronto *Globe and Mail*, said China wanted influence over its neighbors, communist or otherwise, but not control. Its main aim, he said, was "to get rid of US bases that ring China, in South Korea, Japan, Okinawa, and all the way to Thailand." Most of those bases remain today.

Edgar Snow, a journalist who had interviewed Mao Tse-tung, said Mao told him China would not intervene in Vietnam, and "would go to war with the United States only if Chinese territory was directly attacked." But Mao said China would not restore normal diplomatic relations with Washington or join the UN "as long as we maintain a protectorate over Taiwan."

These analyses seemed to be sinking in. In 1966, the Council held a special meeting on "The Challenge of Communist China." More than 2,000 people attended, and the Council took the opportunity to pass out a questionnaire on US policy in Asia. No fewer than 85 percent of the audience favored diplomatic recognition of Communist China. Fifty-one percent opposed US policies in Vietnam, 60 percent opposed bombing of the North and 80 percent favored negotiations to end the war. In other words, Council members opposed the war two years before the anti-war movement filled the streets of Chicago, and they favored recognition of the Maoist government six years before President Nixon made his epochal trip to Beijing.

Japan, that misunderstood nation, was explained by two correspondents based there. Japan might be an American ally, but not in Vietnam, according to Sam Jameson of the *Chicago Tribune*. "We expect Japan to look at things the way we look at them," Jameson said, "in terms of anti-communism, of an international communist threat, in terms of keeping the free world on top. But both the free world and the communist world are 'they' to the Japanese." Japan, unlike Vietnam, faced no real danger from its small communist party, so the Japanese have "reached the logical—from their point of view—conclusion that as long as there is no internal threat of communists seizing control of Japan, there is no threat of communism to Japan."

Richard Halloran of the *New Times*, speaking on "The Illusion of Westernized Japan," reported that Japan takes on the "accoutrements" of the West but not reality, which "is not out front for everyone to see but is behind the scenes." Ostensibly a democracy, Japan is run by an establishment that operates by consensus and "is obliged to be paternal and benevolent. The people, in turn, are obliged to show respect and to be obedient." The economy, ostensibly free-market, was actually "the world's most deftly guided economy," especially in foreign trade, he claimed.

Not all Council speeches were on war, peace, and communism. And not all went off as planned.

Alec Gorshel, a former member of parliament from South Africa and a self-styled opponent of apartheid there, called for Black representation in Parliament. But he defended the rule by the white minority, because whites there had "a fear of being swamped, of being plowed under by a Black majority." For this reason, any party backing a policy that might lead eventually to a Black-led government hadn't "the slightest hope of winning an election."

Barbara Ward, returning to the Council two months after the first manned landing on the moon, pleaded for restraint on the headlong rush of science and technology, and for a halving of the US defense budget, to save "this small, shining, beautiful, blue planet, which is all there is holding human life in the entire cosmos." Life depends on the fragile environment of the earth, just then so clearly seen from space, "and if we bitch them up, my friends, that is it. Let's face it, this is precisely what we are doing."

One potentially exotic speaker never made it to the Council podium. Greek actress Melina Mercouri, the star of *Never on Sunday* and an opponent of the Greek colonels' dictatorship, demanded half the proceeds from her 1968 appearance, which she planned to give to the United States Committee for the Democracy of Greece. The Council balked and cancelled her speech.

One major speech made headlines for the wrong reason. French President Georges Pompidou, on an official visit to the US, came to Chicago to speak at a Council dinner at the Palmer House. It was a delicate time, because of France's Middle East policies and its relations with Israel. Memories of the Six-Day War remained fresh. US-French relations were tense. France had not yet officially acknowledged the role its wartime Vichy government played in the Holocaust. Most immediately, France had just sold 110 Mirage jets to Muammar Gaddafi's Libya.

When Pompidou and his wife arrived at the Palmer House, they were met by 10,000 pro-Israeli demonstrators shouting, "Poo Poo, Pompidou." The demonstrators were nonviolent, but at least six of them jumped in front of the Pompidous as they entered the hotel.

Pompidou was furious. His speech, on environmental issues, went virtually unreported. He called the demonstration "a stain on the face of America," accused Israel of using its religious ties abroad to further its policies, and said Chicago police were "accomplices" of the crowd that "insulted me and my wife." Police officials pointed out that the demonstration was peaceful. Parisian newspapers took the Chicagoans' side, noting that peaceful demonstrations are part of democracy and that Pompidou should have been neither surprised nor angry.

President Richard Nixon, anxious to keep relations from getting worse, flew to New York, Pompidou's next stop, to apologize to Pompidou for the "discourteous and disrespectful" demonstration. But Pompidou cancelled a meeting in New York with Jewish leaders and with the Council on Foreign Relations, perhaps confusing that New York body with the Chicago Council.

—

Charles E. Bohlen was a veteran diplomat and one of the "wise men" who framed America's Cold War policy. He was about to retire when he returned to a Council for a speech that was an overview of American foreign policy from 1929 to 1969. It was both a defense of that policy and a counterpoint to Sevareid's fears of national overreach.

In 1929, he said, isolation from the world's affairs ruled Congress as it did Chicago in those day. "Foreign affairs…did not play a large part in the public life of the nation's capital." But by the end of World War II, there were only two great powers, and Washington realized, "Wherever there was a threat to an important segment of the world, this was a matter of concern not only to the immediate countries involved but also the United States. And this is really the beginning of the post-war policies of the United States."

"This is what history presented us with, and this is what we rose and met," Bohlen said. He ended with a "tribute to the people of this country. To respond to a challenge of which they could in the best of circumstances be relatively dimly aware, of being willing to pay the price which it costs to stand up, and to help preserve part of the world in a degree of freedom, to really do a series of unselfish acts." In the future, "I'm quite convinced that the American people will not recoil from the responsibilities which have been thrust on them by history, and will meet them with the same maturity and good sense that they have met the extraordinary changes in their circumstances in the last forty years."

—

Beyond its money-making charter flights, the Council began to reach out to new audiences, especially in Chicago's business community. For many years after World War II, leaders of Chicago's businesses mostly remained an elusive prey for the Council. The reason, according to former Council President Melvin Brorby, was the continuing toxic power of Colonel McCormick and the *Tribune*. Much of the Midwest and Chicago may have moved beyond isolationism, but its business leaders still feared the *Tribune*. Brorby said when he was president, in 1953 and 1956, "I tried to bring those people into the Council. They were never in it and an awful lot of them had been scared by the *Chicago Tribune* of the words 'foreign' and 'international.'"

"The idea was that the Council was a leftist institution, primarily democratic," recalled one of Brorby's successors, a lawyer named Edward McDougal. "This was its image among businessmen at the time, that it was a liberal institution of questionable principles. And of course, the *Tribune* never passed an opportunity to build up this picture."

There was another reason why the city's CEOs stayed away, according to Richard Templeton, the president from 1958 to 1960. The Council, he said, "had too much of an image in the community of an organization dominated by women from Lake Shore Drive or Lake Forest, who had nice luncheons at the Palmer House so that everyone could see their new hats…and the press coverage was more likely on the women's pages than on the editorial or business pages."

The Council broke this barrier in 1961 when it formed the Chicago Committee, with 220 charter members, made up of the city's senior and most influential business leaders. McDougal persuaded David M. Kennedy, the CEO of Continental Illinois Bank and a future treasury secretary in the Nixon Administration, to be the first chairman of the Chicago Committee, and his prominence drew in the other business leaders. Membership was by invitation only. All speeches and meetings were off-the-record, so "the critical issues of the day can be discussed in the company of known and respected associates." The first speaker was Secretary of State Dean Rusk, whom McDougal enticed to Chicago by saying it was an opportunity to bury the remnants of the isolationism that lingered in the city.

The Chicago Committee was deliberately elitist, that is, it catered to corporate presidents and chairmen—no deputies allowed—and businessmen who were socially allergic to Democrats and women. It included some token Democrats, including Adlai Stevenson, but no women, and drove the point home by meeting mostly at the Chicago Club, which barred women in those days. Some years later, in 1976, Templeton said, "It was set up for a purpose and I think that it has achieved that purpose. But for us to continue on a male chauvinist pig program like this, in this day and age, is insane."

The Chicago Committee stayed all-male until 1978, then began to accept women members. The Chicago Club allowed women as guests, but barred them from membership until 1987, when it invited Hanna Gray, the president of the University of Chicago, to join.

In deference to the business leaders' fear of the *Tribune*, the Committee had an odd structure. It was both in the Council and not in it, a sort of "club within a club," as Templeton called it. Officially, it was autonomous, with its own board of directors and, unlike the Council, offered membership by invitation only. But it was clearly a Council creation and remained affiliated with the Council, which provided meeting space and lined up speakers.

As the Council publication *Notes on World Events* put it, "The idea behind the Chicago Committee was conceived by the Council: it is one in which the Council can take justifiable pride. However, it must be emphasized that the Chicago Committee is completely autonomous and organized by eight of Chicago's outstanding professional and business leaders, only three of whom, coincidentally, are members of the Council." The confusion was deliberate. Alex Seith, later a Board president, said it was "conceived of and sold to the business community as a very exclusive, business-only, highest-level-executives type of thing that would have absolute minimal contact with the Council."

The Committee had two stated purposes: to give high-level briefings to civic leaders, some of whom might end up in government jobs, and to give the Midwest a bigger role in American foreign policy. But as *Notes on World Events* made clear, it had other purposes: to raise the prestige and visibility of the Council, to entice top-drawer speakers, and, not least, to make money. At the time, the Council focused on some forty corporations for donations, but "efforts in this direction have produced rather disappointing results." The Chicago Committee "gave something of specific benefit" to civic leaders, including executives of those same corporations. "It is reasonable to conclude that our appeals for financial support should be more fruitful."

Over the years, the Chicago Committee attracted a roster of top-drawer speakers, some drawn by its off-the-record format. A private memo to CIA Director William Colby in 1974 urged him to accept the Committee's invitation to speak. "This is the most prestigious group of top industrial and business leaders in Chicago," the memo said. "The group is conservatively oriented and probably benignly inclined toward us. The confidential nature of your briefing will be respected."

The Council also became the Chicago sponsor of the national Great Decisions program, run by the Foreign Policy Association and devoted to public education on foreign affairs. Young adult audiences grew, and the Speakers Bureau doubled its activity. The Council moved into larger forums and conferences. It hosted an all-day State Department Regional Foreign Policy Briefing Conference, a program on US-South African economic relations, day-long conferences on foreign affairs for Chicago-area high school students and their teachers, an affiliation with the University of Chicago for non-credit courses on the Soviet economy, and even special programs for foreign doctors at Cook County Hospital.

—

But if the Council brought the world to Chicago, it was deaf to the crisis in race relations that disfigured the city itself. The assassination of Dr. Martin Luther King, Jr. in 1968 ignited rage and rioting in cities across the nation. Some of the worst violence took place in Chicago, which still bears the scars fifty years later. But the Council literally paid no attention. In the months after the riots, it held no programs on racial issues, sponsored no studies, convened no panels, made no attempt to link the crisis in America's inner cities to the nation's image abroad.

"It never occurred to anybody," one veteran of the 1960s Council recalled. "It never entered anybody's mind. We didn't have a sense of the Council as a place that could reach out to domestic issues, even if they impacted foreign affairs."

There was one exception—the Committee on Foreign and Domestic Affairs. Founded as a sort of a farm team for the Chicago Committee, this group of junior leaders used Council facilities but considered itself semi-independent, with membership by invitation only and meetings held in private homes. This committee, more attuned to racial issues, brought in Black speakers such as the Reverend Jesse Jackson and Renault Robinson, a Chicago policeman who founded the African American Patrolman's League.

The Council's racial myopia lasted for a year, until a new executive director, William Graham Cole, took over. Cole spent barely two years in the job and left a lean legacy, but he did see the King riots as a wake-up call to the Council's comfortable and mostly white membership.

"Our range has been thus far been limited to a relatively affluent, well educated, upper-middle-, and upper-class clientele," he said. "We have done little with our Black neighbors, with blue collar workers, and with individuals under twenty. Blacks and union members are presently voters and the young people soon will be."

The most ambitious Council foray into the inner city was the Young Ambassadors program, begun in 1969, to send about a dozen teenagers, mostly African Americans, to Europe for home stays that lasted several weeks. According to reports back to the Council, the cultural clash was severe. The Black Americans were treated as curiosities by white Europeans. Some of the teenagers coped well, others not so well. The program lasted about three years and was quietly axed by Cole's successor, John Rielly.

In 1965, the Council resumed its television programs on Channel 11, Chicago's public TV station. They lasted only one year. As the Executive Committee minutes noted, "Timely issues were discussed, [but] the program tended to generate little excitement."

Various committees discussed ways to make Council programs more relevant, possibly by tying a year's programming to a theme, such as the limits of US military power or the growing gap between rich and poor nations, topics that resonate fifty years later.

"We are no longer a comfortable little Council," Robert E. Wieczorowski, the new president of the Executive Committee, told the annual meeting in 1965. "This is the largest Council in the United States. We should be one of the major open forums in the world."

But it was achieving neither the breadth of audience nor the depth of programs that it needed to educate the public while making its voice heard, Wieczorowski said. More than half of the programs drew audiences of between fifty and three hundred people—too big to allow intensive study, too small to have any broad impact. He suggested the Council aim for a handful of blockbuster programs, drawing a thousand people or more, supplemented by small study groups of thirty people or fewer for "discussion, study and specialization."

In New York, the Council on Foreign Relations drew small prestige audiences but made no attempt to reach the general public, while the Foreign Policy Association drew bigger audiences, but made no impact on policy. Wieczorowski said the Chicago Council had to do both but needed "an overall program which recognizes the need for both depth and breadth."

In 1968, Wieczorowski was succeeded by one of the most controversial figures in Council history, a dynamic and very ambitious

Susan F. Hibbard and William Browne Hale, co-founders of the Chicago Council

Former French premier Georges Clemenceau, left, and General John Pershing when Clemenceau addressed the Council in 1922

Longtime Council leader Walter Lichtenstein was chairman of the Council Board from 1933 to 1935

Melvin Brorby, longtime Council leader and Board chairman from 1953 to 1956

Two Council titans. Melvin Brorby, Board chairman from 1953 to 1956, pins a boutonniere on Adlai Stevenson, Board chairman from 1935 to 1937

Adlai Stevenson, left, former Illinois governor and Council Board chairman from 1935- to 1937 with Richard Templeton, Board chairman from 1958 to 1960

Clifton Utley, the Council's executive director from 1931 to 1942, outside the Council office

A member browses the Council Pamphlet Shop in the 1940s

Indian prime minister Jawaharlal Nehru with Council Board president Meyer Kestnbaum, 1949

Novelist Pearl Buck speaking with Council members in 1951

Louise Wright, the Council's executive director from 1942 to 1952, with Eleanor Roosevelt, 1947

Carter Davidson, the Council's executive director from 1953 to 1960

Ghanaian president Kwame Nkrumah and Council president Richard Templeton at press conference, 1959

Six former Council presidents at the 40th anniversary party in 1962. From left, Clay Judson, Victor Elting, Daggett Harvey, Adlai Stevenson, Walter Lichtenstein and Meyer Kestnbaum

Alex Seith, president of the Council's Executive Committee from 1968 to 1971

UN Secretary General U Thant addressing the Council in 1971

Edmond Eger, Council executive director from 1960 to 1969, and new Council president John Rielly, 1971

Israeli Foreign Minister Abba Eban, a regular speaker to Council audiences, in 1972

West German chancellor Willy Brandt, left, with Council president John Rielly in 1973

Senator Joseph R. Biden, left, at the Council's Atlantic Conference, 1974

Henry Kissinger with Margot Pritzker at a reception following his remarks in 1976

Under secretary of state George Ball with Council leaders Richard Thomas and Herman Smith, 1976

Boris Yeltsin, the future president of Russia, (second from right) with Council hosts Kenneth and Harle Montgomery, and Yeltsin's translator, 1989

Former British prime minister Margaret Thatcher addressing the Council in 1991

James Baker, former secretary of state, with Council member David Rosso in 1992

Polish president Lech Walesa addressing the Council in 1991

Former Soviet president Mikhail Gorbachev and his wife Raisa, with Council Board chairman John Bryan, 1992

Former president Jimmy Carter with Council Board chairman Duane Burnham, 1997

Former secretary of state Madeleine Albright with Council president Marshall Bouton in 2003

President Barack Obama at the Council's Global Food Security Symposium in Washington in 2012

2019 Global Leadership Award Honoree David Miliband with Council Board co-chairs Leah Joy Zell and Samuel C. Scott III, 2019

Council president Ivo Daalder with former defense secretary James Mattis and former Council chairman Lester Crown, 2019

Former vice president Joseph R. Biden speaking to the Council, 2017

young lawyer named Alex Seith. At thirty-four, Seith (rhymes with teeth) was almost as young as Adlai Stevenson had been when he was first elected Council president. Seith, in fact, saw himself in the Stevensonian mold. According to Chicagoans who knew him, he knew that Stevenson used his Council presidency as an entrée into public life and a springboard to a political career. Seith planned to do the same. His dream was to be a senator. Already active in Democratic politics, he felt that he, like Stevenson, could use the Council to achieve political glory.

Seith quickly took over the Council. Eger was still executive director, but Seith sidelined him and usurped his duties, spending three or four days a week at the Council and giving direct orders to the staff. Eger, undermined, quit within a year. Richard Nixon had just become president, leaving many highly qualified, Democratic foreign policy experts looking for a job. But provincialism prevailed. The Executive Committee appointed Oscar Chute, a retired high school superintendent in suburban Evanston, to lead the search committee, and it picked another suburbanite, William Graham Cole, the president of Lake Forest College in suburban Chicago.

Persons involved with the Council at the time unanimously rate Cole a "disaster," a "heavy drinker, elitist, and pompous." Melvin Brorby called him "a complete mistake" who, among his other sins, spent $5,000 to renovate his office.

Seith continued to run the Council, forcing Cole to check every move with him. "What he really was proposing was that I should not blow my nose without his specific permission," Cole recalled in a later interview. "It was really demeaning and humiliating."

"Alex never wanted me, but he never said that," a bitter Cole recalled. "He kept his own counsel very, very skillfully, very shrewdly in this way. But he never really wanted me, and I had not been sitting in this office twenty-four hours before he started his little campaign to get me out of there, and I'm not alone in that conviction."

Cole was fired in early 1971 but was allowed to stay on for six more months. Until mid-year, he sat in his office every day, doing nothing.

Seith served three years as Council president but was eased out in 1971. His successors were Richard A. Hoefs and Herman "Dutch" Smith, remembered by Council veterans as leading business figures and very decent men. Seith kept his Council stationery and used the Speakers Bureau to promote himself around Illinois, but his days of dominance at the Council were over. In 1978, he nearly achieved his dream when he ran a strong senatorial campaign but lost to the Republican incumbent, Charles Percy. Six years later, he tried again but lost the Democratic primary to Paul Simon, who went on to defeat Percy. Seith died in 2010, virtually forgotten.

Under Eger and Seith, the Council took the first steps toward a professional staff. Until 1967, few Council staff members had real foreign policy expertise. In that year, the Council hired a former diplomat named Henry Cox as its director of education. When he left in 1970, it brought in David Mellon, a worldly and cultured educator who had been directing an American college in Switzerland, as assistant executive director and program director.

But in 1971, the Council still needed an executive director. Eger was gone and Cole was going. This time, the search committee searched beyond Chicago and found a young foreign policy expert named John E. Rielly, a native Minnesotan who had worked on foreign affairs with Vice President Hubert Humphrey.

Rielly got the job. As Seith recalled in a later interview, Rielly was "young enough to have energy and old enough to have contacts." Most important, he was the first executive director hired from outside Chicago as a foreign policy professional. He came to Chicago expecting to stay ten years. Instead, he led the Council for thirty years and shaped the next era in the Council's history.

Chapter 6

The Rielly Years

E D EGER DID WHAT HE WAS HIRED TO DO—HE SAVED THE Chicago Council from bankruptcy and left it in solid financial shape. It presented solid programs on foreign affairs, but its focus was as much on charter flights to foreign lands as on the lands themselves. He never had the university contacts, especially at the University of Chicago, nor the camaraderie with foreign policy circles in New York and Washington enjoyed by earlier leaders, such as Clifton Utley and Louise Wright. If the Council thrived financially under his leadership, it languished intellectually. It was the biggest and most important world affairs council outside the east coast, but it had lost its dominance of the diplomatic debate, in Chicago and the Midwest.

John Rielly had bigger ambitions and, in the three decades that he led the Council, largely fulfilled them. As he recalled later, "My goal at the start was to make the Council a force and an actor, a member of the American foreign policy establishment. I wanted to help the United States in its relationship with other parts of the world.

"Until the late 1970s, the American foreign policy establishment was centered on New York, Washington, and Cambridge. By the

1980s, we had a serious organization in Chicago that was part of this establishment." This, Rielly said, was his main achievement.

When Rielly came, the lucrative charter flight program still existed and there was money in the bank—so much that he hired few fundraisers. Over the years he increased the budget but acknowledged that, with vigorous fundraising, he could have done more.

But he unquestionably raised the Council's game. If he kept membership fees low and ran a tight and lean organization, he also used his global contacts and international funding to create a panoply of elite programs: private seminars, youth exchanges, and the Atlantic Conferences, which gave the Council a new and higher global profile.

A former Board member, recalling the early Rielly years, said, "There's no comparison between the Council programs before and after John came. He really got the place moving. He was the first one who had the contacts and background from prior employment to be the lead guy in attracting good people to talk to us. He was very good at dealing with important people. He knew that the Council had to be useful to important people in Chicago.

"Under John, the Council was viewed as more serious."

Rielly left the Midwest as a college student, not planning to return. He studied at the London School of Economics and got his doctorate at Harvard University, then went to Washington to work for the Kennedy Administration's Alliance for Progress, a program to build economic ties between the US and Latin America. A year later, he became foreign policy advisor to Senator Hubert Humphrey, a fellow Minnesotan, and kept that job when Humphrey became vice president and, in 1968, the Democratic nominee for president. Richard Nixon, aided by the Vietnam War, kept Humphrey out of the White House and put Rielly out of a job.

Had Humphrey won, "there's some possibility that I might not have ended up in Chicago at that time," Rielly recalled later. Instead, he went to New York to work in the Office of European International Affairs at the Ford Foundation, then run by President Kennedy's former national security adviser, McGeorge Bundy, whom Rielly had known at Harvard.

A University of Chicago institution called the Adlai Stevenson Institute of International Affairs received a grant from the Ford Foundation. Rielly spent two months in Chicago overseeing the project and meeting Chicagoans. Two years later, when the Council fired William Graham Cole, Rielly, then thirty-eight years old, had Chicago contacts and got the executive director's job.

The *Tribune* gave Rielly a proper Chicago welcome. "The Chicago Council sticks to its pro-Democratic ways," George Tagge, Colonel McCormick's journalistic hatchet man, wrote, noting that Adlai Stevenson had once held the same job and suggesting that Rielly might be added to "the presidential dark horse list." (Actually, Stevenson had been the Council Board president, not the executive director; at the time, that was Clifton Utley.) Tagge also misquoted Rielly as saying the Council should "directly influence" American foreign policy and wrote that Stevenson's pre-war advocacy of interventionism "turned into a nightmare for millions." In post-war Chicago, old grudges died hard.

Rielly, though, brought with him more than a decade's worth of contacts in foreign policy circles from Washington to Boston, and used them to link Chicago to the wider world.

The Ford Foundation had started the Atlantic Conferences, a series of biennial meetings invariably held in lush surroundings that brought together about fifty leaders from North America, South America, and Europe—Africans were not invited for another thirty years—for an off-the-record discussion of common economic and political problems. Ford ran the first two conferences without much success; in 1970, the Foundation asked Rielly and the Council to take them over.

The conferences became an attempt to spread the Council's name in the transatlantic halls of power. The fifty participants included a bare sprinkling of Chicagoans. The other guests were senators, members of parliaments, top journalists, commentators, think tank experts, and foreign ministry officials.

Rielly was a gifted talent scout. Under Ford, the average attendee at the Atlantic Conferences was sixty-nine years old. Rielly ruled that no one over fifty would be invited and used the conferences to spot and court rising leaders. Helmut Kohl was the forty-year-old minister president, or governor, of the German province of Rhineland-Palatinate when Rielly invited him to an early conference. Later, as the chancellor of Germany for sixteen years, he spoke to the Council three times and, in 1988, engineered a $3 million grant from the German Konrad Adenauer Foundation for European Policy Studies.

Later, in the 1980s, he spotted George Robertson, a rough-hewn Scot who got his start in politics protesting the basing of American nuclear submarines in Scotland's Holy Loch. Using the German grant, Rielly had set up a Young Leader Exchange program with Europe, and Robertson, by that time a Laborite member of Parliament, took part. Invitations to the Atlantic Conferences followed. Robertson went on to become British defense minister and then, as Lord Robertson, the secretary general of NATO. Like Kohl, he became a grateful and frequent Council speaker.

So did a very junior senator named Joseph Biden, whom Rielly invited to the 1974 Atlantic Conference in Taormina, Sicily, on the suggestion of Senator Frank Church, who was co-chair of the conference. It was one of Biden's first international outings; he went on to become an expert in foreign policy and, forty-seven years later, as president, the man in charge of reshaping America's place in the world.

Over the years, participants at the conferences included, besides Kohl, three presidents of Germany, two Argentinian presidents, one president each from Chile and Brazil, and a galaxy of foreign and finance ministers, parliamentary leaders, and prominent professors. Most took part before rising to their eventual eminence. Once there, they repaid the early Council support by speaking to Council programs.

The Atlantic Conferences gave the Council entrée into the foreign policy establishment. So did a bigger project, a public opinion poll of Americans, both ordinary citizens and leaders, of their views on foreign policy and America's role in the world. Originally, the poll was run every four years and was called American Public Opinion and US Foreign Policy. It continues to this day, but is now annual, and is called simply The Chicago Council Survey.

The survey, like the Atlantic Conferences, grew from Rielly's contacts at the Ford Foundation. In late 1974, the Watergate scandal has just claimed President Nixon. Gerald Ford became president and kept Henry Kissinger as his secretary of state. Kissinger asked the Ford Foundation to find out if the new administration, in the wake of Vietnam and Watergate, could count on public and leadership support for an active foreign policy. Bundy asked Rielly to do it—but to do it fast, to influence the new Congress.

No such poll had been done before, but Rielly hired the pollster Louis Harris and a professor, Benjamin Page, then at the University of Chicago and later at Northwestern, who delivered the poll by March 1 of 1975. Its conclusion: Ford and Kissinger could forge ahead without fear of a new isolationism. Overall, Americans wanted more attention to domestic issues and opposed sending US troops abroad, especially to Southeast Asia. But, it said, "There is little sentiment among the American public for a retreat from the world—and virtually none among the leaders sampled."

Over the years, the Council had published some small books, including collections of papers presented to the Atlantic Conferences; none received much attention. The unique poll brought the Council the publicity, both in the US and abroad, that Rielly hoped. *Foreign Policy* magazine promoted it, as did network television. Rielly led a Harvard seminar on it. Friendly think tanks in Paris, Bonn, and Madrid translated it. So did the Soviet scholar, Georgy Arbatov, the head of the Institute for the US and Canadian Studies, who distributed it to the Politburo of the Soviet Communist Party and invited Rielly to Moscow to lecture on it.

Suddenly, Rielly said, "the Council was seen as a serious foreign policy organization, offering something to others, not just taking."

Rielly encouraged the formation of world affairs councils in smaller Midwestern cities, and is remembered as a mentor by some of them. Carol Byrne, the former president of Global Minnesota, recalls that Rielly invited her to Chicago when she took the job in 1996 and gave her "a fantastic tutorial, very sage advice" on how to make her organization a part of Minneapolis life.

Rielly also initiated the Ditchley conferences in cooperation with the Ditchley Foundation, a British organization devoted to strengthening Anglo-American relations through conferences on international issues. The conferences were held annually on a home-and-home basis—the Council hosted a conference one year near Chicago; the British did the honors the next year at Ditchley Park, an eighteenth-century manor house in Oxfordshire.

The house itself had a strong Chicago connection, plus a lot of history. In the war and pre-war years, it was owned by Ronald Tree, the grandson of the Chicago merchant king, Marshall Field. Tree was a friend and ally of Winston Churchill, and the wartime prime minister spent many weekends there, especially moonlit nights favored by German bombers; Ditchley was considered safer than either Chartwell, Churchill's country home, or Chequers, the official prime ministerial estate.

After the war, Tree married Marietta Peabody, an American socialite and political activist. While still married to Tree, she became the lover of Adlai Stevenson, by then the US ambassador to the UN. She was walking with him in London in 1965 when he suffered his fatal heart attack.

Like the Atlantic Conferences, the Ditchley affairs produced little memorable work, but were great for networking. The house is considered one of the most beautiful in Britain; for the Americans lucky enough to be invited, it was like spending a weekend at Downton Abbey.

Back home, Rielly worked to establish his authority at the Council and to bring leading Chicagoans, including business leaders, into its activities. Under Seith, the Executive Committee had micromanaged the Council and forced Eger and Cole to get approval for routine initiatives. Rielly made it clear he would run the Council his own way and won.

More important, he also got a commitment, fulfilled in 1974, that the Executive Committee would become the Council Board, that its president would become chairman, and the executive director would become president. The arrangement endures today.

In addition, he also recruited top, and hence busy, business leaders to the Board, replacing directors who were often volunteers with time on their hands to meddle in matters best left to the Council's professional staff. Once, the Board met monthly; under Rielly, it met four times a year.

The Council was big—the biggest in the nation, with 22,000 members—when Rielly arrived. It was beginning to make itself known on the east coast, and then in Europe. With these changes, it became professional.

When Rielly arrived, both the Chicago Committee and its offshoot for young leaders, the Committee on Foreign and Domestic Affairs, had been semi-autonomous. Rielly brought both under Council control.

At the same time, he started a Corporate Service Program, aimed at increasing membership and donations from corporations by catering to their global needs. By the 1970s, Chicago's businesses had burst out of the Midwest to become what was then called "multinational corporations," or MNCs, not yet truly global, but with sales and often offices or factories in other countries. The expansion of

O'Hare Airport into a true international hub had helped foster this. So did the opening of the Saint Lawrence Seaway, which brought ocean-going vessels to Chicago.

The Chicago Committee already included many business leaders, but its programs dealt more with issues of high statecraft. The Corporate Service Program put on meetings and seminars specifically geared to be useful to corporations that stressed how global politics affected their business. Rielly charged corporations $1,000 per year to join; by 1974, two years after it began, the program had sixty active companies.

Through all this, Rielly redefined the Council and its audience. Almost from its founding, the Council struggled with its identity. Was it an elite organization that served Chicago's leaders and its upper crust? Or should it serve the broader community, reach out to schools and neighborhoods, bring the entire city into the foreign policy debate? Its status as a membership organization, open to anyone who wanted to join, argued for the broader mandate. But its history—its founding by a small group of well-traveled and well-heeled citizens, its ties to universities, its efforts to involve the city's leaders—urged a more elite approach.

Eger, Cole, and Seith had reached out in the 1960s to the larger community. The Council sponsored student conferences, a high school speakers' program, and institutes to train teachers in foreign affairs. It staged conferences for college students on specific topics, such as the Middle East. Cole in particular urged cooperative programs with other international organizations, ethnic groups, and Chicagoans beyond the Council's earlier ambitions, including the young African Americans recruited into the Young Ambassadors program.

Rielly had other priorities. He was the first executive director chosen from outside Chicago. He was a product of the national foreign policy establishment and wanted to establish the Council's place in that establishment, both nationally and internationally. At his first annual Board meeting, he looked beyond Chicago, arguing that the

Council's education of its members inevitably influenced national foreign policy.

"It is increasingly important to strengthen programs serving present and potential members," he told the Board. He urged "a significant alteration in the pattern of resource allocation between member and non-member programs. From roughly two-thirds/one-third at the present time, the proposed program would shift this allocation to four-fifths/one-fifth." This meant "some selective cutting back on the secondary education program and on certain community outreach programs," which were replaced by stronger adult programming in the suburbs and an expansion of programs "designed to reach those members with a demonstrated serious interest in foreign affairs (especially in the business, financial, professional, and university communities)." The vision that "the Council's mission is to educate the leadership and the politically conscious citizens about the role of the United States in the world" guided him throughout his Council tenure.

The programs for teachers continued for many years, but most of the other outreach programs, including the Young Ambassadors, died. In the years since, the Council worked to bring more young people and minorities into its membership. High school and college students were encouraged to come to Council programs. But resources were limited, and little effort was made to reach Chicagoans who weren't likely to be members.

In 1987, the Council, prodded and funded by local business leaders, began to operate the World Trade Conference, an annual meeting that had run out of steam. At its first conference, the keynote speaker was Alan Greenspan; a few weeks later, Greenspan was named president of the Federal Reserve Bank, making the Council look like a king-maker. It ran the conference for the next four years, with dwindling audiences and interest. In 1991, it decided to drop the project. "We were glad to be rid of it," Rielly said.

Two other ideas were floated at this time to move the Council on to a bigger stage. One suggested that the Council become a think tank, like the New York Council. The other called for the Council to publish its own journal, such as *Foreign Affairs*, the magazine published by the New York Council.

From its founding, the Council published occasional books, written by outsiders on commission, or pamphlets produced by study groups or conferences such as the Atlantic Conference. Close relations with the Japan-America Society produced funding for study groups on Japan and Asia; three paperback books emerged from these seminars. But unlike the New York Council, it had never had its own resident scholars who published books and articles on the foreign policy issues of the day. The reason was money; the New York Council, the Brookings Institution, and other think tanks had substantial endowments that supported this expensive activity.

From time to time, Council leaders said the organization should branch out into "knowledge creation"—not as a full-scale think tank, but a place where scholars could occasionally tackle specific topics, "to make a contribution to the national discussion of the particular subject." In 1974, a Board member, Augustin S. Hart, Jr., noted that Midwestern foundations had begun to fund research by East Coast think tanks. Hart asked, why not get these foundations to fund research by the Chicago Council, conducted by Midwestern scholars, to create "a limited number of projects which aim to contribute to the national debate on selected major foreign policy subjects?"

Earlier, when Cole was executive director, he urged the Council to become a center of study on cities around the world. Cole's project was called "Cities in Crisis," and was based on the idea that Chicago's problems—of governance, pollution, education, racial and ethnic issues—were shared with other great cities. He proposed hiring four fellows for $25,000 each, to be funded by foundations, to study what other cities were doing about these problems, mostly to help Chicago understand how to solve its own. "There are many lessons to be learned in all of these problems through a careful, comparative study, ranging freely around the world."

The Hart and Cole proposals were good ideas that took thirty years to flower. Shortly after Hart made his suggestion, the Council took on the public opinion survey, and the idea for more targeted research faded away. As for Cole's idea, the money wasn't there, and the suggestion died.

Three decades later came the Global Chicago Center, which studied Chicago's place in the global economy and, a decade after that, the Global Cities Initiative, which studied and compared great cities, as Cole had suggested. By this time, the Council had actually become a think tank, as Hart wanted, with the Global Cities program at its heart and the annual Global Cities Forum as its calling card, but with a team of scholars, both resident and non-resident, researching foreign policy issues of vital interest to Chicago and the Midwest.

In its first year, the Council had missed its chance to publish a journal when it turned down the New York Council's suggestion that it collaborate on *Foreign Affairs*. Another opportunity arose in the early 1970s with the appearance of *Foreign Policy*, a rival magazine funded by the Carnegie Foundation, founded by the Harvard scholar Samuel Huntington and an investment banker, Warren Manshel, and edited by Richard Holbrooke, a future assistant secretary of state. In early 1972, Huntington and Manshel approached Rielly about a "special relationship" between the Council and the magazine.

Both sides were in favor, but for different reasons. Rielly understood the New Yorkers to mean an "intellectual partnership," including recruiting scholarly articles from the Midwest; Huntington and Manshel only wanted to expand circulation of their infant journal by offering Council members cut-rate subscriptions. In the end, Manshel flatly refused any relationship "affecting editorial content, editorial decisions, or any other matter concerning the production and publishing of the magazine." The Council accepted the subscription offer, and Rielly joined the magazine's editorial board and published articles there, mostly on the Council's foreign policy poll. Today,

Council fellows publish regularly in *Foreign Policy*, but the "special relationship" never materialized.

—

The Council celebrated its fiftieth anniversary in 1972. Rielly had revitalized the Council and linked it to the world foreign policy establishment. Membership was high and finances strong.

Not least, the Council and the *Tribune* were on speaking terms, largely because Colonel McCormick and his isolationist editors had died and were replaced by a newer, more international leadership. The *Tribune* bought a table at the Council's anniversary banquet, and the paper's editorial page proclaimed, "The Council has done much to help the Midwest understand the world. As the parts of that world become daily more important to one another, the need for this useful organization seems destined to go on enhanced."

By the time Rielly retired, the Council was holding seminars on globalization and other foreign policy issues at the Colonel's suburban estate, Cantigny. In 2018, the Council saluted a $4 million gift from the Robert R. McCormick Foundation when it named the main hall of its new conference center after its old antagonist, a gesture that doubtless sent generations of Council leaders, and the Colonel himself, spinning in their graves.

—

Rielly's arrival in Chicago coincided with a sea change both in international affairs and the public view of the world and, as a result, the tone of the speeches from the Council's stage. The Vietnam War was ending slowly. With East-West battle lines set, economic issues—oil, trade, floating currencies, and multinational corporations—replaced military matters at the spearpoint of diplomacy. The US and Europe remained allies but never quite trusted each other. Japan rose in the east and China seemed primed to do the same.

Through most of that time, the first question was what the Soviet Union would do. At the start, a second question was what Henry

Kissinger would do. For all of it, a big issue was the seeming decline in American power and hegemony—a premature concern, as it turned out.

Names that fill history books today led Council programs: Kissinger, Willy Brandt, Helmut Kohl, Zbigniew Brzezinski, Abba Eban, David Halberstam, James Reston, Robert McNamara, Kurt Waldheim, U Thant, Richard Holbrooke, Boris Yeltsin; one president named Gerald Ford, future presidents named Jimmy Carter, Ronald Reagan, George H.W. Bush, and Joseph Biden; a panoply of senators and presidential candidates such as Gary Hart, Edward Kennedy, Walter Mondale, Edmund Muskie, Hubert Humphrey, and George McGovern; and even a young Washington correspondent for *The Jerusalem Post* named Wolf Blitzer.

Garrick Utley, the NBC correspondent and son of Clifton Utley, spoke at the fiftieth anniversary dinner, which honored his father with its World Understanding Award. Richard Nixon and George McGovern were running for president and the Vietnam War was winding down, but Utley predicted that, no matter who won, America would pull back from its involvement in the world. He said,

> *"This does not mean that the United States is about to become another isolationist country, the way we were before World War I and World War II...But I do think we can expect, and we should expect, a reaction to set in, the post-Vietnam War feeling or mood or attitude. I'm not going to use the word 'isolationism.' That's too strong, that's a word that belongs to the past. But because we are going to have this restructuring of our national priorities, the work of the Council is by no means at an end.*
>
> *"It has been here for fifty years, has gone through difficult times, and it is going to be here through some more difficult times for another fifty years or so."*

The Council agreed to the point that Rielly organized a series of lectures on "Neo-Isolationism: Myth or Reality." Opening the series, Rielly said the Council's original mandate was to make sure "the proper relationship of the United States in the world would receive a full hearing." He went on,

> *"Today, fifty years later, the mission of the Council remains the same. Today, having fought three more wars in the last three decades, once again a large segment of American opinion finds itself disillusioned with American involvement abroad. Today, once again, a substantial and vocal segment of American society is arguing for a return to some sort of neo-isolationism."*

The post-war Truman Doctrine designed to contain Soviet communism had now been "invoked as the justification for massive American military involvement in Asia. What began as a defensive policy designed to protect Greece and Turkey, later Berlin and Korea, would end up two decades later as an incantation by a tragic president who sought to export the Great Society to Asia."

One of the series' speakers, George Ball, an early opponent of the Vietnam War, said the US should "forget isolationism, new, old, or middle aged." Instead, he said, "Interdependence is no longer a figure of speech but a reality we live with every day…No nation, no matter how large or rich, can afford to go it alone."

At that time, Adlai Stevenson III, the son of the former Council president and US presidential candidate, was running in his first election for the Senate, which he won. In a Council speech, Stevenson rejected neo-isolationism, but warned that containment of the Soviet Union did not extend to involvement in places such as Zaire, Kashmir, or Vietnam.

"To my mind," he said, "neo-isolation would be as dangerous to our national interest and our national security as over-involvement. We must mark out a middle course."

The Council seldom issued policy statements on its own, leaving it to speakers to set the tone. But its monthly newsletter, *World Events*, published an article in 1973 that could have been written a half century later. It was unsigned, but apparently it was written by Frank McNaughton, a former Washington correspondent and Chicago public relations man who, in his retirement, edited *World Events*. Writing in the post-Vietnam years, he laid out the challenges for the Council and the nation:

> *"We are a wounded nation: how badly wounded, only the future will tell. The Council faces…new problems of deeper seriousness [that] call for programs of greater scope and depth and introspection.*
>
> *"How can we restore faith in representative government? No government which is doubted or distrusted by its own citizens…can maintain a proper posture before other nations of the world. There is a great gap in respect for the institutions of government…There are yet too many [citizens] who believe that they hear only lies from their government.*
>
> *"Can we as a people face up to the fact that we have fought and lost a war against a small, underdeveloped nation, a nation that we wrecked but could not defeat?*
>
> *"Can Congress regenerate itself as a governmental institution capable of coping intelligently with moral and social and economic problems of the coming decades?…Can the election processes be cleaned to rid them of rascality and medicine-showmanship? Can some*

> *better system be devised so that the electronic communications media is not abused in the election process?"*

—

Elliot Richardson, the under secretary of state, spoke in defense of NATO, at a time when "the very climate of security which NATO has fostered has seemed to permit many to disregard it or to think it obsolete." To be sure, Richardson told the Council, if the Soviet threat vanished, "There will be no more need for NATO." But the Nixon Administration opposed any cutback in US troop strength in Europe. Richardson promised that the United States would keep its treaty promises to the Europeans, but said, "Our European allies can and should do more to pay for their own defense." Again, the familiar argument for "burden-sharing."

John Connally, the former treasury secretary, went further, and told the Council Washington should insist both Japan and West Germany rearm to meet the Soviet threat. If they did, it would ensure peace for twenty years, when the Soviet people would make the Kremlin "open up their society and become part of the family of nations."

West German Chancellor Willy Brandt said US troops were "the decisive factor" in the Cold War, "and one that will remain indispensable for a future that is at present unforeseeable." But history imposed a "psychological limit" on German military spending; for either the Russians or Germany's allies in the West, "It would not be a good thing for the specific weight of the German armed forces to be considerably strengthened."

Chicago politics nearly scuttled Brandt's speech at the Palmer House. Before Brandt arrived, a Council staffer, Irene Hill, went to City Hall to talk with Colonel Jack Reilly, the city's events coordinator and a right-hand man to Mayor Richard J. Daley, about the city's preparations for Brandt's visit. Reilly hinted strongly that the Council should hire more union workers for the Palmer House dinner. As Hill recalled, she missed the hint and said the workers were not needed.

On the night, city fire inspectors showed up just before the dinner began, threatened to call it off, then ordered the Council to remove some chairs, reducing the size of the audience. The chairs were duly taken away. The inspectors, having made their point, left the hotel, and the show went on.

Zbigniew Brzezinski, then still at Columbia University, claimed the Soviets had achieved "both economic and military parity" with the US, which created "a new sense of vulnerability" among Americans and a "great division and turmoil" which undermined the shared purpose necessary for an effective foreign policy.

Three years later, Brzezinski returned to praise the leaders of both America and Russia in pursuing détente. Both nations showed restraint and a willingness to "step back" from the brink.

Gennadi Gerasimov, a Washington-based Soviet journalist who became, in the next decade, a spokesman for Mikhail Gorbachev, told the Council that Americans still suffered from "Cold War nostalgia" that kept Russia from getting benefits, especially in trade, from détente.

U Thant, the UN secretary general, urged the leaders of the five nuclear powers to meet at the UN to seek solutions not only to the arms race but to other world problems. Four years later, his successor, Kurt Waldheim, a future Austrian president who was later barred from the US for participation in Nazi war crimes, came to the Council to plead for international cooperation.

Waldheim said the world rejected "the idea that peace can be achieved through a balance of power or through superior stockpiles of weapons which, if used, would produce a world holocaust. These ideas belong to the past."

Representative Paul McCloskey of California, a presidential aspirant and a Republican, attacked Nixon's use of presidential power. He urged legislation to curb the ability of presidents to use American armed forces abroad secretly, and to use the Central Intelligence Agency to undermine foreign governments.

Peter G. Peterson was a Chicago businessman who was Nixon's assistant for international economic affairs as well as secretary of commerce, and later became a Wall Street titan and president of the New York Council on Foreign Relations. He had just left Chicago in 1971 when he returned to tell the Council that a post-Vietnam America "must devote more of its resources to the development of its own economy and society." This meant that US allies, both in Europe and Asia, must devote more of their growing resources to sharing the cost of "the security and development of the free world."

Peterson stressed this did not mean a new isolationism or protectionism: "We cannot turn inward economically without turning inward politically [and] we cannot turn inward without encouraging others to do the same."

Some speakers saw the bipolar Cold War world splitting into a multipolar world, some years before this actually happened. Harrison Salisbury, the *New York Times* correspondent and editor, said the Soviet-American "superpower rivalry" was to be joined by three new superpowers: China, Europe, and Japan.

Edmund Muskie, the Democratic senator and former presidential candidate, said the US had lost its dominance in a multipolar world, with a decentralization of power and a "Balkanization of world politics." But this was the result of the rise of stronger nations, many of them US allies, and hence the success of our post-war policies.

"Our present condition resulted from our achievements and that we decided long ago that we didn't want to be in charge of the world—and we didn't want anyone else to be either," Muskie said. "Our objectives were right and our achievements are impressive. So, let us not now sulk about the results. They were foreseeable."

Not everyone agreed. Senator Joseph Biden, the future president, accused Kissinger of trying to impose American will on the world. As the US acted like "the biggest, strongest, most arrogant kid on the block, as the watchman of the free world, we watched the demise of liberty around the globe."

Until 1976, Kissinger dominated US foreign policy. Max Frankel, the editorial page editor of the *New York Times*, told the Council that Kissinger almost seemed to be running for president that year, because the foreign policy debate between the real candidates was mostly about the secretary of state, not about the issues.

Kissinger himself, nearing the end of his role in government, told the Council that the US needed broad bipartisan unity on its foreign policy, similar to the consensus at the start of the Cold War, not a policy that changed with every new administration. He said,

> "The time has come to build a new foreign policy consensus similar in scope but different in content from that which sustained our previous achievements. Democrats and Republicans, Congress and the Executive, government and citizen, must once again conduct the foreign policy debate in the spirit of partnership, recognizing that we are not at war with each other but engaged in a vital national enterprise affecting our future and the world at large."

A year later, Kissinger returned to Chicago to film a special NBC television broadcast, during which he answered questions from a Council audience. A quarter century before globalization and automation became major topics in the Western world, Kissinger warned,

> "All industrial societies are facing some fundamental problems which they have not been able as yet to solve. Most investments in advanced industrial societies tend to be capital intensive and do not necessarily produce the same number of jobs as would be the case in an equivalent period, say, thirty years ago. The computerization of industry tends to bring about a situation in which

> *you can have substantial investment and, nevertheless, no commensurate rise in employment."*

Nearly twenty years before the Cold War ended, many speakers treated it as almost irrelevant in a new multipolar world. Henry Brandon, the Washington correspondent for *The Sunday Times* of London, said US withdrawal from Vietnam and the devaluation of the dollar signaled the retreat of American power in the world, and left a vacuum in American policy making. The old Cold War consensus on the containment of the Soviet Union has disappeared and no new consensus has replaced it, leaving "confusion about American foreign policy around the world."

Not every foreign policy issue in those years dealt with the US-Soviet balance, neo-isolationism, or declining American hegemony. Speakers ranged across the world, from Latin America to Africa, from the first signs of a rising China to nuclear disarmament, from the two energy crises of the 1970s to environmental issues. As always, the Middle East drew alarm.

Abba Eban, by now the Israeli foreign minister, returned to the Council to note that there was progress in every international dispute—between the US and China, between America and Russia, between India and Pakistan—except in the Middle East. "Here and here alone, the taboo and the context of our contact still impedes all progress. Here and here alone do some people profess to believe that you can get peace by remote control."

Two years later, Eban returned to reject any Palestinian claim to Israel. "If they mean Palestine in addition to Israel, perhaps some solution might be reached," he said. "If they mean Palestine instead of Israel, the answer must be no thank you. Israel must not be sacrificed because the Arabs want to control twenty-one states instead of just twenty."

Yehoshafat Harkabi, a former chief of Israeli military intelligence and later an advocate of a separate Palestinian state, said Arab action against Israel would fail because, "For the people of Israel, it is more important that Israel exist than it is important to the Arabs that they destroy it." Still, he worried that "maintaining double standards in modes of administration, [and] withholding full rights of citizenship for the Arabs living in these areas, [might] undermine Israeli democracy." He discounted the danger, because Israeli occupation of the West Bank and Gaza "is only transitory, and these areas will not become part of Israel proper."

Maurice F. Strong, the Canadian secretary general of the UN Conference on the Human Environment, called for international action to end pollution, on land and in the oceans. "A vital element in this," he said, "is the principal that nations accept responsibility for the effect of their activities on the environment of others or the common environment of oceans and atmosphere beyond national jurisdiction." He cited the pollution of Lake Michigan as an example of the challenge worldwide; fifty years later, Chicago's lake is largely cleansed, but the international cooperation that Strong sought is still far off.

Joel Darmstadter and Milton Searl, two researchers at Resource for the Future, a Washington think tank, spoke during the 1973 Yom Kippur War in the Middle East. Only a week earlier, the Organization for Petroleum Exporting Countries had imposed an embargo on oil shipments to Israel's western allies—the first sign of OPEC's power and the oil crises to come. They foresaw the "huge and rapidly growing monetary flows" going to the oil-exporting countries, which were soon to unsettle global financial markets. But the economy, which relied mostly on oil, would remain healthy, they thought, so long as the price per barrel, then $4.75, stayed below $6 in 1985. Unhappily, the price that year was $27.

Frances FitzGerald, a journalist and author, put some of the blame for the jump in oil prices on the US government and its ties to the Shah of Iran. The Shah, she said, used his increased oil earnings to buy arms, mostly from the US, blunting any American opposition.

Europeans, who paid more for oil while missing out on the arms sales, "are in fact subsidizing US defense industries," Fitzgerald said. "Oil prices in the Middle East have always been rigged to serve America's economic and strategic needs."

Over the years, many presidents from around the world spoke to the Council. So did several American presidents—Herbert Hoover, Ronald Reagan, Jimmy Carter—but only before or after their White House years. Only one sitting president appeared on the Council stage in Chicago, when Gerald Ford spoke at the Palmer House in March of 1976. Unfortunately, it was a relatively brief and anodyne speech; he urged "peace through strength," adequate defense spending, support for NATO, and a strong intelligence capacity.

The Council had to wait thirty-six years before it hosted another sitting president, and that was in Washington, not Chicago. In 2012, Barack Obama came to the capital from a meeting of the G8 nations at Camp David, to speak to the Global Food Security Symposium, sponsored by the Council's Global Agricultural Development Initiative. Unlike Ford, Obama brought real news—the G8 and African nations had just agreed to a New Alliance for Food Security and Nutrition, aimed at lifting fifty million people out of poverty through sustained agricultural growth.

If the Council attracted few US presidents, it presented many secretaries of states—Stettinius, Marshall, Dulles, and Rusk in the postwar years, and then an almost unbroken string of secretaries which included Henry Kissinger, Cyrus Vance, Edmund Muskie, Alexander Haig, George Shultz, James Baker, Warren Christopher, and Madeleine Albright. Colin Powell spoke when he was the chairman of the Joint Chiefs of Staff, but his successor as secretary, Condoleezza Rice, appeared before the Council, as did John Kerry.

For all these secretaries, their visits had more to do with politics than foreign policy. All recognized that a constant American engagement with the world could be a hard sell beyond the Beltway; without broad popular support, the wisest foreign policy could end up in the political grave, next to the League of Nations.

Like many future and former presidents who spoke to the Council, Jimmy Carter, then the governor of Georgia, was running for the presidency when he appeared. Carter, speaking only three days after Ford appeared, spent more time criticizing Kissinger, the secretary of state, than the president. Kissinger, he said, was running a secret foreign policy. "Our secretary of state simply does not trust the judgment of the American people, but constantly conducts foreign policy exclusively, personally, and in secret."

Two Democratic senators argued that the US policy toward Cuba was self-defeating and futile. Senator Edward Kennedy argued, "If Henry Kissinger can fly 8,000 miles to Peking as the prelude to a normalization of relations with the People's Republic of China, then surely we can offer to send him 90 miles to Havana to do the same." Senator George McGovern said US opposition only made Fidel Castro a "legend" in Cuba, while the US trade embargo "helped to unify the Cuban people and forced Cuba to seek aid from the Soviet Union, making a Soviet satellite out of a strongly nationalistic revolutionary country."

Nuclear policy dominated many programs in the 1970s. Fred C. Iklé, director of the US Arms Control and Disarmament Agency, said his agency had recently discovered that a nuclear war could destroy the stratospheric ozone level necessary to protect life.

The Cold War's leading attempt to curb nuclear weapons was the Strategic Arms Limitation Talks (SALT), which took place in two rounds between 1969 and 1979. As the SALT II neared completion in 1979, the Council held two debates on whether it should be ratified, between Senator John Culver (pro) and former Defense Secretary Paul Nitze (con), and between David Aaron, an arms negotiation in the Carter Administration (pro) and Edward Luttwak, a leading political scientist (con). At the same time, Senator Edward Kennedy returned to the Council to urge ratification. In the end, the Senate never ratified the treaty, not on its merits but because of the Soviet invasion of Afghanistan.

Under Rielly, some of the most intense intellectual activity took place in seminars and conferences that brought intellectuals from Washington and around the world to meet with leading Chicago businessmen, journalists, and academics. These forums probed the impact of détente on the Atlantic alliance, issues in the Mediterranean and the Middle East and, especially, the implications of a rising Japan, which was the subject of at least three such programs. Closer to home, the Council tapped Midwestern scholars for study groups on international food policy and the relationship among economics, science, and technology. Some of these seminars produced publications, but the emphasis was more on bringing selected Chicagoans into the international debate than in a broader public education.

—

In 1976, the Civil Aeronautics Board changed its rules favoring charter flights by membership organizations, bringing an end to the Council's cut-rate charter flight bonanza. Rielly had expected this for at least five years. The Council had been phasing out such flights, substituting more expensive guided tours, with regular briefings and high intellectual content. The cheap flights had been a boon to membership, which peaked at nearly 23,000 in 1973, but dropped to 13,000 by 1976.

At least one of these tours produced more excitement than planned. A Council group was preparing to leave Egypt in October of 1973 when Egypt and Syria attacked Israel. The Yom Kippur War broke out. Airports closed, curfews were imposed, and the Chicagoans found themselves confined, in only semi-luxury, in the Nile Hilton Hotel.

The war began on Saturday. According to a report written by one tour member, Emma Pencek, "By Sunday noon, the spacious lobby at the Hilton looked like a convention hall teeming with people, dazed, dejected, stumbling around mounds of luggage seeking information, accommodations, and reassurance." By all accounts, the American consulate in Cairo provided no help at all. Attempts to sail out from Alexandria fell through. Finally, after six days, the trapped tourists rose at 3 a.m. and, with a military convoy, rode buses to Alexandria, where a Greek ship ferried them across the Mediterranean to Piraeus, and then to Athens for the flight home.

The Hilton charged the Chicagoans full room rates for their enforced stay, but most of the travelers took the adventure in stride. One of them, Mrs. Charles W. Wyman, wrote the Council that "the tour was fascinating and interesting despite the unexpected war."

Foundations, then as now, funded much of the work of think tanks and world affairs councils. But almost all these foundations, such as the Ford Foundation, were on the East Coast, putting the remote Chicago Council at a competitive disadvantage with its brethren in New York or Washington. The only exception was the Lilly Endowment, based in Indianapolis, which was then interested in international issues and helped finance the Council's early public opinion polls.

For that reason, the arrival in Chicago in 1978 of the John D. and Catherine T. MacArthur Foundation "was a revolution for us," Rielly recalled. John MacArthur made his fortune with the Bankers Life insurance company and left most of his $1 billion fortune to the foundation, making it instantly one of the biggest in the nation. Early funding included a three-year $300,000 grant to the Council to educate the public on national security. From its first grant to the Council in 1981, the MacArthur Foundation became an important source of funding.

Other foundations set up shop in Chicago, such as the Joyce Foundation, the McCormick Tribune Foundation, and the Polk Foundation, and became Council funders. So did an array of foundations around the world—at least thirty-two of them, including six in Germany, four in Spain and Japan, and two in Canada, Italy, and Korea; much of the funding of Atlantic Conferences and the public opinion polls came from these foundations.

But the single biggest gift grew out of Rielly's long courtship of German Chancellor Helmut Kohl, whose government gave the Council a $3 million grant in 1988, to be paid out over ten years. The grant set up the Council's Konrad Adenauer Fund for European Policy Studies, with the income to be used for exchange programs, seminars, and other activities, and the principal devoted to the Council's endowment.

Rielly, although admittedly parsimonious, increased the Council's budget. The travel program—the cheap charter flights before 1976, the guided tours after that—helped. So did corporate sponsor income, which grew tenfold in the decade between 1975 and 1985. Between 1970 and 1985, membership income more than doubled. The endowment itself stood at $6 million, half of it due to Kohl's generosity.

Programming boomed at the same pace. The Council gave its members some 200 programs per year, across various platforms, such as public programs, the Chicago Committee, suburban meetings, and other forums—all with a staff that seldom numbered more than twenty people. Of this twenty, about one-third were secretaries or other support staff.

—

By 1980, the long erosion of the West's industrial economies had begun, but few yet saw it as an inexorable trend. An exception was Tom McNally, a Laborite British Member of Parliament, who told the Council that both the American Midwest and the British Northeast shared low investment and high unemployment, exacerbated by new competition from industrializing Third World nations and, in Britain, from Greece and other relatively slow-growth members of the European Common Market, as it was then. McNally blamed the new British government of Margaret Thatcher for adopting the free-market tutelage of the Chicago economist Milton Friedman.

Another critic of Friedman, the Harvard economist John Kenneth Galbraith, decried the tendency of academics, businesspeople, and politicians to cling to ideology in the face of reality. He singled out supply-side economics, still used as a justification for tax cuts for the wealthy. Business executives "are exceedingly hard-working people now. The notion that they are laying back because of their taxes and have great stores of pent-up energy that will be released by a reduction in taxation is a triumph of ideology over obvious fact," Galbraith said.

In early 1980, shortly after the Soviet invasion of Afghanistan, Secretary of State Cyrus Vance told the Council that the Carter government would keep sanctions on the Soviets until they left that country. But Vance hinted that one of those sanctions, the US boycott of the 1980 Olympics in Moscow, might be eased. In the end, the Soviets stayed for nearly ten years and the Olympic boycott remained.

The Carter Administration imposed another punitive boycott, this time on US grain exports to the Soviet Union. Vance, speaking to the Council a month after that boycott began, was asked about the impact on Midwestern farmers. He brushed off the question: "It is an action which requires sacrifice, but others are going to have to sacrifice and are sacrificing." As it happened, the Midwestern sacrifice was substantial. The boycott helped touch off the farm debt crisis of the 1980s, in which thousands of farms went bankrupt, as did the banks that financed them. Rural life in the Midwest never really recovered.

Vance resigned a month later over the failed attempt to rescue the US diplomats being held in Tehran. His successor, Edmund S. Muskie, told the Council that the Iran-Iraq War, which had begun a month earlier, threatened the breakup of Iran.

"We are opposed to the dismemberment of Iran," Muskie said. "We believe that the cohesion and stability of Iran is in the interest of the stability of the region as a whole."

Two years later, another secretary of state, Alexander M. Haig, Jr., told the Council, during its sixtieth anniversary dinner, that he was dispatching top aides to the Middle East to try to settle three problems there: the Iran-Iraq War, autonomy for Palestinians, and the civil war in Lebanon.

Cardinal Joseph Bernardin, the Roman Catholic archbishop of Chicago, spoke to the Council on the US bishops' pastoral letter on nuclear weapons, and said the church should create a "constituency for peace" to halt the arms race.

A churchman of a different order, the Reverend Ian Paisley, the firebrand Protestant leader of the Unionist forces in Northern Ireland, appeared at a Council lunch with an Ulster Catholic leader, Austin Currie. If the audience expected a verbal brawl, it was disappointed. The two men were part of a Northern Ireland delegation promoting US investment and were under orders to stay away from politics and focus on economic development. Both behaved themselves at the lunch, then cancelled an evening appearance before another Council audience in Wilmette.

By the time the 1980s ended, the Cold War was virtually over. But as the decade began, the Soviet collapse was barely a cloud on the horizon. Marshall Shulman, one of the nation's leading Soviet experts and a frequent Council speaker, said the biggest Soviet problem was its dysfunctional economy, but saw no immediate solution. "Change in the effectiveness of the Soviet leadership may have to await the rise of a younger generation to the top political leadership, and even then, it is not clear whether they will be able to modernize the system against the strong political resistance of the bureaucracy and the population."

Malcolm Toon, a former US ambassador to Moscow, listed Soviet problems—such as nationalism, geriatric leaders, outmoded institutions, and an "inert population only marginally stirred by beating the drums of communism"—but concluded, "There is no storm brewing in Soviet society."

George Ball, one of America's most far-sighted diplomats, agreed that the Soviet economy was "inherently inefficient," but also claimed, "there is little reason to think it is teetering on the verge of collapse or that, short of military action, we could materially shorten its life span."

But Max Frankel, the editorial page editor of the *New York Times*, saw the Kremlin on that verge a decade before it happened. "No sane American would change strategic places with the Soviets," he told the Council. Both the West and China opposed it, its troops were bogged down in Afghanistan, and the East Europeans, led by Poland, were restive.

"The Soviets are stretched as far as could be and still be called a superpower. They are not on the march but reeling from blows."

—

America had its own economic problems. Across the Midwest, once-mighty industries—automobiles, automobile parts, steel, radio and television manufacturing—were toppling before the invasion of Japanese competitors. The growing opposition to Japanese trade practices, and the US government's failure to oppose them, naturally became a new topic in a city that was shedding tens of thousands of industrial jobs.

James F. Bere, chairman of Borg-Warner Corporation and a Council Board member, said in a Council speech he had always opposed trade barriers, but the US auto industry needed protection to survive.

"One cannot entirely blame the Japanese for wanting the best of both worlds—open access to all other markets, plus protection for their own domestic industries," Bere said. "The Japanese seem to feel very confident that our free trade tradition is so ingrained that any real change is unlikely. They are wrong."

Lee Morgan, chairman of Caterpillar Tractor Company, called for a tax on all Japanese imports, and Robert H. Malott, another Council

Board member and chairman of FMC Corporation, complained of closed Japanese markets to his products.

The author David Halberstam agreed. "We should upgrade the issue of trade to national security status," he said. He foresaw the hollowing of American industry, and with it, the middle class, and noted employment growth only of high-wage jobs in finance and low-wage jobs in the service sector.

Some issues had become staples of Council programming. The Middle East—especially Israel and its Arab enemies—was one of them. More Israelis appeared than Palestinians or other Arabs, but the Council tried to keep a vague balance, including through debates. Two professors, Amos Perlmutter of American University and Edward Said of Columbia, appeared together to argue the Israeli and Palestinian side, respectively. So did Dr. Galia Golan of Hebrew University and Hanna Siniora, editor of the Jerusalem newspaper *Al-Fajr*. Rashid Khalidi, a professor at the University of Chicago, said the Intifada of 1989 showed that continued Israeli occupation "is intolerable to the Palestinian population." Uri Bar-Ner, the Israeli consul general in Chicago, rejected any negotiations with the Palestinian Liberation Organization and said the Palestinians could not expect any concessions that would damage Israeli security.

Israeli Prime Minister Yitzhak Shamir portrayed himself to a private Council luncheon as "dedicated to truth," but said peace in the Middle East would come only when Arab governments learned "that they must abandon their hostility and belligerency towards Israel."

—

If the Council drew few American presidents, it became a regular stop for politicians who wanted to be president. Every four years, candidates chose the Council stage for major foreign policy addresses.

In 1976, Jimmy Carter signaled that his foreign policy would steer away from traditional "balance of power politics" or "policies that strengthen dictators" and stress humanitarian values, a goal that foundered with the Iranian revolution and the Soviet invasion of Afghanistan.

Four years later, Ronald Reagan laid out a "grand strategy" without saying what that strategy would be, apart from a strong military and a vibrant economy. But the future president did warn of Marxist activity in the Caribbean, particularly Grenada, a tipoff to his invasion of that island three years later. In the same week, George H.W. Bush, who became Reagan's vice president, broke the candidates' general silence on the Iranian crisis with an attack on President Carter's attempt to release the US hostages there as "bluff, bluster, and political symbolism." As it turned out, the hostages were released on the day that Reagan and Bush were inaugurated.

As the 1984 election neared, Senator John Glenn, also the first American to orbit the earth, accused Reagan of pursuing an inconsistent policy toward Moscow that divided the Western alliance and turned it into "nothing less than a potential disaster." Former Vice President Walter Mondale said that Reagan's sketchy proposals to limit nuclear arms were "encouraging," and called on the president to fill in the details.

Two days later, Senator Gary Hart, still a rising star in Democratic politics, said his foreign policy would be based on "three words: reciprocity, reliability, and restraint; reciprocity in our relations with the Soviet Union, reliability in our relations with our friends and allies, and restraint in our relations with the third world." Joseph Biden said that Carter stressed détente, and Reagan stressed force to manage Soviet behavior; neither succeeded.

In 1988, both presidential nominees, Bush and Michael Dukakis, spoke in Chicago on the same day. Only Dukakis appeared on the Council stage, where he gave a skeptical and conservative appraisal of the new Soviet leader, Mikhail Gorbachev:

> "Just as it would be blind to believe that nothing has changed in the Soviet Union, it is a mistake to suggest

that everything has changed. Mr. Gorbachev is a Leninist. He has not abandoned Soviet goals, but rather seeks to advance those goals through different means... To deal successfully with Gorbachev, the next president must be tough, he must be realistic, he must have good judgment and he must be committed to building a strong defense."

Gorbachev's rise to power and his attempts to reform the Soviet system dominated Council debate in the last half of the 1980s. The eventual Soviet collapse was not obvious, although one speaker saw it coming. Instead, speakers argued over whether the changes in Moscow were real and what the US should do about it.

Robert S. McNamara, the former defense secretary who had been so wrong about Vietnam, did no better in judging the Soviet Union as Gorbachev came to power.

"No illusions should be harbored about the nature of the Soviet system, about its hostility to Western values, nor about the convergence of the two systems," McNamara told the Council. "They're not going to converge, at least not in our lifetimes. They're not going to converge because the Soviet system is not only a country, but it's a cause, and it's based on the proposition that our system should and will disappear.

"The Soviets will not disappear," he said. "We must rid ourselves of the notion that the Soviet economy may collapse, or the equally far-fetched notion that the West either has the power or the duty to contribute in a significant way to the collapse of that economy."

Actually, the possibility of a Soviet economic collapse had been foreshadowed, if not predicted, by Admiral Stansfield Turner, then director of the CIA, in a Council speech in 1977. CIA analysts, he said, saw a "bleak outlook" for the Soviet economy, due to falling productivity, scarce funds, rampant inefficiencies, and shrinking oil production. Past economic growth "is coming to a dead end," he said.

All these internal economic problems were the leading cause of the eventual Soviet disintegration fourteen years later.

Leonard Silk, an economics columnist for the *New York Times*, had recently been in Russia, and talked to the Council on the very day that Gorbachev became the general secretary of the Soviet Communist Party. He called Gorbachev "a new man who seems to be very intelligent, reasonably well read, literate, and flexible, and obviously a good politician in the best American, the best corporate, tradition." Silk predicted that Gorbachev would try economic reforms against huge ideological and bureaucratic resistance "to invent a new way of simulating a capitalist system without being capitalist, without fully freeing up markets, without opening borders to unrestrained trade, without really quite doing it while doing it." It was a good description of Gorbachev's flailing attempts to rescue the Soviet economy before it finally collapsed six years later.

Dimitri Simes, the Russian-born scholar at the Carnegie Endowment in Washington, was more skeptical; he called Gorbachev "a party man: reliable, obedient, and a promotor of the party line." So was another Soviet émigré, former diplomat Vladimir Sakharov, who called the new leadership "young, ruthless, and not likely to change," with Gorbachev himself a traditional Marxist ideologue.

Helmut Kohl returned to the Council in 1986 to give two speeches—one to business leaders on trade relations, and the other on changing East-West relations after the Reykjavik summit between Gorbachev and President Reagan, which he described as "an important milestone in the East-West dialogue." Then he sized up the man whose policies led to Germany's reunification.

"General Secretary Gorbachev is a leader who, like hardly any of his predecessors, is familiar with the inherent limitations of the Soviet system. We cannot yet definitely assess whether the Soviet Union is in reality only seeking to gain time, or whether it is embarking on a new policy of greater restraint in international relations and of a fair dialogue with the West…No opportunity should be left untapped."

Zbigniew Brzezinski, back before the Council in 1987, was more pessimistic. "Gorbachev's current policy," he said, "is designed to make the Soviet Union a more viable, more effective system, more truly competitive with the United States."

The most prescient Council speaker turned out to be William Safire, the conservative columnist for the *New York Times*. Speaking in 1988, Safire reported that the Soviet economy was creaking under increased military spending. He then said, "The next president's greatest crisis could possibly be the beginning of the breakup of the Soviet empire." The next president was George H. W. Bush, who presided over that very breakup.

Boris Yeltsin, the man who inherited that breakup, came to the Council during a barnstorming American tour in September of 1989, sponsored by the Esalen Institute, a New Age outpost in California. At that time, Yeltsin was a member of the Politburo of the Soviet Communist Party, increasingly rebellious, a former Gorbachev ally becoming his most bitter enemy. Two years later, when the Soviet Union disintegrated, Yeltsin became the first president of Russia.

All that lay in the near future. When he came to Chicago, he brought a reputation as a dynamic and undisciplined politician and a heavy drinker. One Italian reporter, exaggerating only mildly, wrote of the trip, "For Yeltsin, America is a holiday, a stage set, a bar 5,000 kilometers long."

Yeltsin's reputation preceded him to Chicago. The Council flew him by helicopter from O'Hare Airport to the Chicago Hilton hotel for a dinner hosted by major Council donors, Kenneth and Harle Montgomery. Yeltsin settled in and told Mrs. Montgomery he wanted a vodka. She looked at Yeltsin's interpreter, an American named Harris Coulter, who doubled as his minder, and he nodded, yes. Ten minutes later, Yeltsin asked for another vodka. Coulter shook his head, no. So, when Yeltsin rose before the audience of 3,000, he was in good shape; he spoke for twenty-five minutes and answered questions for an hour.

He said he wanted to be clear that "I do support Mr. Gorbachev," then proceeded to trash the Soviet leader as a political wheeler-dealer whose actions violated the Soviet constitution.

"I particularly support him strategically in his plans for perestroika (economic reform) and for a renovation of Soviet society," Yeltsin said. Then he accused Gorbachev of so mismanaging perestroika that "we find ourselves in a total crisis—an economic crisis, a social crisis, a crisis of poverty…We have a crisis within the party itself. We are on the edge of the abyss. If we slide into this abyss which is opening up before us, it will take many, many years before we can climb out again."

Henry Kissinger spoke to the Council often, but his best speech came just one week after Yeltsin's appearance, when the former secretary of state analyzed the problems that Gorbachev faced and talked about the new international order after the Cold War ended.

In Russia, he said wryly, "the political system doesn't really work, nor does the economic system. Otherwise, they're not in bad shape." Gorbachev had to find democratic legitimacy in an undemocratic system, Kissinger said. The command economy had ground to a halt but could not be reformed, "because there is a vested interest in that system on the part of the entire nomenclature, the Party, the secret police, the government bureaucracy, and the planning mechanism. Nobody has an interest in making his job dispensable."

Only the black market functioned efficiently, Kissinger said, and it created "an inherently corrupt system" that later blossomed into the era of oligarchs after the Soviet Union collapsed.

Kissinger said that Gorbachev understood these challenges and the need to moderate Soviet power. He continued,

> "The problem of attaining peace with Russia does not just lie with the personality of one Soviet leader, and it isn't even communism alone, but also with the historic

> *difficulty that Russia has trying to live in equilibrium with its neighbors...*
>
> *"How can we get Soviet power to retreat from its borders and, at the same time, not trigger a reaction that may lead us to war if the Soviets feel that their security is threatened?"*

It was a question that obsessed American administrations long after Soviet communism disappeared.

Then Kissinger laid out the global agenda for the years beyond the Cold War.

"With the decline of communist ideology, we have the opportunity to take a new look at international relationships and to discuss the kind of world we want ten years from now," he said. "There is an unusual period ahead of us in which we could construct a new international order." The challenge, he continued, was to,

> *"Define for ourselves a set of relationships whereby the key participants in the international system have a greater interest in maintaining the system than in overthrowing it. This kind of period does not often occur in history. When it does, leadership can make a huge difference.*
>
> *"We are in a unique position right now among the nations of the world in that we can say the shape of the future depends importantly on us, on the ideas and concepts we can form. We must remember that every great achievement was an idea before it became a reality."*

Chapter 7

New World Disorder

THE COLD WAR'S END CHANGED THE SUBJECT. SUDDENLY, the US was no longer declining, no longer just another player in a multipolar world, but the sole superpower, the hegemon, much as in the heady days after World War II. The national debate in the 1990s, in fact, echoed that earlier post-war dialogue. The mighty foe was gone, not only vanquished, but vanished. America and the world faced a clean slate. President George H.W. Bush foresaw a "new world order," but no one knew what that order would be. Once again, everything seemed possible.

After 1945, American leaders, remembering the failures of the isolationist past, created a global order, with the US at its center, that met the challenges of the next forty-five years. From the Council stage, the men and women who shaped that order, including titans such as George Marshall, debated and described what they planned to do. Now, a new generation of leaders, themselves products of the Cold War, argued over the shape of this new era and, especially, America's place in it.

The decade lasted, in essence, until September 11, 2001. What followed that catastrophic day showed that the 1990s, far from building a resilient new structure, deserved the derisive sobriquet, a "holiday from history."

But it was a busy decade. There were the early rise of China, civil war in Yugoslavia, humanitarian disasters in Somalia and Rwanda, the first Gulf War, ethnic cleansing in Bosnia, war in Kosovo, the expansion of NATO and the European Union, the humiliating decline of Russia, the rise and retreat of the UN as a real force for peace, failing states and non-state actors, the Oslo accords, and globalization and the transformative technological breakthroughs that accompanied it.

Lurking in the shadow of these events was America's search for a new doctrine that lived up to our values while respecting our limitations. Were we the world's policeman? Did we have a duty to implant and defend democracy everywhere? Should we use force in a new world in which most wars were within nations, not between them? What did national borders mean anyway, in a time plagued by genocide and swept by globalization? Mostly, should America use its unipolar moment to shape the future globally, or should it focus on its own domestic needs, many of which were neglected during the Cold War, and let the rest of the world carry the burden?

As was so often the case, the American debate swung between a vigorous interventionism and a more modest approach, not isolationist but less engaged. The Truman Administration created a durable foreign policy that was followed by the administrations, Republican and Democratic, that succeeded it. The Bush and Clinton administrations, lacking a single issue and a single foe, experimented but sunk no foreign policy roots.

The Chicago Council, too, struggled to find its place in this fragmented landscape. The Cold War had provided a fulcrum for all its programming; now, suddenly, there were many issues with no central theme. Membership declined to less than 8,000, and the Council's focus broadened. Until then, Council programs had been largely Eurocentric. John Rielly told the Board that the Council's mission remained the same: "to educate the leadership and the politically conscious citizens about the role of the United States in the world." However, the context for this mission had changed, especially as the Council faced new competition from other nonprofit organizations, elite travel agencies, and law and consulting firms that offered seminars on foreign affairs. At the same time, the new economy wiped out some of that audience. As Rielly told the Board, "The number of people with discretionary time and income decreases as downsizing, bankruptcy, and mergers continue to eliminate jobs in every profession."

Helmut Schmidt, the former chancellor of West Germany, spoke a year before the Soviet Union collapsed, but at a time when its end was near. The Soviet economy was getting worse by the day and, with all his challenges, "Gorbachev's period in office may be short and his success rather less than likely now than his failure," Schmidt said. The fading Soviet threat posed "a great challenge for many nations as they search for a future role for themselves and their armies after a forty-year preoccupation with the Soviet threat."

But a new threat loomed, Schmidt predicted—all too accurately, as it turned out. "Islamic fundamentalism may become a worldwide force in the oncoming years, and we better prepare for that. I'm talking about understanding, for the first time, for we to understand Islam."

Europe, especially the European Union, had a key role to play, Schmidt said. He continued,

> *"If the European community gets its integrative act together, she would in the first decade of the next century be the fifth superpower, an economic superpower, certainly stronger than Japan, almost as strong as the United States…It would be advantageous not only for the Europeans, but also for the rest of the world, because I do not think that it's a good world in which you have two communist superpowers, one in China and one in*

the Soviet Union, just one Western superpower in the United States."

Winston Lord, the American ambassador to China, reported on China after the Tiananmen Square massacre. He found "a new chill, a great leap backwards on all fronts, a new emphasis on ideology" and a move away from a market economy. But he predicted that the growing economic problems "will produce within a few years a more pragmatic, humane government that sees the Chinese people and Western countries as partners rather than enemies."

A decade of stagnant or declining median wages had become a political issue. Richard Gebhardt, a Missouri Congressman and former Democratic presidential candidate, accused the government of sacrificing jobs to geopolitics, by refusing to penalize unfair trade practices by allies such as Japan. "Two successive administrations," he said, "have chosen low wages for American workers, and this policy has taken its toll. For millions of middle-income American families… the ladder of economic opportunity has been replaced by a treadmill of frustration."

Al Gore, a senator from Tennessee and future vice president, won the Nobel Peace Prize in 2007 for his campaigning on climate change and the environment. The threat to nature was already on his mind when he spoke to the Council in 1992, warning of the danger that carbon dioxide posed to the balance between man and nature. "The effort to save the earth's environment must become the central organizing principle of the post-Cold War world," he said.

Margaret Thatcher was barely six months out of power as British prime minister when she spoke to the Council at the Chicago Hilton before a crowd of 4,000. The Council seldom pays a fee for any speaker, but it gave Thatcher $50,000, footed by John Bryan, then the Council Board chairman and also chairman of Sara Lee Corporation.

They got their money's worth. Thatcher had been pitched out of Downing Street by her own Conservative Party at least partially because of her growing hostility to the European Union and to a deeper British role in it. After first telling reporters she would "tone down" the anti-EU passages in her Chicago speech, she instead savaged the supranational Union, comparing it to the Soviet Union:

> "Any policy or program which fails to recognize the power of national loyalties is doomed to ultimate failure. Historians will one day look back and think it a curious folly that just as the Soviet Union was forced to recognize reality by dispersing power to its separate states, and by limiting the power of its central government, some people in Europe were trying to create a new artificial state by taking powers away from national states and concentrating them at the center...It is time to recognize, even in Brussels, that the age of empire is over."

Actually, Thatcher delivered two speeches—one for the audience at the Hilton, the other for the British back home. She went out of her way to praise her successor, Prime Minister John Major, for his "firm opposition to a federal Europe" in a speech he had given in Wales. But in fact, Major had criticized a federal Europe only in passing and reaffirmed Britain's place in a unifying Europe. The audience in Chicago heard one speech, which trashed Europe but praised Major. Readers in London understood the underlying speech, which left Major squarely on the spot between the pro-EU majority in his party and the unreconciled Thatcherites. Major had tried to fudge the issue. Thatcher, from a podium in Chicago, laid down the gauntlet.

After the speech, Thatcher went to a black-tie, invitation-only dinner and spent more than an hour shaking hands in the receiving line. Across the Atlantic, her speech helped keep Britain and her party split on Europe, a split that culminated with the British referendum, a quarter century later, to leave the EU.

In 1946, Winston Churchill delivered his famous "Iron Curtain" speech in Fulton, Missouri, announcing that the Cold War had begun. In May 1992, Mikhail Gorbachev, recently ousted as the last Soviet president, went to Fulton to officially bury the Cold War. He flew to Chicago that evening and, before a Council audience, urged Americans and Russians not to "repeat the mistake of 1946, not fritter away the capital of cooperation and mutual trust that was earned with such great efforts."

The Council and the Mid-America Committee co-sponsored Gorbachev's speech. At the evening's end, the corporate sponsors of the two organizations gave Gorbachev a $100,000 check for the Gorbachev Foundation, which he had just established to promote a "spiritual and moral healing" after the Cold War.

Dick Cheney, defense secretary in the first Bush Administration, called for increased defense spending and warned that changes in the Soviet Union were both welcome and dangerous. "No one should assume," he said, "that there is necessarily going to be a peaceful, orderly transition to the future in that part of the world. We cannot ignore potential ethnic conflict and civil war in the Baltics and Moldova and Georgia and Armenia and Azerbaijan and Tajikistan that could well [lead] to serious conflict there."

Colin Powell was the chairman of the Joint Chiefs of Staff and the architect of the Allied victory in the first Gulf War when he came to the Council to talk about America's new role in the world. Four years earlier, he said, he had taken part in a summit meeting with Gorbachev. "I'll never forget President Gorbachev sitting there and saying to the American leaders…'We are conducting a revolution. We are going to take away the enemy that you had counted on for the last forty years.'"

Now, with the 1992 presidential election just past, Powell said, "We Americans stand undisputed as the world's most powerful political, economic, and military nation. The obligation of leadership is ours. The power we have is a power that is trusted throughout the world, and history is counting on us to use it to help secure the post-Cold War world that we helped to create by our vigilance and by our sacrifice over the last fifty years."

Fortunately, he said, the election campaign had revealed "a remarkable degree of consensus across the entire American political spectrum about what our role should be. Our political leaders know this is not the time to start thinking about fortress America." Both President George H. W. Bush and the president-elect, Bill Clinton, "emphasize the importance of honoring our commitments to our allies."

Ten years later, Powell, as secretary of state, made the case at the UN for the US invasion of Iraq. But that night in Chicago, he looked back in satisfaction at the result of the Gulf War and the containment of Iraq.

"Saddam Hussein is an annoying pain," he said, "but he is a threat to no one outside his own borders."

Yegor Gaidar was a leading Russian economist and the designer of the post-Soviet "shock therapy" policies intended to jolt the country's economy into the capitalist future, but which were later blamed for the economic hardship that followed. This result lay ahead, when, in 1993, he told the Council, "One of the most serious problems for the entire civilization is whether Russia will take the road of Germany after the second world war or after the first world war. The security of the world strongly depends on this choice."

Gaidar pointed out that he had problems. One was the post-Cold War decision to slash military spending "when our economy is in its essence a military economy. The military sector is not just one of the many sectors of our economy, it is the central part." Then there was the political decision to privatize the economy quickly, in a country with few skilled managers. "It is possible to change fifteen ministers and bring to the government bright, young persons who support the market, but it is impossible to change 40,000 previous managers of the state enterprises." In addition, there was the hyperinflation—

nearly 9 percent per week. "So, it is very difficult to expect efficient financial stabilization of Russia in the next few months," he concluded.

Three weeks later, Warren Christopher, the new secretary of state in the Clinton Administration, praised the determination of Boris Yeltsin, now the president of Russia, to privatize companies, halt inflation, and stabilize the ruble.

"One of our highest foreign policy priorities [is to] help the Russian people build a free society and a market economy," Christopher said. "The stakes are monumental. If we succeed, we will have established the foundation for our lasting security into the next century. But if Russia falls into anarchy or lurches back to despotism, the price that we pay could be frightening."

The Cold War's end left Germany no longer on the eastern fringe of the West, but suddenly surrounded by friends, or at the least ex-enemies—and not very comfortable about it. Richard von Weizsäcker, the German president, or constitutional head of state, warned not to expect more from Germany than it could give.

"Let no one be in doubt," von Weizsäcker told the Council, "Germany is not the leading power in the European Community, it is not the senior partner, and it is not the first among equals either. Germany would not want such a position, could not hold such a position, and what is more should not be pushed into such a position." The reason, he said, was "the experiences and lessons of history—the horror committed in its name." For the same reason, Germany was loathe to join any NATO military action outside the NATO area. "While there is no lack of German support for conflict settlement the world over, there is no German finger on the trigger," he said. "Would you want it otherwise?"

Zbigniew Brzezinski was out of government and back in academia when he returned to the Council in 1994 to proclaim "the new world order" had been replaced by "global turmoil." The end of the Cold War "has not created an enhanced stability but has opened the doors to new forms of disagreement, collision, and conflict on the world scene," he said, from Europe to Russia to a nuclear North Korea to the "Islamic crescent." Russia in particular had "neither a democracy nor a free-market system, and the sources of instability are becoming stronger. The imperial impulse is rising."

That left it up to the US, "as the only global superpower," and its Western allies, to be the core of stability. But "the victorious West is not projecting a relevant message to much of the rest of the world capable of mobilizing its enthusiasm and support." The problem, he said, was not power, which the US had, but a shortage of moral leadership. Like Arnold Toynbee fifty years earlier, Brzezinski saw a powerful but morally unmoored America, rich in material goods but without the philosophical center traditionally filled by religion. He continued,

> *"Increasingly, much of the world perceives the West as essentially becoming preoccupied with what might be called a state of permissive cornucopia, a preoccupation with one's own well-being, a sense of heathenism and moral relativism, which is replacing either fundamental religious beliefs or moral imperatives...We are the first society in the world in which values are no longer transmitted from parents to children, first of all, reinforced by the schools and buttressed by the church. But we are a society in which values are instilled indirectly, largely by television, and the values that are thereby installed are not necessarily morally compelling."*

For the US to stabilize this new global turmoil, it "must be actively engaged and capable of projecting a vision that is compelling, attractive, [and] that simultaneously legitimizes the American leadership and generates support for it."

He had doubts about the commitment of this leadership. "I do not think that our present leadership is isolationist—far from it," he said. "But I do think it is minimalist in its interpretation of America's world role. It is prepared to do the least that is necessary but not more than that."

Les Aspin had been defense secretary until the US debacle in Somalia forced him out. This clearly was on his mind when he spoke to the Council in 1994 on the new post-Cold War role for the US military and the place of American "values," as he put it, in this role. The question, he said, was "the use of the US military in unlikely situations around the world, and…whether we should use US military in these unlikely places."

The military exists first of all to protect America's security, Aspin said, but increasingly it was being called upon to protect American values, to end starvation in Somalia or genocide in Yugoslavia. During the Cold War, he said, no one wanted American forces "to go in there and sort it out because…you didn't invite one side of the Cold War in without risking involving that region in the Cold War." Now the world was demanding American intervention, but it usually involved an internal fight within one country, not a war between two countries. He emphasized that this was "a huge, huge difference… The American military during its existence has been involved in preventing fights or dealing with fights across borders."

Aspin cited in particular the so-called "CNN effect." Until then, the media's coverage of far-off events had been a relatively stately affair, with battles and atrocities reported at a distance, for the morning newspapers or evening telecasts, giving governments the time to digest the news, prepare responses, and consider action. Cable news, exemplified by Cable News Network, or CNN, changed all that. Suddenly these events became immediate, appearing in real time on television sets across the nation, repeated and rehashed hour after hour, robbing officials of precious time to consider options and prepare a coherent response. Often, viewers at home knew as much about major events as the leaders who dealt with them: both were getting their news from CNN.

"You see the people who are starving," Aspin said. "You see the ethnic cleansing going on. You see the ambulances coming, and it's all on camera and the feeling wells up—we ought to do something. Something's got to be done…But CNN can build up pressure to bring the troops in, and it also can build the pressure to pull all the troops out." This had happened in Somalia. In the end, the military found itself doing police work, which it was not trained to do and didn't want to do.

"But the United States of America has values," he continued, "and in the post-Cold War world, if it doesn't stand up for these values, when is it ever going to stand up for them?"

Aspin suggested one solution—that US forces only intervene with a UN mandate—but he didn't sound as though that really settled the problem.

Aspin also opposed the expansion of NATO to include the former East Bloc countries, not because it would anger Russia, but because "what does it say about the ones you leave out? Are you saying that it's OK that the Russians had better not attack the ones that we've decided to let in, but it's OK to attack the ones that are left out?" The question exploded in Ukraine twenty years later.

—

James Baker had been secretary of state in the Bush Administration and a major shaper of the post-Cold War order in Europe. Now, he said, "The principal responsibility for the changed world we live in lies in the ordinary men and women who seek freedom, who struggle against the darkness of totalitarianism, and who rise up to seek liberty for themselves." It was seemingly a call for US intervention to defend values.

But like Aspin, Baker bemoaned the impact on foreign policy making of the communications revolution:

"Faxes, cellular phones, satellites, all of these things that reduce the time it takes to convey information from one side of the world to another. CNN, in particular, has made news very much a real time business and radically shortened the time that governance and policymakers have for decision making... When we have foreign policy by television, we have no foreign policy at all, unless you want to subscribe to the theory that America should be the policeman of the world."

Klaus Kinkel, the German foreign minister, told the Council, "The most urgent task is...to make democracy and the market economy irreversible in Central Europe, Russia, and Ukraine. Otherwise, we could slip back into a 'cold peace.'" Mostly, he said, "Russia must feel it belongs," through a partnership with the European Union, and "a special security partnership with NATO." This stopped short of membership in either organization, he said, but "Russia's links with the Western world are in any case already so close that it cannot afford to sever them."

Jack Matlock, the former American ambassador in Moscow, told the Council that the US helped bring the Cold War to an end, but the collapse of the Soviet Union itself was an internal affair led by Gorbachev. "Gorbachev recognized the Soviet Union needed a period of cooperation with the Western world if it was to reform," he said. "Everything he did was in his interpretation of the interest of the Soviet Union...So far, as the end of communism in the Soviet Union, we had only an indirect effort. We didn't aim to bring it down, though we never cared for it, and we were not unhappy to see it collapse. But that was done from within, primarily as a result of decisions made by Gorbachev."

Matlock said that, under Yeltsin, "Much of the power of decision making has seeped out of Moscow and to the people now in the provinces, particularly the elected governors. Many of the businesspeople are not about to submit to Moscow rule again in the way they had to in the past." Under Vladimir Putin, both these governors and businesspeople lost this independence.

With the collapse of the Warsaw Pact, the expansion of NATO to the ex-communist nations jumped to the top of the agenda.

Anthony Lake, President Clinton's national security adviser, told the Council in 1996, "NATO can do for Europe's East what it did for Europe's West fifty years ago. It can prevent a return to local rivalries. It can strengthen democracy against future threats. It can provide the conditions for fragile market economies to flourish."

Poland, Hungary, and the Czech Republic were the leading candidates for NATO membership and Robert Hunter, the US ambassador to NATO, urged their admission. "What we are being asked to do will irrevocably bind the United States to European security," he said, and continued,

> "It will impose new demands and, yes, some added cost. It will entail an enduring commitment to the security and stability of Central Europe. It will mean taking seriously the concerns of Russia and trying to answer them… In time, we want those who stand in Chicago, in Frankfurt, in Warsaw, Prague and Budapest, in Bucharest, and the Baltic States—and yes, in Kiev and Moscow—all to be able to say that what NATO has done has made their futures more secure."

Joseph Biden, then a senator, agreed that expanding NATO would bring historic benefits and failure would bring historic risks. "The desire to be a part of NATO has less to do with their immediate concerns about their security and more to do with their desire to be tethered to the West," Biden said. He continued,

> *"If we cannot provide a clear path, lead the way to nations that historically are western nations, who have as a consequence of a call of history been on the wrong side of a line for five decades, if we do not accommodate their yearning in some very meaningful way, they will work out their own accommodations.*
>
> *"I cannot say that I am absolutely certain that expanding NATO will not damage relations with Russia. But I believe, based on history, based on reality, and based on pragmatism, that it has the potential to…generate a dynamic debate within Russia that leads them to the conclusion that security in the gray zone of central Europe is not their enemy but their ally. And I could be wrong about that."*

Basically, Biden said, the US had no choice but to move into the historical vacuum of central Europe. "I believe every time the United States has concluded it is not a European power, we have been thrown into a European conflict. We are a European power."

Chaim Herzog, the former president of Israel, spoke to the Council five months before his death, and more than five years before 9/11. Much of his speech dealt with Israeli politics after the Oslo Accords, but he warned, "The major problem of the world in the Middle East today is not necessarily our problem with the Palestinians or with our neighbors. The major problem facing the world today—and it faces you just as much as it faces us—is the possible link-up of Islamic fundamentalism with weapons of modern mass destruction.

"Fortunately," he continued, "the one power that is really aware of the problem and that is trying to do something about it is the United States. But what is in danger is not only the state of Israel, but all the neighboring states—Saudi Arabia, Jordan, and so forth—to neighboring states to Iran and to Iraq."

A lineup of foreign leaders graced the Council stage in the 1990s without adding much to the post-Cold War debate. They included presidents—such as Kim Young-sam of South Korea; Václav Klaus of the Czech Republic; Jacques Chirac of France; Mary Robinson of Ireland; Eduardo Frei Ruiz-Tagle of Chile—and prime ministers such as Jean-Luc Dehaene of Belgium, and foreign ministers such as Lamberto Dini of Italy. Their speeches were bland orations that mostly boasted of progress in their countries and called for closer cooperation with the US. Experienced audiences knew that the most interesting speeches were often given by out-of-office politicians, such as Aspin or Baker, who were free to speak their minds.

Even Helmut Kohl, the German Chancellor who returned to Chicago in 1997 to speak at the Council's seventy-fifth anniversary, confined himself to platitudes. He gave thanks for American aid to Europe after World War II and made a plea to the US to stay close to Europe even as it shifted its attention to Asia. This echoed a familiar phobia among Europeans, and especially Germans, that the US would abandon Europe.

By contrast, one of the most remarkable speeches came from Robert McNamara, the former defense secretary and master planner of the Vietnam War. More than twenty years after that war ended, he wrote a pained book taking blame for the war and came to Chicago on a *mea culpa* trip to talk about it.

"We were wrong, terribly wrong," McNamara said, "and I believe therefore that we owe it to future generations to explain why." He then listed "eleven major causes for our disaster in Vietnam," a list that should hang in every policy planner's office.

First, he said, the US government misjudged the threat of North Vietnam and the Viet Cong to the US. Second, it misjudged the South Vietnamese, seeing them as fighters for democracy in our own image. Third, it underestimated the power of nationalism to motivate people. Fourth, it was ignorant of the history, culture, and politics of the region. Fifth, it overestimated high technology in modern warfare. Sixth, it failed to bring Congress and the American people into a full and open debate on the war. Seventh, it didn't level with the people when the war began to go bad. Eighth, "we don't have the God-given right to shape every nation in our own image or as we choose." Ninth, it failed to win real cooperation from other countries. Tenth, it forgot that, in life, "there may be problems for which there are no immediate solutions, certainly not military solutions. We may have to live in an imperfect world." And finally, the executive branch simply wasn't organized to deal with the complexities of the war.

"Now that this bloody century has come to a close, we have an opportunity to view the future with new hope," McNamara said. "The Cold War has ended. We have the lessons of Vietnam before us, so they can be learned and applied."

As the next decade showed, they weren't.

—

As McNamara said, the Cold War indeed was over. Globalization was about to become the dominant world theme, and Thomas Friedman gave Council audiences the first full description of what lay ahead. Friedman, the *New York Times* foreign affairs columnist, spoke to the Council in 1996, three years before his first book on globalization, *The Lexus and the Olive Tree*, was published. Critics complained that that book presented too rosy a picture of the global future as an inevitable and mostly positive force that would reward the nimble—both countries and people. His speech foreshadowed that upbeat view but was much more nuanced about the costs.

"We are seeing a new global architecture being produced," Friedman said. "We've gone from a world of superpowers to a world of supermarkets, and it's increasingly the power of markets and their impact on global politics…Whoever gets their economics and politics right will be rewarded with investment capital to grow by these supermarkets."

This was the new efficiency and discipline that he celebrated in *The Lexus and the Olive Tree*. But then he added:

> *"Whoever doesn't get it right will be left as roadkill on the global investment highway, and half of you are destined to be roadkill... The most interesting conflicts in the world today are between the winners and losers within countries. It's the people who get it, who have the knowledge, skills, the business skills, the marketing skills, to tap into this newly integrated world and profit from it. And it's the people who don't. It's the communists versus the oligarchs in Russia. It's the unions versus the industrialists in France. It's the Pat Buchanan forces versus the rest of the Republican party in this country."*

All this led not only companies but governments to downsize. He continued,

> *"So they are shrinking their social safety nets right at the same time that a whole new group of people are being thrown onto the market, and that's what's creating this turmoil...At a time when all these pressures are creating winners and losers and more are left behind, if we take away our social safety nets, as we shrink them radically at exactly the same time, I think it can create a very explosive social situation."*

Anthony Lake, a former national security adviser for President Clinton, spotted another "very explosive situation." Speaking a year before 9/11 happened, he said his nightmare was "the very real possibility of a catastrophic terrorist event using weapons of mass destruction," produced by "a new kind of semi-private terrorism in the world, what I would call existential terror." Before, terrorists operated within organizations such as the Irish Republic Army, serving clear political goals, and hence were easier to monitor, as opposed to the new private terrorists, who acted "out of a sense of weakness, out of a sense that they are powerless in the face of Western power and Western temptations."

Madeleine Albright spoke to the Council only three days before the Clinton Administration ended and she stepped down as secretary of state. Her speech has not stood the test of time.

She saw Russian President Vladimir Putin as "more pragmatic than democratic," someone who understood "that Russia cannot prosper in isolation from the West." Besides, "the Empire struck out. It will not strike back. The Russian people know too much of freedom ever to let it go."

She praised the establishment of normal trade relations with China, because "it encourages China to play a constructive regional and global role…Beijing is moving resolutely toward integration into the world economy."

Finally, she got the incoming Bush Administration wrong. "I expect," she said, "that the new administration will not depart dramatically from the current administration's approach on most issues. There will be much continuity."

Six months later, John Rielly gave his farewell address as Council president. He said the "central question in our work at the Chicago Council" remained as it had been since 1922—America's role in the world. This was changing, and for the worse, with an "increasing unilateralism" which undermined America's traditional global leadership. The Clinton Administration, by calling America "the indispensable nation," had begun this unilateralism, he said, and the Bush Administration had exacerbated it by abandoning treaties on arms control and the environment and taking an "openly confrontational stance with China."

—

The Council marked its seventy-fifth anniversary in 1997 with a gala banquet and a speech by German Chancellor Kohl. The *Chicago Sun-Times* saluted it as "one of the nation's largest and more prestigious world affairs organizations." And the *Tribune* had nothing but praise for its one-time ideological foe.

"For seventy-five years, the Chicago Council has been the primary outlet for that influential slice of Chicago with a strong foreign-policy itch," the *Tribune* wrote. "We're proud as punch to be home to such a world-renowned fixture, even if it defies simple description… Part watering hole for policy wonks, part networking opportunity for Chicago's ever growing international trade community, part travel agency and part intellectual singles bar, the Council over the years has served as a magnet for visiting world dignitaries, and the crème de la crème of foreign policy experts."

The "intellectual singles bar" referred to the Young Professionals program, an attempt to draw in younger members. The Young Professionals were founded in 1987, as the successor to the previous youth program, the Council Forum. It provided lectures on current events but also parties and trips. Speakers of that era tried to keep their remarks short, being very aware that the networking—the real point of the evening—was yet to come. As former Council Vice President David Mellon told the *Tribune*, "There's something about telling daddy that I met him at the Council on Foreign Relations that sounds better than saying he picked me up at a bar."

—

Programming remained strong and the Council's budget stayed in balance, but increasingly, challenges loomed. Ever since World War II and a growing supply of international news, the Council had lost its local monopoly on the foreign affairs debate. Now new rivals appeared, even as the economy gnawed away at the Council's constituency.

By the seventy-fifth anniversary, the changes in the travel program had cut Council membership to less than 8,000, far below its high of 23,000. Chicagoans who once had to join the Council to get a cut-rate charter flight had more choices now, and the membership that boomed with the charter era plunged when it ended. The times were changing, and not always to the Council's advantage.

As John Bryan, the new Board chairman, reported in 1994, "The end of the Cold War destroyed a simple and clear threat, which helped the popular membership focus on foreign policy matters. This, combined with more competition for the intellectual attention of the people today, have caused a decline in general membership."

Three years later, Bryan's successor, Duane Burnham, told the Board, "Changes in corporate America have had an enormous impact on the Council. There are at least ten people among our Board of directors who have changed their position last year because of retirement, firings, and voluntary resignations."

A year later, Burnham reported that mergers and acquisitions were gobbling up Chicago companies, many of them Council supporters. "The number of large companies based in Chicago that play an active role here has been reduced and is likely to be further reduced." For a Council that relied heavily on corporate support, this was ominous.

Rielly himself noted other challenges. In a report to the Board, he said that there was increasing competition in programming from other organizations, all putting on internationally themed programs for their clients, even as the Council's natural audience—the corner-suite people with the time and money to spend on its programs—shrunk through downsizing and mergers.

Rielly suggested expanding program offerings to new issues and regions, with "more attention to immigration, population, terrorism, and the environment, and focusing more attention on leaders and issues related to Central and East Europe, India, Indonesia, Mexico, and Brazil." The need was there: Europe still dominated Council programming. Other issues, such as immigration, barely registered. The real diversification had to await the new millennium and new leadership.

Then there were homegrown challenges from other clubs. The Economic Club, the Executives' Club, and the Chicago Chamber of Commerce focused more on domestic issues and business topics. With the economy becoming more global, all competed with the Council for top speakers.

The biggest competitor was the Mid-America Committee (MAC), a nonprofit world affairs council started in 1966 by Thomas Miner, a former Council Board member, as an adjunct to his for-profit consulting business. Miner had excellent contacts in Washington and specialized in bringing in government officials, both American and foreign, for off-the-record briefings for Chicago businesspeople.

By the early 1980s, competition from MAC had become a major concern of the Council. The two organizations had overlapping interests, overlapping audiences, and even overlapping boards; some Chicago executives belonged to both boards and were getting tired of supporting both. Rielly estimated that MAC and the Council's Chicago Committee and Corporate Service program "have 98 percent of the same constituencies and do the same sort of thing. This is the only community in the United States where there was such a situation—where a commercial entrepreneur, a consulting firm, is doing the exact same thing that a nonprofit organization is doing."

Occasionally, MAC and the Council hosted joint programming, like the Gorbachev dinner. More often they competed for the same speakers or even poached each other's speakers; a dignitary coming to Chicago for a Council dinner was grabbed by Miner for a MAC lunch.

At a 1983 Board meeting, one director, John D. Gray, complained, "These are two organizations competing head-on, and this community does not need two. There isn't room for both of them."

No one, including the board members of MAC and the Council, seemed to disagree. But it took another twenty years to solve the problem.

As if the homegrown challenges weren't enough, the Council faced new rivalries from New York. The Council on Foreign Relations (CFR) and the Asia Society were both established institutions with a national reach, and the Council had co-sponsored programs in Chicago with both. But in the mid-1990s, both stepped up their Chicago activities in a way that threatened the Council's membership and funding.

Membership in the New York CFR is by invitation only. It already included some Chicagoans, mostly academics and former government officials—not the big donors that a nonprofit needs. Under its new president, Leslie Gelb, the CFR began recruiting corporate and financial executives, and the head of its corporate program commuted regularly to Chicago.

According to Rielly, several members of the Chicago Council Board encouraged this CFR drive. But Burnham, while worried, noted that Chicago business leaders already felt there was too much overlapping between the Council and its Chicago rivals. He said, "Anything that contributes to a further proliferation of effort here is likely to be strongly resisted by the business community."

In the end, Burnham seemed to be right. The CFR still has national members, including Chicagoans, and still puts on four or five programs in Chicago each year, mostly dinners for its Chicago-based members. But it never recruited the corporate heavy hitters it had hoped, and the threat died away.

The Asia Society had bigger ambitions. It already had offices in Washington, Houston, and Los Angeles and, in the 1990s, planned new offices in Chicago and Seattle to provide more intensive programming in Asia than the Council offered. Rielly opposed this, as he had with the CFR campaign, mostly by urging Chicago's corporate leaders to steer clear of the New Yorkers.

Marshall Bouton, who later succeeded Rielly as the Council president, was then the executive vice president of the Asia Society. He talked with leading Chicago universities and corporations, including Motorola, and found mostly skepticism. The Asia Society needed solid financial backing—$250,000 per year for three years—from Chicago donors to make a Chicago office possible. That funding never appeared. Then the 1997 Asian financial crisis hurt the Asia Society's overall funding, and the idea died.

—

As the new millennium approached, it was time for a change. It had been a decade since the Cold War ended and China and India opened themselves to the world. But Council programming still focused on Europe. The Council served its corporate clients with programs on the global economy. But it largely missed the other half of the picture: Chicago itself, like the world, had changed.

The Council had been founded to bring news of the world to Chicago and to help Chicagoans understand their place in that world. At its founding, the city was an industrial behemoth, shipping its products into the world but isolated, by distance and culture, from that world. An important city certainly, but a provincial one.

Now, three-quarters of a century later, Chicago had lost much of its industry but had become a hub of the new global economy. Its homegrown businesses were global corporations now. Its universities both drew students and scholars from around the globe and scattered their ideas and research around that globe. Chicago law firms helped write the constitutions of new post-Cold War nations. Its LaSalle Street markets helped finance the global economy. Its consulting firms advised companies and nations on the mysteries of capitalism. New technology put the city into instant contact with London, Tokyo, and Singapore. Mostly, waves of immigrants, primarily from Mexico, had revived the city with new energy and new money.

Chicago was a different city, with a different place in the world. Before, it was more place-based, the capital of the Midwest, a more self-sufficient city, with its own money-center banks and evolving futures market. Now, it was part of the global mesh, less dominant perhaps, but a hub on the global value chain. Once removed from the world, Chicago now was part of the global landscape. Indeed, it was one of the commanding heights on that landscape.

The Council struggled to keep up with all this. It ran its programs for younger members, brought in speakers such as Thatcher and Gorbachev, and sponsored training sessions for teachers. But it remained Eurocentric, focused on issues of statecraft in a world dominated more now by economics than by strategy. If Chicagoans were more involved internationally than ever before, this did not translate automatically into the vital interest in foreign affairs that drove the Council for most of its history.

All this was underlined by a 1998 report called *Global Chicago*, written by the author of this history, and commissioned by the MacArthur Foundation, whose president, Adele Simmons, was the daughter of Herman (Dutch) Smith, a former chairman of the Council Board. The report argued that Chicago's many global assets, such as its corporations and ethnic communities, did not add up to a global city. This was partly because these assets operated alone, seldom cooperating, as "islands rather than an archipelago," and partly because the city remained midcontinental in its mindset—it did not see itself as the global metropolis it really was. To be a global city meant thinking like a global city, and someone had to bring all these fragments together into a conceptual whole.

The Council should be doing that job, the report said. It saluted the Council as "one of the oldest and strongest world affairs councils in the nation. If Chicago is more international in its outlook than it was twenty-five years ago, the Council deserves much of the credit." But because it "stands at the center of the foreign policy debate in Chicago," it should be "a key player in a broadly-based effort to reach out to Chicago's various foreign policy communities and lessen the fragmentation between them."

The report urged the Council to work more with ethnic communities and globally minded, non-governmental organizations; to present shorter and sharper programs tailored to a younger generation which was already getting its foreign news online; to work more with Chicago-area members of Congress to influence foreign policy, and to improve its antiquated website and data base.

Too many of the Council's regulars were "older, relatively well-to-do, and of European descent," and attended meetings in luxury hotels or starchy establishment centers such as the University Club, it said. Too often these meetings were seen as "elite" or "stuffy" by younger or more diverse Chicagoans, who simply didn't feel welcome.

The report led to the founding of the Global Chicago Center, funded by the MacArthur Foundation and housed at the Chicago Kent College of Law. At its start, it was mostly a website, a calendar of global activities and organizations in Chicago. In 2002, new Council leadership merged it, along with its ideas, into the Council.

That lay ahead. Rielly retired in 2001 and was saluted at a farewell banquet by a Council grateful for his thirty years of leadership. His old friend, Lord Robertson, the secretary general of NATO, came to salute the outgoing Council president. Marshall Bouton left the Asia Society to become the new president. He arrived in Chicago on August 13, 2001. Four weeks later, on September 11, 2001, the twin towers of the World Trade Center and the Pentagon were attacked.

A new era for the nation and the Council had begun.

Chapter 8

Millennium

JOHN RIELLY'S THREE DECADES SAW THE CHICAGO COUNCIL become, as he had hoped, a recognized institution in the American foreign policy establishment. But it was still a lean organization, with a staff of only seventeen people and a tight budget of $1.7 million. Marshall Bouton was a builder and, under his leadership, the Council burgeoned. When he retired after twelve years as president, the Council, already the biggest and most active world affairs council west of the East Coast, had a staff of about fifty and a budget of $11 million. More importantly, it took its first steps toward becoming a think tank. It shifted its traditional focus to a global outlook, with a new emphasis on Asia, and especially China. It tapped Midwestern expertise on global issues, such as agriculture, immigration, and trade. It even changed its name, to become the Chicago Council on Global Affairs.

"We've taken the Chicago Council to a whole new level of reach and reputation and impact," Bouton said in an interview when he retired. "We put the Council on the map of important and influential international affairs organizations in the United States."

A study of think tanks agreed that Bouton "transformed the Chicago Council's identity from an elite local forum for the discussion of ideas to a generator of new thinking for national debates on global affairs that could take advantage of its strategic position in the Midwest."

Bouton, a native New Yorker, got his doctorate in political science from the University of Chicago, but had spent little time in the city when he took the Council job. In his early years, he had been an aide to the American ambassador to India and worked on South Asian affairs for the Pentagon. He had been with the Asia Society in New York for twenty-one years and was the executive vice president there for eleven years; he guided its expansion in the US and Asia. Anxious to run his own organization, he was looking for a new challenge when the American foreign affairs network went into action.

First, Bouton got a call from Kenneth Dam, a University of Chicago law professor, former deputy Treasury secretary, and Council Board member, asking him if he would be interested in the Council presidency. At the same time, Michael Moskow, the president of the Chicago Federal Reserve Bank and another Council Board member, called Carla Hills, the former US special trade representative, seeking her ideas about Rielly's successor. Hills, an old friend, called Bouton. Dam added his support for Bouton. By the spring of 2001, he had the job.

Bouton came to Chicago with transformation on his mind. The Council needed a new global focus, especially toward Asia, and Chicago needed a world affairs organization to match its status as a global city. "Asia had risen," he recalled. "Chicago needed to contribute to the national discourse, to provide a voice. Chicago was a big city, a business powerhouse, but also the birthplace of isolationism. If there was a place that needed to make a statement about its place in the globalizing world, it was Chicago."

He got the job done, but it took time. Used to the frenetic, competitive thrust of New York, Bouton found Chicago a conservative place, where progress depended on cooperation and consensus, not competition. Increased funding came hard. The name change took five years. Some supporters felt the Council's proper role lay in its programs, not in diving into a research field dominated by East Coast think tanks.

But 9/11 helped. Four weeks after he arrived, on a brilliantly clear Tuesday morning, three hijacked airliners slammed into the two World Trade Center towers and the Pentagon; a fourth crashed into a Pennsylvania field as its passengers and their hijackers fought for control. The airborne drama lasted an hour and a half. It changed the mentality and mission not only of the country, but of its people, including members of the Council, who dealt with these issues. Suddenly, the twenty-first century had begun.

Bouton, seeking to give the Council new relevance, seized the opportunity. The 9/11 tragedy, as horrible as it was, "enabled me to hook my aspirations for this place into something that everybody could grasp." At an early Board dinner, he said, "The Council's role is the same but also different from the past. We live in a changing America in a globalizing world. The United States is a nation of nations, but at least until September 11, it sometimes saw itself as apart from the world. On September 11, we crossed a threshold into a new era."

Before that September ended, the Council held public programs, attended by hundreds of persons, both in the city and the suburbs, on the attacks and what they meant. Bouton scheduled panel discussions on "Immigration and America's Future: After the Attacks." The annual Chicago and the World Forum debated "Islam and the West." The Corporate Service Program discussed how terrorism had changed global business. Working with the Chicago Federal Reserve Bank, a series of breakfast seminars asked how terrorism was affecting trade, finance, and economic growth.

Bouton told the Board that he planned to devote three-fourths of the Council programming over the next year "to what has happened and its impact on our society and role in the world." With many Americans too frightened to fly, he closed down what was left of the travel program. At the same time, he hired a vice president for development to invigorate the Council's sluggish fundraising operations to pay for the growth ahead.

The challenges from the Asia Society and the New York Council on Foreign Relations had been settled by the time Bouton arrived. But the local challenge from the Mid-America Committee (MAC), festering for twenty years, remained. As one of Bouton's first orders of business, it was quickly solved.

Board members of the two organizations, who were often the same people, agreed that the feud was costly, confusing, and bad for Chicago. Within two months of Bouton's arrival, talks of a merger—in reality, an end to MAC—began. The biggest issue was the future of MAC's president, Tom Miner. By March of 2002, agreement had been reached to merge MAC into the Council and rename the Council's Corporate Program the Mid-America Committee; it soon reverted to its original name. Miner signed a non-compete agreement and got a one-year consultancy at the Council. Six MAC Board members joined the Council Board; one of them, Lester Crown, became the Council Board chairman for ten years, by far the longest-serving chairman in Council history.

Bouton also quickly brought the Global Chicago Center into the Council. As the travel program disappeared, so did the Ditchley Conferences. Bouton sponsored two more Atlantic Conferences, but they had been losing attendance and were ended. The Chicago Committee was replaced by the Global Economy Roundtable, a closed forum for local business leaders led by Moskow, the former president of the Chicago Federal Reserve Bank, who used his national contacts to draw in top economists and business thinkers.

Focused on growing the Council, Bouton experimented with new programs. Some succeeded, others didn't.

From the start, Bouton wanted to give the Council a voice—nationally and locally—that influenced public policy. The goal was a full-fledged think tank, but the Council lacked the money to bring in resident researchers. So, it staged a series of task forces in which groups of local experts and leaders spent months discussing a single topic to produce solid and widely publicized reports.

An early task force, on a foreign policy to reflect America's global primacy, foundered on misunderstandings. But another, on immigration into the Midwest, produced "Keeping the Promise," a report that helped set the agenda for the immigration debate to come. Future task forces dealt with the Midwest's place in a national energy policy, foreign direct investment, integrating Chicago's huge Mexican community into the city's political and economic life, and equipping Chicago to compete in the global economy. One of the most remarkable was a task force on the role of American Muslims in the nation's life after 9/11. All zeroed in on emerging issues and made recommendations that remain valid today.

The Global Chicago Center worked with WTTW, Chicago's public television station, on a series of short programs dramatizing Chicago's ties to a globalizing world: after sixteen segments, funding ran out and the programs ended. But the Center also sponsored a series called the *Heartland Papers*, booklets by academics on modernizing the rural economy, Mexican immigration, the future of biomass in renewable energy, and the restructuring of Midwestern higher education.

The Center also published a 2004 book, *Global Chicago*, financed by the MacArthur Foundation and spinning off the earlier MacArthur paper that led to the Center's founding. Its contributors analyzed how globalization had changed Chicago's economy, demographics, education, arts, and even its politics. Published by the University of Illinois Press, it was the first attempt anywhere to assess the impact of globalization through the lens of its effect on one city.

Instead of sponsoring conferences abroad such as the Ditchley Conferences, Bouton organized major conferences in Chicago, with mixed results. As he said later, "I misunderstood Chicago's thirst for attending conferences."

In 2003, the Council kicked off a series of conferences on the global economy with a two-day program on trade, set for September 15 and 16. It was timed to immediately follow a major meeting of trade ministers in Cancun, Mexico, on the progress of the Doha round of world trade talks. The Cancun meeting itself broke down in total disagreement; it was the beginning of the end of the expansion of the multilateral trading system.

Bouton's timing could not have been better. Many of the speakers at the Council conference flew straight from Cancun, full of anger and insights. For content, the conference was a triumph. But it drew a meager audience, possibly because Chicago's business community did not see the link between trade policy and business, and lost $100,000.

The traditional debate continued over the Council's role in Chicago. Was it an elite forum on foreign relations that catered to its members, or a civic institution that reached out to unserved Chicagoans, including persons not likely to become members? Bouton reached out mostly to immigrant communities, especially Chicago's vast Mexican population, not only with the task forces on immigration, but with meetings with leaders from Mexican, Korean, Chinese, and Filipino communities in their own neighborhoods.

An early goal was a younger and more diverse audience. This was achieved almost from the start. Audiences that had been mostly white and mostly older became more mixed, especially with Asians, as the Council programming expanded geographically.

Not all these initiatives stood the test of time. The outreach to immigrant communities, for instance, failed to gain the interest of more than a handful of leaders. But taken together, these ideas raised the Council to a more ambitious level and increased its visibility.

By 2004, Bouton was arguing that if "Chicago is our primary constituency," it was also vital to influence policy nationally and internationally and tap into expertise and leadership across the Midwest. With the folding of the Mid-America Committee, the Council dominated the Chicago foreign policy debate. The national and Midwestern campaigns were harder sells.

Bouton told the Board the Council "must become a significant producer of information and insights on the great issues of our time." In other words, it needed to become a think tank. Because it lacked the money for this, he said, "the Council will operate as a 'virtual' think tank, tapping the expertise on various issues in Chicago and Midwestern universities, businesses, local and state governments, media, and other fields."

By 2010, the virtual think tank existed and one of its reports, on America's foreign agricultural policy, led to a change in that policy, brought in millions of dollars in funding, and established the Council as a true think tank. The first two senior fellows were Moskow and the author of this history; for both, it was a retirement job. Catherine Bertini, the former head of the UN World Food Program, came on next, and split her time between the Council and Syracuse University. The first full-time fellow was Roger Thurow, a former *Wall Street Journal* correspondent who wrote a series of books on global hunger issues for the Council.

The Council also needed a regional footprint, Bouton said. "At present, the Midwest lacks a non-university-based organization that brings the interests and concerns of the region to bear on policy-relevant discourse in the nation and beyond."

The *Heartland Papers* filled part of this need. So did a series of meetings on the Midwest, which were held in Chicago and other cities. So did briefings on major regional issues, such as trade or immigration, for journalists from Midwestern newspapers. So did attempts to strike up a conversation across state lines with community colleges. But the Council never established a permanent regional presence, and the programs gradually faded away.

Despite this uneven progress, the changes by 2010 were visible, with a swing toward transnational and global issues. In 2003, 22 percent of all programming dealt with Europe, 17 percent with Asia, and 20 percent with transnational issues. By 2010, Europe commanded only 3 percent of the program, compared to 23 percent for Asia and 38 percent for transnational issues. Membership was up to 6,000 from 4,000. The number of programs had increased by 38 percent, and total attendance by 62 percent.

For the first time, the Council began working with City Hall. Early Chicago mayors such as Big Bill Thompson hated foreigners, especially the British. Mayor Richard J. Daley cared only for local politics and his successors were almost as parochial. Daley's son, Richard M. Daley, talked local like his father but had a global outlook, and presided over Chicago's emergence as a global city.

Bouton, well connected in China, had already set up a "Chicago-Shanghai Dialogue" a series of meetings with leaders of that city in 2004. Two years later, he sponsored Daley's first trip to Shanghai, a jaunt that led to more contacts, including a Chicago meeting in 2014 between trade and commerce ministers of the two countries. The occasion was a session of the Joint Commission on Commerce and Trade, a US-Chinese body whose annual meetings were almost always held in Washington or Beijing; the Chinese conclave was only the second in twenty-five years outside the capitals.

Most dramatically, the Council changed its name. In 2006, after eighty-four years as the Chicago Council on Foreign Relations, it became the Chicago Council on Global Affairs. Bouton had pressed for the change since his arrival, but it took five years to persuade the Board to do it.

Partially, the Council changed its name because, in the global era, nothing was truly "foreign." Its strategic plan saw a "historic shift in the fundamental dynamics of world affairs—from a world dominated entirely by nation-states to one increasingly shaped by global forces operating independently of nation-states. To many observers, the term 'foreign' is at best anachronistic in this age."

Another reason for the name change was mentioned only in passing. It ended the perennial confusion, dating to the Council's founding, with the New York-based Council on Foreign Relations. The Chicago Council was simply tired of being seen, wrongly, as a branch office of the New York Council.

With the name change came a new mission statement. The old statement said the Council was "an independent, nonprofit, nonpartisan organization committed to building global awareness in Chicago and the Midwest and contributing to the national and international discourse on the great issues of our time." The new statement added it intended to "influence the discourse on global issues through contributions to opinion and policy formation, leadership dialogue, and public learning."

Mostly, it planned to "create intellectual capital through studies and publications produced by research teams, task forces, and individuals including Council fellows." It would do this by focusing on five major themes: the global economy, democratization, sovereignty and intervention, global institutions, and changes in American society.

The goal was to reach "key constituencies beyond Chicago"— national and international policy makers, media, think tanks, foundations, and global business leaders, plus policy makers and leaders across the Midwest. "These," it said, "are precisely the constituencies in which the Chicago Council is now least well known. To the extent the Council is now known beyond Chicago, it is almost entirely in limited foreign policy circles in Washington and other capitals as a speakers' platform in Chicago and the sponsor of the quadrennial public opinion survey."

The 2010 strategic plan also emphasized the Council's ties to the Midwest. It not only proposed to act as the voice of the Midwest but promised to tap foreign policy expertise across the region.

All this was supposed to happen by 2010. As noted above, it took longer than that, but the seeds definitely had been planted.

—

John Mearsheimer was a political science professor at the University of Chicago and the leader of the realist school of international relations. Witty and provocative, he had been a frequent speaker at Council events for many years when, in 2006, he and a Harvard colleague, Stephen Walt, published an article in the *London Review of Books* called "The Israel Lobby and US Foreign Policy." The article argued that the powerful Israeli lobby in Washington exerted an unwarranted influence on US foreign policy, with results that damaged American interests in the Middle East.

The article stirred immediate controversy. Mearsheimer and Walt were accused of anti-Semitism, which both denied. They claimed they supported Israel's right to exist and, in fact, said that the Israeli lobby, and especially the American Israeli Public Affairs Committee (AIPAC), were only doing their job as a lobby, like the National Rifle Association. But they argued that AIPAC, like the NRA, "has helped produce policies that are not in the US national interest."

Mearsheimer and Walt expanded the article into a book with the same title. The Council often presented authors of books on foreign affairs; as frequent Council speakers, Mearsheimer and Walt were invited automatically, apparently without consultation with Bouton.

Then the storm began. Details remain disputed, but the clearest account is the open letter that Mearsheimer and Walt wrote to the Council Board, describing what happened next.

First, they said, Mearsheimer heard from Council schedulers that it had received protests about their appearance. Then, Mearsheimer received a call from Bouton.

Mearsheimer wrote that Bouton "said he felt 'extremely uncomfortable making this call' and that his decision did not reflect his personal views on the subject of our book. Instead, he explained that his decision was based on the need 'to protect the institution...This one is so hot,' Marshall maintained, that he could not present it at a Council session unless someone from the 'the other side'...was on stage with us."

Bouton suggested turning the speech into a panel or debate. Mearsheimer refused, so Bouton cancelled the event.

The details of what happened behind the scenes are shrouded in conflicting stories. Mearsheimer and Walt saw it as a case of censorship and intimidation, and "surely not the way the Council normally conducts its business. This is undoubtedly why Marshall, who is a very smart and decent man, felt so uncomfortable calling us to say the event had been cancelled. He knew this decision was contrary to everything the Council is supposed to represent."

The incident received national attention, including a story in the *New York Times* and protests from other academics. Other venues also cancelled speeches by the authors, including the City University of New York, but the Council shared in the criticism.

Years later, both Mearsheimer and Walt have spoken to Council audiences, although not about the Israeli lobby. Relations between the leading world affairs body in Chicago and the city's best-known international relations scholar have been restored. But it was the most painful moment in Bouton's presidency.

—

Ten days after 9/11, Gareth Evans, the president of the International Crisis Group and former Australian foreign minister, praised the US response to the attacks as "gritty, determined, measured, and recognizing very clearly that the response just had to be cooperative and multilateral, not just a unilateral one, with the US going it more or less completely alone." The attacks themselves, he said, stemmed from an irrational "blind hatred of modernism, of the impact of globalization. The unhappy reality is that the US is the natural international target of this kind or resentment."

Pervez Musharraf, the president of Pakistan, presented his country as a leader in the fight against terrorism. "Pakistan is against terrorism in all its forms and manifestations, wherever it occurs," he told the Council. "We are part of the international coalition in the fight against terrorism." On the same trip, he told the *Chicago Tribune* that Al Qaeda "is on the run" and said he "guessed" that Osama bin Laden was dead; US Navy Seals killed the Al-Qaeda leader in Pakistan nine years later.

Jack Straw was the foreign minister in the British Labor government, which sided strongly with the Bush Administration in the lead-up to the invasion of Iraq. Five months before the invasion, Straw told the Council, "Dealing with weapons of mass destruction, particularly with Iraq's possession of weapons of mass destruction, and with international terrorism, are part of an overall strategy to try and make the world a safer place. We have to deal with all of these threats in order to deal with any one of them."

Saddam Hussein's government, he said, was "a prime example of a regime which despises our values…The Iraqi regime should be left under no illusions of the consequence of noncompliance, of the depth of our resolve." As Straw spoke, anti-war demonstrators protested outside, but John Madigan, the Council Board chairman and host at this program, assured him they "could not possibly be from Chicago."

Thomas Friedman, the *New York Times* columnist, agreed with Evans on the cultural roots of 9/11. "In every household there are two or three young people not working. They have nothing to do. They go to the mosque; radical preachers fill their heads with crazy ideas. Everything is the fault of the Americans. And that is a big part of the 9/11 story in my view."

Friedman, who later supported the US-led invasion of Iraq, had doubts when he spoke to the Council. He said it was not "a crazy argument" that Saddam Hussein had "to be taken down for the sake of the world." But he said Saddam had been deterred for the previous ten years; overthrowing him was not enough.

> *"If you are for taking Saddam Hussein down, you have to be for nation building. You have to be for a prolonged American occupation of Iraq to build, and nurture, and put together a more Arab, Islamic, progressive, Iraqi state. What worries me about the Bush Administration is that these guys are really good at smashing things, OK? But I am deeply suspicious about their ability to build anything."*

Madeleine Albright, now out of office, returned in September 2003, when the Iraqi invasion was just beginning to sour, to say it was going badly:

> *"We didn't need [international support] to win the war, but we do need it to win the peace because the weapons of mass destruction we expected to find have not been found. The Iraqi cheers we hoped would greet us have been few and far between. The oil revenues we believed would pay for reconstruction are insufficient. The enemy we thought we defeated has come back to fight in a less conventional way, and the international terrorists we sought to intimidate have instead been drawn to Iraq by the chance to shoot Americans.*
>
> *"The president said that the terrorist threat to America and the world would be diminished. But our occupation of Arab land has become a recruiting tool for Osama bin Laden. So, Iraq has become a far more imminent danger to Americans now than it was prior to the conflict."*

A month later, Condoleezza Rice, the national security adviser, came to the Council to argue that, even though no weapons of mass destruction had been found, Saddam Hussein intended to use them:

> "Right up until the end, Saddam lied to the Security Council. And let there be no mistake, right up to the end, Saddam Hussein continued to harbor ambitions to threaten the world with weapons of mass destruction... [Saddam] is the only tyrant of our time to possess weapons of mass destruction. He has maintained his ties to terror. We have no evidence that he was involved in the 9/11 attacks, but the prospect can't be put aside. The threat [he presents] is so catastrophic that it is not a threat that can be maintained."

A year later, Rice, sobered and less optimistic, was back to say that the US was trying to build "a free, democratic, and successful Iraq as a beacon and a catalyst in the Middle East." But she acknowledged that this "will require a commitment of many years, across many fronts. We will have the makings of a failed state in Iraq, like Afghanistan was in the 1990s, and it could become a base of operation for terrorists."

"Americans must be prepared for violence to continue in Iraq," she said. "Even after a government is formed, there will be no Iraqi equivalent of VE Day or VJ Day. Peace will be secured as more and more Iraqis recognize that the democratic process is open to them and that politics, not violence, is the best way to achieve their interests. This is how democracy will conquer terrorism, but it will do so gradually."

Rice's appearance was part of a White House public relations offensive to counter growing disillusionment with the war in Iraq. Soon after Rice spoke, Defense Secretary Donald Rumsfeld came to the Council to assert America's Afghan policy "clearly is a booming success," and "the rise of democracy in Iraq will deny terrorists a base of operation."

"If I read the media," Rumsfeld said, "I'd have to be discouraged. But if I look at the progress, one has to be hopeful."

As for Afghanistan, the president himself, Hamid Karzai, came to the Council to tell a sold-out crowd that his country was on the path to recovery, with five million children in school, a new constitution, and an economy that was growing at a 25 percent pace annually.

"It is possible to have democracy in our part of the world," Karzai said. "It is possible to have institutional reform in our part of the world."

—

Dick Prall was a rock guitarist from a small town in Iowa who worked on the Council's programming staff but lived for the music that he and his band played in bars around Chicago. The owners and employees of some of these bars shared Prall's interest in foreign affairs. Out of this came GOAt, the tortured acronym for Globally Occupied Attention, an initiative that brought the Council a lot of favorable publicity and also one of its most controversial moments.

At the time, the Council was trying to overcome its reputation as a stuffy establishment club offering boring lectures to wealthy senior citizens. Chicago teemed with well-educated and well-traveled young people who seldom came to Council programs. Prall's inspiration was to take the Council to them.

GOAt staged lively debates on foreign policy issues in the music rooms of Schubas Tavern and other bars, in the early evening before the bands came on. The bars served beer before and during the debates. Debaters were limited to five-minute arguments followed by long question-and-answer sessions. The bars loved it, because many of the attendant thinkers were drinkers. The Council got unaccustomed praise from the entertainment pages of Chicago's press. Costs were low; the bars donated the space and most of the debaters were local experts and required no travel stipend. But GOAt recruited few new members for the Council and, when Prall left Chicago to make music back in Iowa, the program died.

One GOAt program became a *cause célèbre*. John Yoo was a former legal counsel in the second Bush Administration and a defender of the use of torture; he argued that the president was not bound by the War Crimes Act based on the Geneva Conventions. Yoo had just written a book, and Prall invited him to debate with Douglass Cassel, a leading human rights lawyer then teaching at the Notre Dame Law School.

The debate was open to the public but, on Yoo's insistence, no recording was allowed. The program was about to begin when four persons who had purchased tickets entered, took a table, stripped off their street clothes to reveal orange jumpsuits, put on hoods, and stood on their chairs. The Council, unnerved, agreed to let them stay only if they sat down and promised no outbursts or protests. True to their word, the four sat quietly—even when Cassel maneuvered Yoo into a remarkable statement:

> *Cassel: If the president deems that he's got to torture somebody, including by crushing the testicles of the person's child, there is no law that can stop him?*
> *Yoo: No treaty.*
> *Cassel: Also, no law by Congress...?*
> *Yoo: I think it depends on why the president thinks he needs to do that.*

Two weeks later, *Revolution*, the newspaper of the Revolutionary Communist Party, published the Cassel-Yoo exchange. Other publications picked up the story. It turned out that the protesters, deceptively well behaved, had tape recorders under their jumpsuits. Yoo, feeling betrayed, demanded an apology. Prall argued there was no way the taping could have been prevented, short of frisking the paying customers. Bouton, assured that Yoo had actually said what he said, backed Prall, and the incident eventually died down.

—

Paul Krugman, the Nobel Prize-winning economist, came to the Council in 2003 to rail against the Bush-era tax cuts and the danger that the resultant budget deficits would bring on a new recession. Asked when this recession would happen, he said, "I don't know, but if you want to guess, I'd say three in the afternoon on May 30, 2008." He was off by about six months. In passing, he praised a new book on bankruptcy by a then-obscure law professor and future senator, Elizabeth Warren.

On his path to the White House, Barack Obama spoke to the Council three times: in 2004 as a Senate candidate making his first major foreign policy speech, again in 2006 as a senator, and in 2007 as a presidential candidate. Obama had made his name in foreign policy circles with his early opposition to the Iraq War, and all three Council speeches continued his criticism of the Bush foreign policy.

In 2004, he warned Iraq could "disintegrate into chaos, [and] will plant the seeds of an even greater and more poisonous radicalism." He urged international attempts to curb Iran's nuclear ambitions and accused the administration of wasting three years by refusing to negotiate with North Korea, "in the name of a misguided sense of moral purity."

In 2006, he called for a "phased redeployment of US troops from Iraq," while opening a dialogue with Iran, policies he carried out as president. He quoted polls indicating a swing toward isolationism in America and warned, "We can't afford to be a country isolationist in the twenty-first century. Nine-eleven showed us that, try as we might to ignore the rest of the world, our enemies will no longer ignore us, so it is absolutely vital that we maintain a strong and active foreign policy."

In 2007, he declared "the American moment is here," but the challenges—an end to the war in Iraq, countering global warming, nuclear non-proliferation—required not only American leadership but strong alliances.

"America cannot meet the threats of this century alone," he said, "but the world cannot meet them without America. We must neither retreat from the world nor try to bully it into submission."

Tony Blair, the former British prime minister, had given a major speech in Chicago in 1999, laying out the rationale for international intervention, especially on humanitarian grounds. But he gave that speech to the Economic Club, not the Council, a case of a big speaker who got away. Ten years later he was back, but before the Council this time, to defend his intervention theory after it had been put to the test in Iraq and Afghanistan.

"Iraq, though measurably improved from two years ago, remains fragile," he said. "Afghanistan is proving to be a battle needing to be re-waged. My argument is that the case for the doctrine [of intervention] remains as strong now as it was then, and that what has really changed is the context... The struggle can only be won by the long haul."

Thomas Pickering, perhaps America's most distinguished diplomat, in his own critique of the Iraq War, told the Council, "As we have found out at our peril, force is there to be used only in the most extreme circumstances, only as a last resort." Saddam Hussein did not present a "clear and impending danger" to the US, and it was wrong to go to war there without exhausting the diplomatic remedies.

Pickering said it was time to begin negotiations with Iran. So did another veteran of Middle East diplomacy, Dennis Ross, who said the key to these negotiations was economic sanctions, which depended on full cooperation from European nations. "[Iran's] economic lifeline is found in Europe. If you want to change their behavior, you have to affect the Europeans."

Radosław Sikorski, the Polish foreign minister, laid out the differences between Russia and the West that served as a guidepost to the next decade. "The European Union is about overcoming borders," he said. "Russia clearly has shown that it is in a different century, in the eighteenth or nineteenth century, where a border dispute was the norm. Russia has thrown out an ideological challenge because it says we can do it different, and it works, and what are you going to do about it?" He continued,

> "Russia has again chosen a model of politics, not through a representative mechanism...but through internal mo-

bilization against an external enemy. I think we now have Russia speaking overtly in a language that is confrontational with the West and with the United States in particular. Russia is saying openly that we do not accept American leadership. The unipolar moment is over."

The challenge is not nuclear annihilation, he said, "but piecemeal, below the radar," including lobbying and other modern techniques.

Joschka Fischer, the former German foreign minister, cast a bleak eye in 2008 on the previous eight years, in both the US and Europe. "The last eight years were devastating for the United States," he said, because of the Iraq War. But Europe also, despite the enlargement of the European Union and NATO, "was not able to restructure itself to become a real power. Part of the present weakness and disunity on the European side is due to the fact that we managed enlargement, but we failed to streamline our institutions," to create a common foreign and security policy and to create joint economic institutions. Now, with the 2008 economic crisis and recession, we were "stuck in this gap."

The most successful initiative of the Bouton years dealt with food and agriculture, especially the overwhelming hunger and poverty in sub-Sahara Africa. The initiative linked Chicago expertise, Gates Foundation money, and a friendly administration in Washington. It produced a shift in American policy and, in the process, established the Chicago Council as a think tank.

From the time he arrived, Bouton wanted to do a major project on agriculture. In 2006, a Council task force produced a report calling for reforms in American farm trade policy. One of the cochairs was Catherine Bertini, the former head of the UN's World Food Organization.

About that time, the Bill & Melinda Gates Foundation, aware of the growing hunger crisis in Africa, wanted to help develop Third World agriculture. The leader of the project, Rajiv Shah, hired Bertini as an adviser. Shah need an organization to take the lead and Bertini, fresh from her Council task force, suggested that she and Shah fly to Chicago to talk with Bouton.

Over lunch at the University Club, Shah said the US government had done little in overseas agricultural development since the Green Revolution, which had done so much to reduce hunger. The problem now was acute in sub-Sahara Africa, he said, and he wanted to get the government involved again. For this, he needed a white paper to present to the transition team of the candidate who won the upcoming election. This was in April of 2008; the election was in November. In other words, Bouton was handed a six-month deadline. Shah promised Bouton that Gates would come up with the money by June.

Armed with this promise, the Council went to work. Once again, Bertini co-chaired a task force with Dan Glickman, the former secretary of agriculture. Robert Thompson, a professor at the University of Illinois, led an experts' group. Shah delivered $1 million in June— blinding speed, by foundation grant-making standards. One Gates official who put the grant together was Alesha Black, who later joined the Council as head of its food program.

The white paper was ready by November. The transition team liked it, because it argued that the emerging global food security crisis would impact American national security. Bertini and Glickman met members of Congress, including Senator Richard Lugar, the Indiana Republican, who discussed the report with Hillary Clinton, then the new secretary of state. Clinton responded by telling Lugar, "This will be our blueprint." President Obama signaled his agreement in his inaugural address when he pledged to poor nations "to work alongside you to make your farms flourish and let clean waters flow, to nourish starved bodies and feed hungry minds."

Suddenly, the Council's report had become administration policy. Not long after, Clinton announced a nine-point plan called Feed the Future that followed the Council's work almost point by point. Among other things, it put women at the center of this strategy, a priority for Bertini. A month later, the Council staged the first of its annual symposia in Washington on global food and agriculture.

Gates, impressed, gave the Council a three-year $3 million grant—one of the biggest in Council history—and the Council set up its Global Agricultural Development Initiative, or GADI, led by Lisa Moon, who had worked with Black on the original grant. The Council opened its first Washington office, to keep pressure on Congress. Obama included the Council's Feed the Future plan in his foreign aid bills, which Congress passed during his administration. In 2016, just before Obama left office, Congress authorized a separate Global Food Security Act, funding it for eighteen months; in 2018, the Trump Administration and Congress authorized it for five years, at $1 billion per year, in effect institutionalizing it as an American program.

In the meantime, GADI became the Global Food and Agricultural Program, to get the word "food" in its name. Moon left the Council and Black took her place. Roger Thurow co-authored a book on hunger under Council auspices, then left the *Wall Street Journal* to become a Council fellow and author of later books on food and nutrition, in the US as well as Africa. With continued Gates funding, the program had eight employees, plus consultants and non-resident fellows.

All this showed that, despite doubts, Chicago could have a globally-recognized think tank. It proved the Council could influence policy. It gave the Council access in Washington and in other think tanks. As a study of think tanks said, it "positioned the Chicago Council as both a locally grounded and a nationally relevant policy organization." Before, the Council was typical of outside-the-Beltway institutions that had "excellent regional reputations but…had to build a national brand to break into the crowded national field of think tanks." The food security project helped the Council "burnish its national reputation through its direct impact on global policy."

Most notably, as Bouton said, "this became an issue on which the Council credibly established itself as a leading national think tank."

—

As the 2000s turned into the 2010s, the tone of Council speeches changed in an unsettling way. The Bush foreign policy, almost universally lamented by speakers, was history, but few seemed enthusiastic about President Obama's stewardship.

The Council had reacted fast to the 9/11 disaster. Then, when Lehman Brothers collapsed in the waning days of the Bush Administration and the recession began, it did it again, with a rapid series of programs, framed by the program director Niamh King—a series especially valuable to Chicago's business community.

The 2008 crash hung over many programs, even as the recession receded. There was an underlying current of unease about inequality, the power of money in politics, a dysfunctional economy, and a gridlocked Congress. Abroad, the focus continued to swing away from Europe and toward Asia and its trouble spots, such as China, Afghanistan, and Korea.

Robert Reich, a member of Obama's economic transition advisory board and a University of California professor, told the Council in 2010 that, officially, the recession was over. "Do you not feel better?" he asked. "It just shows how large a gap exists between academic economics and the lives of most people, because most people don't feel that the great recession is over."

Instead, he said, most of the post-recession gains had gone to the top 1 percent, leaving the rest behind. The result was that "there is not enough aggregate demand out there from the great middle class or working class." Nor were things likely to get better. Globalization and automation had stolen "a lot of routine jobs and even factories. If you don't have the right education, the right training, the right connections, if you're not in the right place, globalization and technology are not your friends. They are your enemies…The long-term challenge is not jobs, per se. It is wages."

All this has political consequences, Reich said. An anemic and unbalanced economy "generates a politics of anger and resentment because so many people are so insecure and so anxious and so fearful. They are easy targets for demagogues who want to use their fear and channel it into a politics of resentment that blames immigrants, that blames international trade."

Gary Becker, the Nobel Prize-winning economist at the University of Chicago, told the Council, "the American dream will continue to live" if there were reforms in five areas: in education, he called for voucher programs and charter schools; in immigration, he urged a point system for skilled immigrants; in entrepreneurship, he favored cuts in taxes and regulations; in government, he urged tougher budget controls, mostly through reforms in Social Security and Medicare; and in taxes, he called for a move away from income taxes toward consumption taxes.

Al Gore, the former vice president, said that an unprecedented galaxy of global challenges was transforming the world, and all were out of control. Gore, in a speech entitled "The Future," cited "six drivers of global change": globalization, the digital revolution, climate change, genetic engineering, the shift of global power from west to east, and the seizure of American politics by big money. Once, technology led to higher productivity and better jobs; now, he said, it was destroying jobs.

Chuck Hagel, the former Republican senator from Nebraska and later defense secretary in the Obama Administration, lamented, "We've lost confidence in our institutions and we've lost trust in their leaders." The greatest threat, he said, was not terrorism but "global instability, because everything flows from that."

Peter Orszag, the former director of the Office of Management and Budget, said the recession "left scars that may be permanent. These included the growing inequality in earnings and wealth, with more money going to capital and less to labor." This in turn led to political polarization.

Orszag had worked for President Obama. Edward Lazear had worked for President George W. Bush, but he was no more optimistic. The post-recession problem, he said, was the Obama Administration's tax and trade policies, which blocked business investment.

Francis Fukuyama returned to the Council to contrast the democratic American political system, based on checks and balances, with the autocratic Chinese system, based on internal controls over the leadership. Speaking in 2011, he used an eerily prophetic example to make his point: "There's a more rigorous vetting system to get promoted within the communist party hierarchy," he said. "I mean, Donald Trump can run for president and anybody can run for president, but the Chinese would never let Donald Trump get into the [party's] Central Committee. You can guarantee that."

Ahmed Rashid, the Pakistani journalist and frequent Council speaker, said the fighting in Afghanistan was "a crying shame and a crying waste of money and blood and toil by the US. It is all to do with Iraq, taking the eye off the ball, not being sufficiently engaged in Afghanistan." The only solution, he said, was that "the US will have to talk to the Taliban."

Those talks failed. Two years later, Rashid told the Council, "I blame the Americans more than the Taliban" for the failure. The reason, he said, was "paralysis in Washington," with the State Department pushing concessions and the Pentagon blocking them. Now, American policy was more united, but "the Taliban are refusing to come back to the table."

—

Václav Klaus was president of the Czech Republic, a former student at the University of Chicago, a committed Thatcherite, and a fervent opponent of the European Union, even as his country was cementing its membership within it. To the Council, he decried the "large-scale centralization, excessive bureaucratic regulation, unnecessary standardization, and harmonization of the whole continent." He also opposed "the creeping but constantly expanding green legislation. The greens must be stopped from taking over much of our economy under the banner of such flawed ideas as global warming.

"For someone like me who lived for half a century under communism," he said, "the most important point is Europe should return to democracy, which can exist only at the level of nation states, not at the level of the whole continent."

Anne Applebaum, a *Washington Post* columnist and the wife of Radosław Sikorski, said that, despite Klaus, all central European nations were committed to European values and, unlike Britain, had no desire to leave the EU. Russia, on the other hand, was reverting to authoritarianism, with a suppression of civil society, targeted violence, and media control. "Russia," she concluded, "is threatened by countries that have made the transition to democracy."

Chris Hill, the former US ambassador to South Korea, told the Council the new North Korean leader, Kim Jong-un, "is about as not-ready-for-prime-time a leader as you will see anywhere in the world. I don't think there's any evidence to suggest that he has a clue about what he's really doing. I think he's more of a cult figure or a third-generation cult leader."

Hill warned against a repeat of the "bellicose statements" that the Bush Administration launched against the North Koreans, because "they were really harming the fabric of the US-South Korean relationship," by making Washington the cause of instability, not Pyongyang. "We're not going to be able to solve this problem if we're not going to get on the same sheet of music as the South Koreans," he said.

As always, Council speakers debated America's leadership role in the world. Increasingly, they saw this role diminishing.

Kishore Mahbubani, the Singapore diplomat and scholar, said the rest of the world was rising to Western standards of middle-class wealth and governance, and was poised to share global governance with the West. Mahbubani called this "the great convergence," a world with 193 nations sailing on the same ship, but without a captain.

Washington resisted this, he said, but the rest of the world—what he called the 88 Percent—was ready to move forward. "If you need optimism," he said, "you have to go outside the West. If you look at the world through the eyes of the 88 Percent, things have never looked so good."

Richard Haass, the president of the New York Council on Foreign Relations, called himself "a card-carrying member of the foreign policy establishment," so was surprised to advocate for a retreat from US "overreaching" abroad. This didn't mean an end to American leadership, he stressed. "There's no alternative to a world that is led by the United States. The alternative to a world without American leadership is a world that is not led."

But America had so many problems at home—government debt, shabby infrastructure, inadequate education, a broken political system—that had to be fixed to underwrite this continued American leadership. "We can only shape that world out there if we get it right at home. If we get it right, this could be a second American Century. If we get it wrong, it won't be anybody's century."

The big example of overreaching was the US war in Iraq and the country's continued involvement in the Middle East. "The Middle East has become a distortion of American foreign policy," Haass said. When the Berlin Wall fell in 1989, it would have been "inconceivable" that we would spend "the lion's share" of the next twenty-five years on Iraq and Afghanistan. "But that's what we did."

Robert Kagan, a prolific author and senior fellow at the Brookings Institution, insisted that nothing short of American leadership was vital to world stability. "We're situated to maintain this world order for many years to come," Kagan said. "Yes, America will decline someday, but not yet. We have to push back against this mood that it's time to retrench. Let's not forget how bad the world can get and the role that the US has played all these years. We can persist—if we have the will to do it."

America has filled this role since 1945, he said. "This is the Era of American Order. History tells us that these orders aren't self-sustaining but have to be sustained by a leading power. You dare not imagine that you can pull America out of the equation and everything remains the same."

—

As the decade ended, the Council tempo increased. The Council had instituted a hiring freeze when the 2008 financial crisis hit, but it weathered the ensuing recession well. Much of this was due to good advice from Lester Crown, the Board chairman, who understood what was happening and knew the economy would be hit. By pulling back early, the Council was able to resume its growth in 2009.

Among other activities, its Global Chicago Center co-sponsored, with the Chicago-based consulting firm A.T. Kearney, a listing of global cities. Chicago came in eighth. Such listings became common in later years, but this was one of the first, and got global attention.

If the Council couldn't afford many full-time resident fellows, it began bringing in visiting fellows for briefings and speeches, under specially funded fellowships. The Dr. Scholl Foundation, led by Board member Pamela Scholl, focused on China, and usually brought in a leading Chinese scholar each year. The family of former Board chairman Augustin "Gus" Hart endowed the Gus Hart Fellowship, which brought an emerging leader from Latin America to Chicago for a week of workshops, interviews, briefings, and the annual Hart Lecture.

The Koldyke Fellowship, honoring longtime Board member Patricia Koldyke, originally brought in emerging leaders active in social transformation. In 2015, it became the Koldyke Global Teachers Program, giving five teachers in the Chicago region a year of intense background education in global affairs, including foreign travel. When Bouton retired in 2013, the Council established the annual Marshall M. Bouton Asia Fellowship, and hosted a prominent Asian scholar or policymaker in Chicago for a week of meetings with local leaders and a Council lecture.

One of the most successful programs, Emerging Leaders, aimed to do what the Council did for Adlai Stevenson and his generation: train younger members for public service. Begun in 2008, it offered projects and programs to give its up-and-comers a deep background in global issues. It seemed to be working. In its thirteenth year, it had produced two members of Congress—Illinois Democrats Raja Krishnamoorthi and Sean Casten—plus a judge, an ambassador, a state legislator, and all-star architect Jeanne Gang. Less spectacularly, it armed a new generation of business and social leaders with a world view beyond Chicago.

The Council still shied away from capital campaigns, but a fundraising drive in 2005, called the 21st Century Fund, brought in $5.275 million. Its think tank activities began attracting notice and money, including $1 million-plus funding from the Gates and Ford Foundations, and from two local foundations, MacArthur and McCormick. The latter was the legacy of the Council's old sparring partner, Colonel Robert R. McCormick.

For years, no single gift matched the $3 million that John Rielly received in 1988 from the Adenauer Fund. That changed in the new millennium. The Gates Foundation gave more than $11 million over the years, all for food and agricultural programs. The McCormick Foundation gave more than $10 million for a variety of programs, including $4 million in 2018 for the 21st Century campaign.

Northern Trust, an original corporate member which joined in 1951, was still active and was probably the leading corporate donor in Council history. As the Council's centenary neared, Shirley Ryan was both the longest-serving active Board member and a major donor. Kimberly Querrey, a Board member, gave $1,525,000 for the Young Professionals Program. Leah Joy Zell, a Board co-chair, gave $1,988,000 over the years, including $750,000 to support one of the Council's early fellows, Phil Levy, an economist focusing on the global economy.

Apart from these gifts, Bouton's tenure saw two major shifts in funding. One was a growth in the membership of the Board, coupled with increasing pressure on Board members to become bigger and regular donors. The other was the inauguration of annual dinners. From the start, Board member John Manley and his wife Mary underwrote each of these dinners. The first dinner, in 2004, brought in $100,000; by the time Bouton retired, they netted $1.5 million.

The public opinion survey got a much-needed revival. In the early 2000s, it still appeared every two years, but without much notice. When Rielly started it, it was the only such survey on foreign policy issues and claimed headlines when it appeared. Over the years, other and livelier surveys challenged it. It remained a solid, well-constructed poll. But by 2011, it was getting little attention and the Council seriously considered ending it. But before it did, it gathered an all-day roundtable of pollsters, academics, and journalists to debate whether it was worth saving.

Roger Cohen, the *New York Times* columnist who was in Chicago for a Council speech, sat in. He listened for a while and then said that the Council, competing in the digital world, put out a boring and dated survey and wondered why nobody paid attention. "You're not visible enough and your 2010 title ["Global Views 2010"] was terrible," Cohen said. "You buried a ton of interesting things. And other things were really repetitive. You need more incisive analysis. Every two years isn't going to cut it. You need more. The media always wants a story, so give them one. And don't limit yourself to American media. Location doesn't matter anymore. You have content, get it out there. Japan! China! *Times of India*!"

It was worse than that, Cohen said. The Council's website was outdated, and the organization virtually ignored social media, such as Facebook and Twitter; at the time, it had forty-five Twitter followers.

The Council had a choice—drop the survey or get serious. It got serious. From that session came the decision to bring the Council's communications into the twenty-first century, and with an expanded staff to handle it. Dina Smeltz, a veteran director of Middle East and European research for the State Department, became the first senior fellow for public opinion. Later, in 2014, the Council created an advisory group of top academics across the nation to help frame the questions; not coincidentally, the same academics began citing the poll in their books and blogs. The survey became annual, and a drumbeat of spot surveys on timely issues, often done in collaboration with pollsters from Russia, Mexico, and Korea, put the Council back in the news.

———

In 2012, both NATO and the G8 group of nations planned summits in the US. President Obama insisted that they be held simultaneously in Chicago. But G8 summits traditionally touch off violent protests. The last thing that Obama needed in an election year was blood in the streets of his hometown, so the G8 meeting was moved to Camp David. The NATO summit remained in Chicago. Despite some small protests, it was a modest success for the city and a triumph for the Council.

From the start, the Council was involved in the summit planning and became a virtual partner to the city organizers. It sponsored public events and speeches by visiting leaders, held joint press conferences with city officials, posted a special NATO website, lined up interviews for visiting correspondents, and prepared a brief on the alliance's importance. All the preparations went smoothly, and the Council shone.

The summit paid one unexpected dividend for the Council. The US ambassador to NATO at the time was Ivo Daalder, a Dutch-born academic, author, and former director for European affairs at the National Security Council. Daalder had spoken to the Council in 2003, his only visit to Chicago. In 2012, he came two times before the summit, then brought his wife Elisa for the summit.

"We arrived here from Europe," he recalled. "It was May, about seventy degrees. An easy drive in from the airport. Then we drove on Lake Shore Drive to Wrigley Field, and we saw the Oak Street Beach—a beach in the middle of town!" They sat in the owner's box at Wrigley field and Daalder (a Washington Nationals fan first, and only later a Cubs fan) led the crowd in the traditional seventh-inning stretch rendition of "Take Me Out to the Ballgame." After the summit, "we spent an extra twenty-four hours here. As we were flying out, I said, 'I could live here.' She said, 'Me, too.'"

The first Obama Administration was ending and, with it, Daalder's planned four-year term as NATO ambassador. Bouton's retirement was announced in June, one month after the summit. A search firm hired by the Council approached Daalder in Brussels. Daalder, already impressed by what he had seen of the Council at the NATO summit, called Louis Susman, a Chicago lawyer, Council Board member, and, at that time, the American ambassador to Britain. He asked Susman whom he should call at the Council, and Susman said, "Lester," referring to Lester Crown, the Board chairman. Then Susman called Crown and said, "Lester, don't waste your time with a search firm. I've got the guy for you."

Daalder visited Chicago in October and again in January. After lunch during that trip, Crown offered him the job. On July 1, 2013, Daalder took over as president.

Chapter 9

All Over Again

At 10 a.m. on the morning of November 9, 2016, Ivo Daalder called a snap staff meeting in one of the big work rooms in the Council's new offices in the Two Prudential Plaza building. Daalder, like the rest of the staff, was reeling from the results of the presidential election day before. The US had only one president, he said, and that president was Donald Trump, a fact that recast the Council's mission. Speaking with more confidence than he felt, he said that the Council had been founded more than ninety years earlier to keep America open to the world and engaged in the world's affairs.

And now it would have to do it all over again.

A month later, Daalder sent out a memo saying in more formal language what he told the staff that day.

> "The basic contours of the international order that have shaped the global environment since the end of World War II—an order based on free trade, strong alliances, democracy, and the rule of law—are being called into question... The deep divisions showcased by the presiden-

tial election raise profound questions about the country's continued willingness to bear the burdens of global leadership. The future is more uncertain than at any point in my lifetime.

"While these developments are unsettling to many, they also provide an opportunity for an organization like ours—which was founded in 1922, at a time of growing isolationist sentiment—to promote an active American engagement in the world. Our mission has never been more important. And our location in the middle of the country, where blue states turned red and provided Mr. Trump his margin of victory, gives us a special responsibility to promote our mission with renewed vigor and confidence.

"For the past seventy years, when America's global engagement was supported across the political spectrum, our main role was to provide a platform to discuss how the United States should engage the world, not whether it should. Today, we need to go back to our roots... We must do so as an organization that remains strictly independent and nonpartisan. But we do have a point of view, and we should not hesitate to promote those views."

Later, in "An Open Letter to the Midwest," Daalder wrote, "We are nonpartisan but not neutral. We believe in ideas and we believe in engagement. We have fought isolationism before, and we will do it again."

In fact, it was less a return to 1922, when the Council provided information on world affairs, than to the late 1930s, when it became the battleground between two clashing views of America's role in the world. As before the Council took no stand on specific issues or personalities. But for the first time in its history, it was challenged by the American foreign policy of the day—a policy that, while less isolationist than nationalist and exceptionalist, jeered at everything the Council believed.

It was not a battle that Daalder had expected to fight when he arrived in Chicago three years earlier, in 2013. Bouton had been Mr. Inside, building the Council in size, budget, programs and reach. Daalder was Mr. Outside, a public intellectual, the author or co-author of eight books, comfortable on the podium and on television, with global contacts and a public persona. Bouton had raised the Council's profile, especially nationally. Daalder was determined to raise it higher, and internationally.

In an interview shortly after he arrived, Daalder said he wanted "to make Chicago the go-to place when you want to know about foreign policy…to enhance [the Council's] visibility in Chicago, the country and, more important, the world. I want the Council to play a bigger and bigger role as a convening organization, to bring different parts of the city together to talk about how the city can engage globally."

Later, in a memo to the Board that he called "Vision 2022," Daalder recognized the nation's polarized politics, its digital dependence, and its fragmented culture. The Council needed "to adapt to these changes while taking full advantage of the opportunities they present." This was necessary both to make the Council "one of the premier global affairs organizations in the country and the world," and to help launch its Second Century Campaign, a major fundraising drive.

First, the Council moved out of its outgrown office on South Michigan Avenue into a large and more modern office that occupied a full floor in Chicago's Prudential Plaza. Off the lobby, it set up a new conference center, the Robert R. McCormick Foundation Hall, which held 299 persons and thus carefully avoided the cut-off point in Chicago's fire code for crowds of 300-plus persons. Before, most programs were held in venues such as the Chicago Club; the new center removed this cost. It also allowed modern communications, including live-streamed programs, which instantly enlarged its audiences. A modern broadcasting studio was located next door.

If Roger Cohen's scolding of the Council led to an invigorated public opinion survey in the Bouton years, his derision of the Council's digital presence paid off in the early Daalder years. Its communications and digital reach grew with the use of Twitter, interactive reports, live-streamed events, an improved website, podcasts, and other efforts, all overseen by a communications staff that grew quickly from one person to nine. All this became an unexpected weapon when the Covid-19 pandemic hit in 2020.

The survey went from biennial to annual and expanded its cooperation with polling organizations in other countries, including the respected and courageous Levada Center in Russia.

Daalder became the Council's public face; he regularly appeared as a speaker and panelist around the world and on television talk shows, frequently wrote articles for publications such as the *Financial Times* and *Foreign Policy*, and maintained a column in the *Chicago Tribune*.

Second, the Council's think tank activities grew beyond its nutrition program. Mostly, it ignored the issues—the Middle East, for instance—where the East Coast think tanks commanded the field, and concentrated on the global issues such as trade, cities, agricultural, immigration, energy, and transport, where Chicago and the Midwest had a comparative advantage. Daalder's vision saw "centers of excellence" working on these issues, "with a small in-house research and administrative staff, supplemented by a larger network of non-resident fellows and associates on whom we can draw for research and expertise."

The Global Chicago Center became the Global Cities Initiative, focusing on the growing connections and common challenges of major cities around the world. One of the Council's first resident fellows, Phil Levy, anchored its work on the global economy. Other fellows, resident and non-resident, worked on climate change and urban resilience, water issues, national security, and immigration.

When he arrived in Chicago, Daalder knew he wanted to stage a defining annual event, a signature forum to put Chicago and the Council on the global map, as the annual security conference had done for Munich. Glenn Tilton, Lester Crown's successor as Board chairman, suggested a focus on global cities, and the Chicago Forum on Global Cities was born. With the *Financial Times* as co-host, the three-day forum began in 2015 and was held every year after, although the Covid-19 pandemic forced it to be held virtually. In its fifth year, it received a $5 million gift from Chicago's Pritzker Foundation and was renamed the Pritzker Family Forum on Global Cities.

Other major gifts came in. The McCormick Foundation, already a major donor, gave $4 million in 2018, a grant that led to the renaming of the McCormick Hall in the conference center. UL, the former Underwriters Laboratory, committed more than $3 million for the Global Cities Forum. AbbVie joined it as a lead sponsor of the Forum, giving $3 million over the years.

Notably, the family of Lester Crown gave $10 million to honor Crown's ten years-plus as Council chairman. The gift set up the Lester Crown Center on US Foreign Policy, which was to do research on foreign policy issues, establish an annual lecture, convene a national security roundtable, fund the Council's public opinion survey, and beef up its digital capacity.

With the Forum, each of the Council's most recent three presidents had established flagship programs: Rielly's public opinion survey, Bouton's food and agriculture program, and now Daalder's Global Cities Forum. The Forum enabled the Council to cement a relationship with the *Financial Times*, a leading global newspaper, and to establish itself as a place for debate on critical issues between mayors and urban experts.

By 2016, a survey published by the University of Pennsylvania ranked the Council as the world's number one "think tank to watch."

—

The foreign policy landscape changed totally on that election day in 2016. But the contours were already changing when Ivo Daalder arrived in Chicago in 2013. Globalization was here, and its impact was felt across society and across the world. America, the traditional land of opportunity, had become the most unequal of the major nations. In 1922, Chicago was an isolated and unworldly factory town: now it was a global city. China, humiliated for centuries, throbbed with ambition. Russia, so recently prostrate, glowered with a new nationalism. The scars of the 2008 recession refused to heal. Iraq and Afghanistan bled the nation's military, treasury, and reputation; problems bequeathed by the Bush Administration remained unresolved by the Obama Administration. Many blamed the old order in Europe and America for this state of affairs and demanded a break with the past. A new force called populism questioned the verities that had guided the world since World War II.

All these omens, well before the Trump ascendancy, were audible from the Council stage for those who cared to listen.

Daalder set the tone with his inaugural speech to the Council. Speaking two months after his arrival, he said the country faced the "paradox of American power"—the decline of its global influence even as it remained, by far, the world's most powerful nation.

America was not weaker, but power had diffused across the globe, he said. It also was diffusing internally, as power moved from capitals to global cities such as Chicago, which "are increasingly important actors on the global stage. We can't leave foreign policy just to Washington. We here in Chicago, including here at the Chicago Council on Global Affairs, are an integral part of our nation's foreign policy and global engagement."

But this was no reason to abandon a policy that had worked for seventy-five years. "We need to remain—indeed, intensify—our global engagement...We cannot ward ourselves off from this world by building bigger fences or bigger guns."

Anders Fogh Rasmussen, the Danish secretary general of NATO, warned of just such a retreat. "I am concerned by a tendency to retrenchment," he said. "For a superpower like the United States, retrenchment is not an option." With their "global reach," Americans remained affected by any crisis, no matter where it occurred.

Martin Wolf, the *Financial Times* columnist and the leading economic journalist of his era, told the Council that a post-recession lack of demand, plus globalization, caused "a massive deindustrialization," that led to changes in work and lower pay, and generated an "appalling mess" and "a colossal transformation."

"People feel cheated," Wolf said, and continued,

> *"People feel despair and anger, and you can see this in our politics. There's a profound disillusion of the populace with their elites. There's always been a bargain—the populace will accept your (the elites') status because you seem to know what you're doing. But once you screw up monstrously… What we see in the United States and Europe reflects this disillusion with the elites, who retain power only if they deliver what the non-elites think is a fair deal."*

Francis Fukuyama, the Chicago-born political scientist, made his name in 1989 with an essay, "The End of History," which argued that liberal market democracy had vanquished all opposing systems, especially fascism and communism, and would henceforth be the goal for all nations. Twenty-five years later, he told the Council that achieving this goal—"getting to Denmark," as he put it—was harder than he had thought it would be. A century of relatively good government was breaking down and being replaced by "political decay. A gap has opened between the demands for government and the ability of government to deliver."

In America, Fukuyama said, the nation's system of checks and balances was seizing up. Designed to divide and restrain power, it now enabled narrow special interest groups to use the courts and Congress to block all positive action—a "vetocracy," he said. "A rule by veto."

Other speakers charted the economic and political reasons for the breakdown in the American dream. The journalist Hedrick Smith blamed it on "the revolt of the bosses"—a forty-year campaign by corporate and business interests to squash organized labor, erase regulations, and promote a massive redistribution of income and wealth. "We're two Americas now," Smith said, "divided by power, divided by money, divided by ideology."

Chrystia Freeland, later the Canadian foreign minister, had just been elected to Parliament when she spoke to the Council on plutocrats and populists, a new world of unsustainable inequality, and of the "alpha-geeks" against everyone else. The Industrial Revolution "required a whole set of political and economic adjustments to make it work," Freeland said, and now we needed to do it again.

The main problem was the rise of the "plutocrats," the 1 percent at the top, a new class of men who were both global and parochial, "staying in the same hotels in Beijing or New York, eating the same food in Dubai or Palo Alto, seeing the same people," who assumed the same superiority and entitlement and were now "getting to the tipping point where they pull up the ladder."

Jean-Claude Trichet, the former president of the European Central Bank, assured the Council that the European Union had survived its post-recession financial crisis and the strains on the euro, and was now stronger than ever.

"I draw your attention to the resilience of the European endeavor," Trichet said. "What we are doing is very bold…Fifteen years after [the euro was introduced], in the worst crisis since World War II, its governments and its central bank took bold decisions, and the euro remains credible as a currency."

George Friedman wasn't so sure. An author and chairman of Stratfor, a geopolitical forecasting and intelligence corporation, Friedman warned that old historical demons were stirring in Europe, propelled by an economic imbalance between a northern Europe dominated by Germany and a southern Europe beset by depression and high unemployment.

Once again, Friedman said, Germany is "Europe's basic flaw," a country that was "economically powerful and geopolitically fragile," and now able to manipulate the single currency, the euro, to benefit German exports.

A result, he said, was the rise of nationalist and populist parties, on the left in Greece, on the right in France and other countries, with secessionist movements in Spain and "a massive de-legitimation of main-stream parties," coupled with a "rise of hatred" among "a massive, intelligent, and embittered class" of Europeans who saw impoverishment and realized, "this isn't temporary, this is my life." Friedman spoke just a year before the British referendum plunged Europe into the Brexit crisis.

David Rothkopf, the editor of *Foreign Policy* magazine, saw a nation trapped in fear and insecurity, and blamed both the Bush and Obama administrations for inflicting long-term damage to America's standing in the world.

The Bush Administration, he said, overreacted to 9/11 and turned a manageable threat into an era of fear. But Rothkopf said President Obama was "deliberative to a fault," and "seems steadfast in his resistance both to learning from his past errors and to managing his team so that future errors are prevented. It is hard to think of a recent president who has grown so little in office."

A panel of experts involved in the search for post-9/11 justice also condemned both the Bush Administration for its bungled handling of the Guantanamo Bay prisoners and the Obama Administration for its failure to right these wrongs.

"There's been no action to close Guantanamo, no action to change legislation," said career ambassador Thomas Pickering. "There's little sense that the government is ready to pick up on this."

"Such a disappointment, such a disappointment," agreed Thomas Sullivan, a Chicago lawyer who represented eight of the Guantanamo prisoners. "My basic attitude is a deep, severe disappointment in the president—an Illinois lawyer—not having the gonads to step forward and say, 'God damn it, we've got to get these people out of there.'"

Unsurprisingly, Timothy Geithner supported Obama. Geithner, who was Obama's treasury secretary, told the biggest Council audience in two decades, at 3,300 persons, at the Auditorium Theater, that the administration, acting in the wake of the 2008 financial crisis, was "able to do a set of things that were remarkably effective in getting the economy growing again." Mistakes were made, he said, but post-crisis reforms "give us the prospect of an enduring period of stability."

Adam Posen, the president of the Peterson Institute for International Economics, also looked on the bright side of the world economy. The US was grappling with its post-recession problems, while "China's development is a good thing for humanity. The threat from China is exaggerated." A half-century of American dominance was ending but was being replaced by a more balanced world with rising middle classes and low inflation. Latin America and Poland "are sticking to pro-market policies." The federal debt was manageable, and the fear that American jobs were moving to low-wage places "is a labor fallacy. It's just not true."

Paul Krugman, the Nobel-prize-winning economist and *New York Times* columnist, agreed, but only to a point. "High-paying jobs," he told the Council, "have mostly not been lost to overseas competition. They've mostly been lost to technology. It just takes a whole lot fewer auto workers to produce a car than it used to."

But trade and globalization increased inequality, Krugman said, "not because high wage jobs have moved overseas but because low-wage jobs have moved overseas. This means reduced opportunities for low-education workers." Because of the rise of trade with Mexico and China, he said, "Wages are probably several percent lower for high school graduates without any college education."

As America churned in uncertainty, attention turned to China. Evan Osnos, the former Beijing correspondent for the *Chicago Tribune* and *The New Yorker*, painted a picture of a hungry and ambitious China. "The China I encountered," he said, "is splintering into a billion different individual stories." Suddenly, ambition had become a driving force, as people asked, "What do I want? What must I do?"

From this was emerging a "Chinese dream," or, rather, two dreams. The Chinese government aspired to a restoration of Chinese greatness in the world, Osnos said, while the Chinese people sought "a greater control over their lives" and, increasingly, a moral underpinning for what had been a restless drive for riches.

The Scholl Fellowship brought Chinese scholars to the Council each year. Some of them were surprisingly blunt. Yu Yongding, a senior fellow at the Chinese Institute of World Economics and Politics, said the Chinese economy was distorted by over-investment and over-reliance on exports. "Now," he said, "the once successful growth model has run out of steam." Faced with choking smog, ubiquitous waste, and lackluster foreign demand, China needed to change its growth pattern.

In addition, he said, "China's banking system is quite heavily protected," encouraging a "misallocation of resources." He urged a more equitable income distribution and an effort to cut the nation's huge trade and foreign currency surpluses.

Zhang Weiying, a professor of economics at Peking University, was an outspoken free-marketer. In Chicago, he urged a shrunken state-owned sector in China, plus deregulation, and the rule of law. The secret to a growing economy, he said, was wealth creation, which depends on innovation, which depends on entrepreneurialism. Government and an industrial policy were definitely not part of this equation, he said.

The Council's cultivation of its Chinese connection paid off in 2014 when top trade negotiators for America and China came to Chicago for the annual meeting of their Joint Commission on Commerce and Trade. It was only the second time it had been held outside Beijing or Washington.

At a public forum sponsored by the Council, Penny Pritzker, the US commerce secretary and a Council Board member, warned that massive US investment in China would not necessarily continue if China did not meet American concerns over "sanctity of contracts, transparency, rule of law, intellectual protection, and other issues." These concerns, she said, "are beginning to take their toll."

In response, Chinese Vice Premier Wang Yang said China knew it was thriving in an American-led world trading system. "We accept the rules," he said. "We have neither the ability nor the intent to challenge the United States." In 2014, these words reflected the conventional wisdom; a half-decade later, the US-Chinese relationship had changed utterly.

John Mearsheimer, the University of Chicago political scientist, saw this coming. Returning to the Council for the first time since 2007, Mearsheimer warned that China's growth put it on a collision course with its neighbors and ultimately, the US.

Mearsheimer, a leader of the realist school which holds that every nation is on its own in a Hobbesian world, said, "The best way to survive is to be the most powerful…to be the biggest, baddest dude on the block." This meant that China would try to dominate Asia, in the same way that the US dominates the Western Hemisphere. Given America's interest in Asia, this means an eventual and inevitable clash.

"Can China grow peacefully?" Mearsheimer asked. "The answer is no."

Chris Hill, the former US ambassador to South Korea, earlier told the Council that Kim Jong-un, the new leader of North Korea, was "not ready for prime time." Hill returned in 2015 to revise that view. Kim was "very much in control," Hill said. Despite that, the North Korean regime would fall "sooner or later," and the US and China had to be ready to help any reunification with South Korea.

Two former secretaries of defense, Leon Panetta and Robert Gates, both told the Council that one of the hardest parts of their jobs was dealing with Congress. Panetta, a former congressman, said, "The major issues facing this country—[Congress] is not going to deal with them." He blamed much of this on the partisanship engineered by a former speaker of the House, Newt Gingrich, exacerbated by gerrymandering, the flood of special interest money, and "the media's sound-bite mentality."

Gates, who served both Bush and Obama, said he was finally driven out by his "private frustration, anger, and disgust" with a dysfunctional Washington. "Every day, I was at war with Congress," Gates said. Congress was "inquisitional, uncivil, incompetent, micromanaging, parochial, egotistical, thin-skinned," and filled with politicians who "put reelection before the national interest" and prized sound bites over progress.

"Television cameras have the same effect on members of Congress that a full moon has on werewolves," he said.

—

When the Council was founded in 1922, the Middle East was a trouble spot. Nearly a century later, that had not changed.

David Miliband, the former British foreign secretary, was the president of the International Rescue Committee when he spoke in 2014 about the civil war in Syria, which he called "a war without end and a war without law." He called for a sort of Marshall Plan to help neighboring countries dealing with Syrian refugees.

Miliband did not suggest Western military intervention but said the Syrian situation "exemplifies something about us"—a post-Iraq, post-Afghanistan, post-financial crisis mentality in which the West turned away, for fear that "at worst, we will do more harm than good when we venture abroad."

Carlotta Gall, the former *New York Times* correspondent in Kabul, told the Council that Osama bin Laden had been protected by the notorious intelligence arms of Pakistan. The US kept the raid that killed bin Laden a secret from the Pakistanis, for fear they would tip him off.

Pakistan, ostensibly a US ally, "is behind the resurgence of the Taliban and behind the fighting against our troops," Gall said. With US troops being withdrawn from Afghanistan, "we have to look straight at what Pakistan is doing and what is our policy going forward."

Husain Haqqani, a former Pakistani ambassador to Washington, seemed to agree. He called his country a deeply dysfunctional nation, with its dysfunctions willingly financed over years by a heedless US. It was time to "take away the crutches," Haqqani said. "The US has to get out of the old paradigm in which it gets influence by giving aid. You don't. If [Pakistan] is not going to change, who's asking you to write the checks? The US has to understand that foreign policy is more than who to take to lunch and who to bomb."

Two American veterans of the Israeli-Palestinian dispute pronounced a plague on both sides—and especially on the Israeli prime minister, Benjamin Netanyahu. Roger Cohen, the *New York Times* columnist, told the Council in early 2017 that any peaceful settlement there—what he called a miracle—depended on Netanyahu's defeat in an upcoming election. Cohen, a Zionist himself, called Netanyahu's Israel "a perversion of Zionism" and said the Israeli leader never "had a serious belief in a two-state solution." The Palestinians were "in complete disarray," he said, and the Gaza Strip was "a factory for violent extremism."

"Making peace can still be done," he said. "Work very hard, sweep away the slogans—and don't forget the miracles."

Martin Indyk, the former US special envoy for Israeli-Palestinian negotiations, spoke two months later, barely three hours after

Netanyahu won the election. The revival of the peace process "was barely on life support before this election…Now, the chances are slim to none."

Netanyahu's victory meant there would be no progress toward a two-state solution—and "the alternative to a two-state solution in my view is no solution," he said. "There has to be a separation and creation of a Palestinian state. But we can't get there from here."

The 2014 Gus Hart Fellow was Yoani Sánchez, a rarity in Castro's Cuba, a thirty-nine-year-old independent journalist who used technology, imagination, a global network, and courage to get blogs and tweets to thousands of followers both inside and outside Cuba. She painted a bleak picture of her homeland.

"We are a country of whispers," Sánchez said. "Nobody speaks out loud. The revolution is dead. It was six feet under when I was born. Where is the Cuba that we were promised? My mother was born under Castro. I was born under Castro. My nineteen-year-old son was born under Castro. That's three generations of Cubans who have been deceived."

Jeb Bush, not yet an official presidential candidate, came to the Council in early 2015 to give the first foreign policy address of that campaign. The speech, a ringing endorsement of American global engagement, may have been a high point of his campaign, which died a year later. "I am my own man," Bush said, acknowledging that his brother's administration "made mistakes in Iraq for sure." But most of his fire was aimed at the "inconsistent and indecisive" leadership of President Obama.

"America does not have the luxury of withdrawing from the world," Bush said. "Our security, our prosperity, and our values demand that we remain engaged and involved in often distant places. We have no reason to apologize for our leadership and our interest in serving the cause of global security, global peace, and human freedom."

John Beyrle, the former US ambassador to Moscow, called for a steady engagement with Russia, even if the policy of Russian President Vladimir Putin made it "orders of magnitude more difficult."

Beyrle said this did not mean a new Cold War, but rather the resumption of an age-old struggle within Russia between the "Westernizers," Russians who saw their nation's future inside the wider Atlantic world, and the "Slavophiles," who saw Russia as a unique civilization and viewed the outside world with hostility.

At the moment, he said, the Slavophiles "have a grip on the lever of power," and this would not necessarily change if Putin left office.

—

Increasingly, the Council programs swung from a single speaker to a panel or debate format. Daalder, a proponent of sending lethal defense weapons to help Ukraine fight the Russian incursion, faced off against Jane Harman, the president of the Woodrow Wilson Center in Washington.

"Foreign military elements are in a country that hasn't invited them," the Council president argued. "That's formally known as an invasion. It's a foreign power occupying a country that isn't theirs… So how do we respond? We should give the country that's being invaded the means to defend itself."

Harmon responded that economic sanctions "are the better tool. Is our strength in our economy—or is it weapons against a Russian army that is right next door?" She drew a parallel with World War I, which began "through a series of miscalculations. I worry about World War III, what with all this saber-rattling by Russia."

George Osborne, the former British Chancellor of the Exchequer, told the Council that the policy of humanitarian interventionism, proclaimed in Chicago by Tony Blair seventeen years earlier, was "long gone. In its place is a resignation that it is never worth getting involved—that the price of intervention is never worth paying." But because the West did not intervene in Syria, he said, "hundreds of thousands were killed. Millions displaced. Neighboring countries destabilized. The taboo on the use of chemical weapons broken. The emergence of a terrorist state. Russia back as a major player in the Middle East. And a refugee crisis that has fueled the rise of extremism across Europe.

"Yes, my political generation knows the cost of intervention—but we are also beginning to understand the cost of not intervening. It doesn't make our countries more secure."

Secretary of State John Kerry spoke to the Council two weeks before Donald Trump won the presidential election. He warned, "Whatever happens in the next two weeks, our country is going to have to…remember that every action we take is being carefully observed by our global allies and adversaries, and that what they see will have a direct impact on our future ability to lead."

Kerry recalled the day in 1937 when President Roosevelt came to Chicago, just after the passage of one of the Neutrality Acts, and decried those "who said that to remain safe, America should close its eyes to the storm gathering abroad and avoid making an enemy of Hitler." As history was soon to demonstrate, Roosevelt's every word was proven true.

"As I enter my final three months as secretary of state, I am as convinced now, as FDR was then, of the need for peace-loving people on every continent to band together to reject the apostles of hate, the authors of aggression, and the manipulators of truth who threaten to hold us back and do us harm."

—

In June of 2016, Britain voted to leave the European Union. Less than five months later, Donald Trump was elected president. The two events transformed the debate.

For a century, policy—especially foreign policy—had been dominated by elites. Now, suddenly, came a revolt from below, a mutiny by outsiders against the right of these elites to run the world. The insurrection targeted the verities that had guided American and Western policy for decades: alliances, trade, open economies, multiculturalism, a growing supranationalism, and the new economic tsunami called globalization. With the digital revolution, the elites lost control of the debate. In the last half of 2016, they lost control of governance.

For the Council, this rebellion posed a special threat. Overnight, a new force called populism strode onto the stage. Like the isms of old—isolationism, fascism, communism—it challenged the way that the Council and its members viewed the world. The Council itself was an elite organization and saw itself as such. Now its vision of itself and its world was under assault on its own turf. Trump owed his election largely to the defection of much of the Midwest from mainstream politicians such as Hillary Clinton to a new worldview, rooted in the implosion of the Midwestern industrial economy and fed by social media and a mix of nationalism, nativism, and the politics of resentment.

The Council struggled to make sense of what all this meant. Much of the programming following 2016 dealt with populism, immigration, trade, America's retreat from the world, and an economy that left behind so much of Chicago's own backyard.

Fareed Zakaria inaugurated the Council's new conference center in the interim between the Brexit vote and Trump's election, but he foresaw the rough water ahead. The US, he said, stood at the center of global order, but now, "for the first time really, you have a candidate who is arguing for something very different, for an upending of that order, for a dismantling of that system."

The greatest foreign policy challenge, he said, lay not in Syria or some distant place, "but what happens in Washington." Future historians might "look back and say the United States in the early twenty-first century did an extraordinary job of transforming and globalizing the world, but they just forgot along the way to globalize the United States of America."

Dan Balz, the veteran political correspondent for the *Washington Post*, credited Trump with "the good luck or the sheer genius to do a hostile takeover of an existing party." The election, he continued,

> "Was about a recognition that a whole part of the country felt alienated. It was a combination of economics and national identity and the kind of cultural tension that's at the root of some of the changes we are going through... The country needed to recognize the depth of these divisions. You can't ignore them; you can't ignore a whole part of the country that has a different view of things."

Jeffrey Garten, a professor at the Yale School of Management, saw a backlash against globalization, which he felt was already slowing down. Yascha Mounk, a Harvard lecturer, warned against the belief that, just because a country was affluent and had had a couple of fair elections, "We no longer have to worry about democracy. That is now scary, really turning out to be a mistake." On the same program, Larry Diamond, a senior fellow at Stanford University, warned, "We are in a dangerous new era. The democratic recession has intensified. I think there is an emerging global crisis of confidence in democracy."

Panels or discussions dealt with such issues as cyber-security and hacking, immigration, the growth of populism and the future of trade.

All this broadened the ideological span of programs—within limits. No Trump Administration official accepted the Council's many invitations to speak to a public meeting. Dan Coats, then the director of national intelligence, spoke to a private off-the-record meeting with donors in October of 1917, but no one in the new Administration would face an open meeting.

Throughout its history, the Council had always found it easier to get critics of government policy than spokesmen for that policy. Even by that standard, the Trump Administration's reluctance to speak up for its own policies was extreme.

The Global Cities Forum began in 2015, while Brexit and Trump were still clouds on the horizon. By 2017, the realization was growing that, in the new era of populism, cities might be on their own. Gillian Tett, the US managing editor for the *Financial Times*, told the Forum that there was a tension between "the economic and cultural importance of cities on the one hand and their lack of political power on the other." Independent city states were unlikely, she said, "but our national politics and our cosmopolitan city politics are diverging… Certainly we saw that in the Brexit vote in the UK. We saw it in the vote here."

Martin Wolf, the economics columnist for the *Financial Times*, contrasted "the growing tribalism in the nation and the outward looking metropolis of London. The people who voted for Brexit in significant ways were voting against London."

The reason, he said, is that "we have not succeeded in persuading a large part of our populations that the global order has worked to their benefit…The Brexit referendum captured this stress." Cities won't "rise up and say, give us independence," he said, but they did have to "take the argument to their countries" by persuading them that the existence of great cities benefits the country as a whole.

Yascha Mounk wrote a book called *The People vs. Democracy* and returned to the Council to talk about it. The problem internationally and in the US, he said, had three roots: the stagnation in living standards for ordinary people, the increasing multi-ethnicity in societies, and the explosion of social media. As a result, people were confused and had "a feeling that the political system isn't listening to them. So, when people say this, they say, 'Let's try something new.'"

Edward Luce, the Washington commentator for the *Financial Times* and a frequent Council speaker, said people were simply losing faith in democracy, both as it existed in the West and as a goal in China and other countries:

"The glue of democracies is trust. That trust barometer has been plummeting pretty steadily in the last two-thirds of a generation. When you lose trust, when you lose faith, you tend to turn to agnosticism, you stop caring, you stop voting, you stop participating in civic activities. You turn to atheism, not believing in the system anymore. We are nonbelievers, and you see people exploiting it very skillfully."

Madeleine Albright, the former secretary of state and the author of *Fascism: A Warning*, returned to the Council to talk about the roots of fascism and also about "certain trends that are worrisome." She defined fascism as "an identification with a tribalist nationalist group at the exclusion of others, a sense that democratic institutions don't matter, and that a free press is not a major part of what is needed...I decided to write because of what I was seeing." What she saw included a swing to identity politics.

In her book, Albright called Trump "the first anti-democratic president in modern US history." She did not go so far in Chicago, but she criticized Trump for praising the regressive leaders of Poland. "People are wondering who we are," she said. "Why we're not talking about what our value system is, who's filling that vacuum now that we're no longer doing that?"

Another frequent speaker, Francis Fukuyama, agreed with Albright that the focus of global politics had moved from economic issues to identity politics. This, he said, encouraged "specific grievances of specific groups...It begins to erode a kind of sense of common citizenship because the emphasis is really on what makes people different. It makes governance very difficult because it requires this effort to find common ground with people that you've identified as being quite different from yourself."

Daalder and James M. Lindsay, the director of studies at the Council on Foreign Relations in New York, published *The Empty*

Throne, a book highly critical of Trump's foreign policy. Since World War II, they argued, the US had exercised global leadership through alliances and the rules-based international order. Now, they said, Trump had abandoned this leadership and left the throne empty.

When they spoke to the Council, Daalder said Trump "came to the presidency with a fundamentally different view about American foreign policy and how the United States should act in the world. It's often described as isolationism. That's not really what it's about. It's essentially whether or not the United States advances its interests and values by leading in the world."

It was a glum assessment, but they closed by arguing, "the good news is that it's not irreversible." The next administration, they said, could "recommit to the fundamentals of the rules-based order and the re-establishment of strong relationships with our allies and friends and with a commitment to diplomacy to get that done."

—

On Wednesday morning, March 10, 2020, the Prudential building management told its tenants, including the Council, that a case of Covid-19, a new and potentially deadly flu-like disease, had been reported in the building.

The next day, Thursday, the Council cancelled all in-house programs for the spring, including one for that very night. The shut-down eventually lasted into 2021. Staff members cleared out their desks, installed Council devices on their home computers, and went home.

So ended the Council's pre-pandemic world. But it shifted quickly to the new reality. On Thursday, it asked former Council fellow Phil Levy to do an online program, the first full video program in its history. Levy agreed and, on Friday, Daalder interviewed Levy in a Zoom program watched by one hundred persons.

Altogether, twenty-five live programs were cancelled; some speakers, including Albright and Chicago Mayor Rahm Emanuel, agreed to do later programs on Zoom. Others, including former National Security Advisor Susan Rice, who had a new book she hoped to sell and sign in person, declined. By the year's end, the Council had staged 131 programs, all digitally, and in the process opened up a whole new future.

Basically, the pandemic showed the Council could reach beyond Chicago to connect with a broader national and international audience more cheaply than before. Before, it had to pay to fly in speakers from the Beltway and foreign leaders to spend an hour on the Council stage—that is, when these poohbahs could spend the day or two to make the trip. Now, bringing them in took no more time nor money than a Zoom call.

One example was *World Review*, a weekly program in which Daalder spent forty-five minutes every Friday morning talking with three top journalists on the East Coast or in Europe on the big global stories of the past week; time differences made it hard to include journalists in Asia in these conversations. With minimal marketing, *World Review* attracted a regular audience of 500 or more, and was likely to remain a permanent feature.

A digital approach, in fact, was integrated into everything the Council did, even when the pandemic ended. Some in-house programming returned, to serve members in Chicago and to restore the social networking much prized by those members. But even these could be hybrid affairs, with some speakers on the stage and others on a screen, working as seamlessly as the evolving technology permitted.

This included the Council's signature event, the Pritzker Global Cities Forum. In 2020, the usual three-day, Chicago-based program was scrapped in favor of a series of digital programs presented throughout the year. Eventually, the Council hoped to restore the in-person Forum but, again, mixed with digital presentations.

All this changed the concept of Council membership and of its fundraising. Before, it relied heavily on local philanthropy and on dues from members who benefitted from public programs. Even before the pandemic, local membership had stagnated. With digital, global participation grew. So did the global possibilities for financial support.

An immediate effect of the pandemic and the recession it caused was a 25 percent reduction in Council revenue. It emerged from 2020 with a balanced budget but with a hiring freeze and other economies. The global shutdown of travel helped cut expenses; so did the shift to digital programming. But both corporate and individual giving fell, forcing the Council to look for new funding sources.

The pandemic affected other think tanks and world affairs councils, of course, and all shifted quickly to digital operations. But the Council found it had two advantages in this competition. The first was its sheer technical capacity. The new broadcast center and the expanded technical staff gave the Council an up-to-date digital reach that it quickly exploited. The second was the kind of research and studies that its think tank was doing. The traditional Beltway think tanks, such as Brookings, focused on the headline issues and talked about them with their natural audience, which were the policy makers on their doorstep; the wider public was mostly shut out of this conversation. If this was a claustrophobic world, it was also a powerful one, and one that the Council, located a thousand miles away, couldn't crack. Instead, the Council aimed to influence the public debate by focusing on niche issues that the other think tanks missed and marketed them to a broader audience. One example was its food and agricultural program. Another was its work on cities. Another was a new program on post-Trump foreign policy. Policy makers listened to these reports, because no one else was doing this work, and so did the general public.

The Council's public opinion survey was part of this niche impact. Everyone knew of the deep partisan splits dividing the country, but nothing illustrated it so strongly as a much-cited 2020 survey that asked Americans to list the top threats to the country's vital interests. Republicans said the top five threats were China, international terrorism, immigration and refugees, domestic violent extremism, and Iran's nuclear program. Democrats listed the Covid-19 pandemic, climate change, racial inequality, foreign interference in US elections, and economic inequality. In other words, Democrats and Republicans saw the world through entirely different eyes, differing not just on solutions but on the problems.

—

The 2020 killing by police of George Floyd, a Black man in Minneapolis, ignited both peaceful protests and violent looting across the nation, not least in Chicago. Thousands of protesters marched through the Loop. At the fringes, looters smashed store windows and ransacked their shelves. It was the city's worst racial crisis since the 1968 riots.

In 1968, the Council had literally ignored the racial turmoil in its own city. In 2020, that wasn't possible. The protests had come to the Loop, to the Council's front door. More to the point, it was a new era and a different Council, more diverse in its programing and membership, more attuned to the impact of racial inequalities at home on the nation's foreign policy, and more sensitive to its own role as a major civic institution.

On the day after the first protests, the Council's senior management met to chart the organization's response. The first was a livestreamed panel, "Confronting Systemic Racism and Inequality," designed and moderated by Ertharin Cousin, the former director of the UN's World Food Program, and now a resident distinguished fellow at the Council. The program, held the day after Floyd's funeral, went beyond his death to discuss racial inequities in health care, education, the criminal justice system, and the economy. More than 1,400 persons registered to watch the program. Another series, moderated by Samuel C. Scott III, the Black co-chair of the Council Board, aimed at determining corporate responsibility for racial equity.

Beyond that, the Council wrestled with a proper response. A consultant was hired to address diversity issues. But what did this mean? A full-scale focus on racial issues, similar to the concentration on terrorism that followed the 9/11 attacks? More diversity in its hiring practices? In programming? In vendors? In membership? Clearly, this was a work in progress that would stretch well into the Council's second century.

As before, the racial issue forced an examination of the Council's very identity. Throughout its history, it had been an elite organization. If its programming and membership had diversified, it still aimed at an intellectual elite. Earlier attempts to connect directly with the city's Black population had not worked. The Council never had been a service organization, with a mission to overcome racial divisions.

But, as Daalder said, the Council operated in a diverse and troubled Chicago. If it hoped to establish a stronger international presence, it still was the Chicago Council, a part of the city, affected by its inequities and responsible to do what it could—through programming, staffing, and other measures—to deal with those inequities. Mostly, it still had its original mandate to explain the world to Chicago, and racial issues had become central to that world.

"We will," Daalder said, "make sure that the issues that shape our city, our nation, and our world are brought to the fore in all that we do. And so we will take a closer look at the deep fault lines in our society…We will continue to bring disparate voices, including especially of those who have suffered so greatly to ask questions, provide perspectives, and offer solutions."

If the Council had its limits, it also had its responsibilities. How it balanced these realities would help shape its future.

—

As he had on the morning after the 2016 election of Donald Trump, Ivo Daalder held a staff meeting—virtual this time—after the 2020 election to reaffirm the Council's role in the new, post-Trump world. The election of Joseph Biden promised something different—possibly a return to America's traditional leadership role, possibly a rethinking of that role—but the four years with the Trump Administration had reshaped the landscape.

The United States remained a deeply divided nation, much more divided than anyone realized four years earlier. As the recent Council poll had showed, Americans differed not only in their opinions but in their facts. For all this, he said, the Council's role remained the same, to help people understand what was happening in the world and how the United States could be an active and positive force in that world.

"We are part of the independent, fact-based, nonpartisan conversation," he said. "It is not our role to unite the country, but we can help, by bringing people together to civilly discuss our differences."

Looking back on the damage of the past four years, he said, "We can be angry and sad. But the reality is, we're in this for a little longer."

—

Back in 1972, when the Council celebrated its fiftieth anniversary, Garrick Utley looked across the post-Vietnam landscape and said, "the work of the Council is by no means at an end." Fifty years later, that burden remained.

In its century, the Council had changed. It was the biggest world affairs council west of New York and Washington. It had become a think tank as well as a forum. Its reach, once confined to Chicago, was global. At its birth, it relied on a few wealthy and worldly volunteers; now it was highly professional. Then it was run by Polly Collier working alone in an office that cost twenty dollars a month to rent; now it sprawled across a full floor in the Prudential towers. Women had been important since the founding, with Susan Hibbard as a co-founder. Ninety-six years later, a woman, Leah Joy Zell, became the first female co-chair of the Board; the other co-chair was Samuel Scott, the first African American to hold that position.

But at its centenary, the Council would have been recognizable to its founders. It was still a serious, outward-looking organization catering to the influential minority of Chicagoans with a deep interest in global affairs. Audiences were younger and more diverse, but the membership still remained older, whiter, richer, and more educated than the city around them. The average Council member was fifty-two years old. Three quarters of the members were white, more than half had master's degrees or higher, and nearly half earned more than $150,000 per year.

The Council came to life at a time when the main threat to the US was its own aloofness from the world. It charted the changes through World War II, the Cold War, Vietnam, the fall of the Berlin Wall, the rise of China, 9/11, the Iraq War and, most crucially for Chicago, the end of the industrial era and the arrival of globalization.

Much—too much—remained the same. The Council was founded in the wake of the great 1918 flu pandemic and groped into its second century in the shadow of the Covid-19 pandemic. Just as World War I exposed the blindness of American isolationism, so did Covid-19 lay bare the exclusions and frailties of the new global economy and the global society.

The Council was founded to fight isolationism, particularly potent in Chicago; now it fought a national spasm of nativism and nationalism, fueled largely by the resentments of a post-industrial Midwest. At its founding, it saw itself as the fount of information on world affairs in a news-starved provincial city, even if two of Chicago's newspapers had foreign correspondents; now, no Chicago paper had foreign correspondents and, for Chicagoans craving fresh insights into a still-troubled world, the Council remained the only game in town.

The Council still tried to balance its programming and refused to endorse either policies or people. But as Daalder said, it was nonpartisan but not neutral. It held to its founding verities: a belief in the rule of law, in democracy, in the power of reason, facts, and free debate to steer America through a world that never seemed to be in repose, even when the nation seemed ready to jettison those verities. Mostly, at its centenary, the Council reaffirmed that America's proper view is outward, that its proper role abroad is active involvement, and that its proper policy in a still dangerous world is openness.

Acknowledgments

My thanks go first of all to Bruce and Martha Clinton and to Bob and Susan Arthur, whose magnanimous matching gifts made this book possible, and also to Pat and Ron Miller and to Adele Simmons, for their generosity and support.

This history grows from the enthusiastic help of my colleagues at the Chicago Council on Global Affairs. Ivo Daalder, the president, supported this project from the start. Special thanks to Niamh King, and also to Audra Berger, Jenny Cizner, Shana Chandler, Bob Cordes, Anna Edwards, Dzena Berbic, Catherine Bertini, Bridget Brogan, Natashur Brown, John Cookson, Evan Fazio, Marcus Glassman, Brian Hanson, Mandy Hatfield, Kim Heys, Alex Hitch, Ellen Janowski, Craig Kafura, Susan Kahan, Juliana Kerr, Sarah Kowalczyk, Phil Levy, Claudette Lexsee, Jon Macha, Brittany McGhee, Karrie Miner, Rachael Mizuno, Kelly Norton, Kara O'Keefe, Lisa Park, Jennifer Petersen, Julia Polszakiewicz, Honore Raz, Brandon Richardson, Ros Roberts, Samantha Skinner, Cecile Shea, Dina Smeltz, Ana Teasdale, Iain Whitaker, and Victoria Williams.

I was fortunate to be able to interview the three men who led the Council for the last fifty years—John Rielly, Marshall Bouton, and Ivo Daalder. Many other persons involved in the Council's history, including past and present employees and Board members, generously agreed to be interviewed, most in person, some by telephone or email. They are Lester Crown, Adele Simmons, John Manley, Michael Moskow, David Rosso, Newton and Josephine Minow, Arthur Cyr, David Utley, Jonathan Utley, Irene Hill, Sharon Houtkamp, Rachel Bronson, Kennette Benedict, Carol Byrne, Alesha Black,

Niamh King, Joel Henning, Kenneth T. Jackson, Henry Kisor, Jack Schnedler, Adlai Stevenson III, John Mearsheimer, and Dick Prall.

In the early 1970s, John Rielly and his colleagues, David Mellon, Nora Dell, and Dennis Allred, conducted a series of interviews with past Council leaders for an oral history project. These interviews provided a trove of Council history, especially of the years just before and after World War II. Those interviewed include Melvin Brorby, Clifton Utley, Alex Seith, William Graham Cole, Walter Fisher, Roberta Ellis, Louise Wright, Edward McDougal, Daggett Harvey, Harriett Welling, and Richard Templeton.

Nikki Shields and Meg Teaford, the granddaughters of the Council's co-founder, William Browne Hale, made their grandfather's papers available to me and shared their family history. Ms. Shields gave me the picture of her great aunt, Susan Hibbard. Debbie Kaiser, David Strong, and Robert Strong, the grandchildren of Walter Strong, added to my knowledge of their grandfather's meeting with Mussolini. Gary Johnson, president of the Chicago History Museum, provided the Chicago history of 1922 that appears at the start of chapter one. Kenneth Janda of Northwestern University shared his memories of Kenneth Colegrove. Paula Dell generously shared old Council pictures left by her late stepmother, Nora Dell. Ted Kaufman clarified President Joseph Biden's relationship to the Council.

The Council's papers, dating to the founding meeting, are by far the most valuable source for this book. They are archived in the Special Collections section of the Richard J. Daley Library at the University of Illinois at Chicago, and I'm grateful to Peggy Glowacki, the manuscripts librarian, and her team, for their help and hospitality to me. My special thanks to Michael Reed, a fellow Council history buff, for his help in photocopying the thousands of documents from these archives.

Thanks also to Christa Cleeton at the Seeley G. Mudd Library at Princeton, where Adlai Stevenson's papers are stored; to Anna

Hocker at the Schlesinger Library at Radcliffe College, for providing the papers of Louise Wright; to Kevin Leonard, the archivist at Northwestern University's library, for steering me to papers stored there, for helping dig up early *Chicago Tribune* references to the Council, and for unearthing an early history of the Council; to Lee Grady, the reference archivist at the Wisconsin Historical Society Archives, and to Liz Antaramian and her team at the archives center at the University of Wisconsin Parkside, for help in accessing the papers of Clifton Utley.

Priscilla Roberts at the University of Hong Kong very generously shared her work on think tanks, plus her collection of files from the Northwestern University library dealing with the Chicago Council.

Special thanks go to the good people at Agate Publishing who made this book so much better. They include the publisher, Doug Seibold; Naomi Huffman, who edited the manuscript with care and insight; Jane Seibold, the production editor who shepherded the book through page design, layout, and printing; and Morgan Krehbiel, who fashioned the cover design.

To mark the Council's fortieth anniversary in 1962, it commissioned a history of its first four decades from a University of Chicago graduate student named Kenneth T. Jackson. It was an inspired choice. Jackson went on to become one of the nation's most distinguished historians, the Jacques Barzun Professor of History at Columbia University, and a former president of the Society of American Historians, among many other honors. I have drawn heavily on his work, especially material from his interviews with the Council's early founders and leaders, many of whom were still alive then.

Bibliography

Appelbaum, Binyamin. *The Economists' Hour: False Prophets, Free Markets, and the Fracture of Society.* New York: Little, Brown and Company, 2019.

Bailey, Thomas A. *The Man in the Street: The Impact of American Public Opinion on Foreign Policy.* New York: The Macmillan Company, 1948.

Ball, George W. *The Past Has Another Pattern: Memoirs.* New York: Norton, 1982.

Briscoe, Jerry. *A Study of the Chicago Council on Foreign Relations.* Unpublished dissertation. Chicago: University of Chicago, 1949.

Daalder, Ivo H. and James M. Lindsey. *The Empty Throne: America's Abdication of Global Leadership.* New York: Public Affairs, 2018.

Davis, Kenneth S. *The Politics of Honor: A Biography of Adlai E. Stevenson.* New York: G. P. Putnam's Sons, 1967.

Dyja, Thomas. *The Third Coast: When Chicago Built the American Dream.* New York: The Penguin Press, 2015.

Foreign Notes, 1925-1951. Chicago: Chicago Council on Foreign Relations, 1925-1951.

Harley, John Eugene. *International Understanding: Agencies Educating for a New World.* Stanford: Stanford University Press, 1931.

Jackson, Kenneth T. *Chicago Council on Foreign Relations: A Record of Forty Years.* Chicago: Chicago Council on Foreign Relations, 1962.

Johnson, Walter, edit; Carol Evans, asst. edit. *The Papers of Adlai E. Stevenson: Beginnings of Education, 1900-1941.* Boston: Little, Brown and Company, 1972.

Jones, Chester Lloyd, Henry Kittredge Norton, and Parker Thomas Moon. *The United States and the Caribbean.* Chicago: University of Chicago Press, 1929.

Judt, Tony. *Postwar: A History of Europe Since 1945.* New York: The Penguin Press, 2005.

Kusch, Frank. *Battleground Chicago: The Police and the 1968 Democratic National Convention.* Chicago: University of Chicago Press, 2004.

Labat, Sean Joseph. *Creating Consensus: Chicago and United States Foreign Relations During the Early Cold War, 1945-1950.* Unpublished dissertation. Chicago: University of Illinois at Chicago, 2002.

Longworth, Richard C. *Global Chicago: Two Reports on Chicago's Assets and Opportunities as a Global City.* Chicago: The John D. and Catherine T. MacArthur Foundation, 1998.

Macmillan, Margaret. *Paris 1919: Six Months That Changed the World.* New York: Random House, 2001.

Madigan, Charles, edit. *Global Chicago.* Urbana: University of Illinois Press, 2004.

Martin, John Bartlow. *Adlai Stevenson of Illinois: The Life of Adlai E. Stevenson.* Garden City: Doubleday & Company, 1976.

McGann, James G. "2015 Global Go To Think Tank Index Report." Philadelphia: University of Pennsylvania, 2016.

McKeever, Porter. *Adlai Stevenson: His Life and Legacy.* New York: William Morrow and Co., 1989.

Mearsheimer, John J., and Walt, Stephen M. *The Israel Lobby and U.S. Foreign Policy.* New York: Farrar, Straus and Giroux, 2007.

Miller, Donald L. *City of the Century: The Epic of Chicago and the Making of America.* New York: Simon & Schuster, 1996.

Notes on World Events. Chicago: Chicago Council on Foreign Relations, 1952-1970.

Rhodes, Ben. *The World As It Is: A Memoir of the Obama White House.* New York: Random House, 2018.

Rippy, J. Fred. *United States and Mexico.* New York: Alfred A. Knopf, 1926.

Schneider, James Covill. *The Anxieties of Neutrality: Chicago Public Opinion and American Foreign Policy, 1939-41.* Unpublished dissertation. Madison: University of Wisconsin-Madison, 1979.

Schultz, Bud. *The Price of Dissent: Testimonies to Political Repression in America.* Berkeley: University of California Press, 2001.

Selee, Andrew. *What Should Think Tanks Do?* Stanford: Stanford University Press, 2013.

Smith, Richard Norton. *The Colonel: The Life and Legend of Robert R. McCormick.* Boston: Houghton Mifflin Company, 1997.

Steinweg, Isabel. *The Chicago Council on Global Affairs: A Foreign Policy Think Tank in the Midwest.* Trier: WVT Wissenschaftlicher Verlag, 2009.

Taubman, William. *Gorbachev: His Life and Times.* New York: W.W. Norton & Company, 2017.

Wilburn, Mark Steven. *Midwestern Interventionism and the European Crisis, 1935-1941.* Unpublished dissertation, Ohio University. Ann Arbor: University Microfilms, 1987.

World Events. Chicago: The Chicago Council on Foreign Relations, 1971-1990.

Notes

In the notes that follow, "UIC" denotes material that can be found in the Chicago Council archives, housed in the Special Collections section at the Richard J. Daley Library at the University of Illinois at Chicago.

Introduction

2	**"We take it to be self-evident":** Council brochure, UIC, Nov. 1, 1923.
4	**"It was felt that at the time":** John Eugene Harley, *International Understanding: Agencies Educating for a New World*, 1931.
4	**"isolationists differ from others not so much":** William Browne Hale, "Our International Commitments," undated.
6	**"the primary outlet for that influential slice":** *Chicago Tribune*, Apr. 25, 1997.
8	**"the foreign policy problems of the United States":** Maurice F. X. Donohue in a letter to Daggett Harvey, July 30, 1953.
8	**"Because we are going to have this restructuring":** transcript, "The Presidential Campaign and American Foreign Policy," UIC, June 27, 1972.

Chapter 1: Beginnings

9	**"The year 1922 saw a sunburst":** Gary Johnson, "Chicago in 1922," Oct. 30, 1917.
9	**"On February 20 of that year":** Council meeting minutes, UIC, Feb. 20, 1922.
11	**"After all, are not knowledge":** Walter Johnson, *The Papers of Adlai E. Stevenson: Beginnings of Education, 1900-1941*, 1972.
11	**"Chicago was a hotbed of isolation":** John Bartlow Martin, *Adlai Stevenson of Illinois: The Life of Adlai E. Stevenson*, 1976, p 97.
11	**"Chicago was long an isolationist citadel":** Thomas Bailey, *The Man in the Street: The Impact of American Public Opinion on Foreign Policy*, 1948, p 109.
12	**"The Council was a vital place":** George W. Ball, *The Past Has Another Pattern*, 1983, p 12.

12	**"to communicate the patriotic American viewpoint":** Richard Norton Smith, *The Colonel: The Life and Legend of Robert R. McCormick*, 1997, p 194.
14	**"had often been in those old days the token woman":** Harriet Welling in an oral interview with Nora Dell, July 7, 1976.
15	**"imposing Southern gentleman":** Welling to Dell, July 7, 1976.
15	**"At the Council's first public meeting":** Council meeting minutes, UIC, Mar. 18, 1922.
15	**"on the theory that the people in general":** Council meeting minutes, UIC, May 31, 1922.
16	**"the most remarkable body of agreements":** Council meeting minutes, UIC, Mar. 18, 1922.
17	**"it was concluded that any attempt to battle":** Jerry Briscoe, *A Study of the Chicago Council on Foreign Relations*, unpublished dissertation, 1949, p 8.
17	**"desires to offer a forum":** transcript, UIC, undated.
17	**"nonpartisan but not neutral":** from author interview with Ivo Daalder, July 30, 2018.
18	**"a pro-Bolshevik field day":** Graham Aldis in a letter to William B. Hale, Jan. 30, 1928.
18	**"he opposed in general any participation":** Council meeting minutes, UIC, Mar. 31, 1922.
19	**"let us reason with each other":** Kenneth T. Jackson, *Chicago Council on Foreign Relations: A Record of Forty Years*. Chicago Council on Foreign Relations, 1962, p 11-12; speech text from *Chicago Tribune, Chicago Daily News, Chicago Herald-Examiner, Chicago Daily Journal, Chicago American*, UIC, Nov. 10-29, 1922.
20	**"The Clemenceau program left the infant Council":** Council meeting minutes, UIC, Dec. 21, 1922.
20	**"The British statesman, whose work":** Jackson, p 12; speech text from *Chicago Tribune, Chicago Daily News, Chicago Herald-Examiner, Chicago Daily Journal, Chicago American*, UIC, Nov. 10-29, 1922.
20	**"Attendance ranged from sixty persons":** *Chicago Daily News*, UIC, May 16, 1924.
20	**"minus fifty dollars, this being the approximate difference":** Council meeting minutes, UIC, Mar. 22, 1922.
20, 21	**"'war communism' policy of crash nationalization":** *Chicago Tribune*, UIC, Apr. 12, 1922.
21	**"Black folks all over the world":** transcript, UIC, Feb. 21, 1926; unattributed newspaper clippings, UIC, Feb. 21, 1926.
21	**"Count Richard von Coudenhove-Kalergi":** unattributed newspaper clipping, UIC, Nov. 29, 1928.
21	**"But a British diplomat":** *Chicago Tribune*, UIC, Sept. 13, 1929.

21	**"A former Hungarian foreign minister"**: *Chicago Tribune* and *Chicago Daily News*, UIC, 1923.
22	**"Mussolini had just taken power"**: Jackson, p 13; unattributed newspaper clippings, UIC, 1926-27.
22	**"Walter A. Strong, publisher of the *Chicago Daily News*"**: *Chicago Daily News*, UIC, Dec. 4, 1926; speech text, Walter Ansel Strong Papers, Newberry Library archive; email between author and David Strong, Nov. 6, 2018; email between author and Robert Strong, Dec. 4, 2018.
22	**"Often the Council staged debates"**: transcript, UIC, Apr. 3, 1926.
22	**"Nobody used the word 'globalization'"**: transcript, UIC, Apr. 11-12, 1924.
22	**"In the post-war years"**: transcript, UIC, Apr. 11-12, 1924.
23	**"Major General John F. O'Ryan"**: transcript, UIC, Jan. 13, 1923.
23	**"join in publishing a quarterly magazine"**: Council meeting minutes, UIC, June 8, 1922.
24	**"Some early notes suggest"**: Jackson, p 7.
24	**"Actually, Addams, while an early member"**: Eloise ReQua in a letter to Adlai Stevenson III, Illinois Institute of Technology Chicago Kent Law Library, May 24, 1964.
24	**"Debate continued on the issue of nonpartisanship"**: Council meeting minutes, Feb. 1, 1928.
24	**"'any whom the spirit moveth'"**: transcript, UIC, Mar. 18, 1922.
24	**"an address that promises to have dramatic"**: Council annual report, UIC, May 26, 1925.
25	**"The Council's first and most successful publication"**: Council meeting minutes, Apr. 17, 1925.
25	**"will be to print the principal international news"**: *Foreign Notes*, Apr. 29, 1925.
25	**"All sold well, but by the time"**: Jackson, p 14.
26	**"The Council, which began with 176 charter members"**: Clay Judson in a letter to Graham Aldis, UIC, May 20, 1929.
26	**"On October 29, 1929, several hundred Council members"**: Jackson, p 16.

Chapter 2: The Great Debate

28	**"the council had turned"**: James Covill Schneider, *The Anxieties of Neutrality: Chicago Public Opinion and American Foreign Policy, 1939-41*, unpublished dissertation, University of Wisconsin-Madison, 1979, p 83.
29	**"The Council's fortunes crashed"**: Jackson, p 17.
29	**"Council membership cost five dollars"**: Walter Lichtenstein in a letter to Theodore W. Koch, UIC, Sept. 28, 1933.
29	**"Clifton Utley was a tall"**: Jackson, p 17.

29	"there was an abysmal ignorance": *Chicago Daily News*, June 26, 1973.
30	"this may have been unfair": Jackson, p 17.
30	"'things happen rapidly here in Geneva'": Alice Benning in a letter to Graham Aldis, UIC, Aug. 10, 1931.
30	"'my getting the directorship'": Clifton Utley in an oral interview with John Rielly, Nov. 21, 1977.
31	"'the Middle West was the most negative part'": transcript, Council meeting, June 27, 1972, p 10-11.
31	"'It is no longer a question'": *Chicago Daily News*, Oct. 11, 1931.
31	"From the start, the Council tried": Council meeting minutes, UIC, May 27, 1930.
31	"'a dreamer, an exceptionally gifted speaker'": Richard von Kühlmann, transcript, UIC, Feb. 4, 1933.
32	"'speaker representing the National Socialist point of view'": Council meeting minutes, UIC, Sept. 22, 1933.
32	"'Just tell the truth!'": *Chicago Tribune*, UIC, Nov. 15, 1933.
32	"A week later, Schönemann gave": *Jewish Telegraph Agency*, Nov. 28, 1933.
33	"'It would be suicide for Germany'": transcript, UIC, Mar. 20, 1937.
33	"'Their history shows that they will take advantage'": transcript, UIC, Oct. 27, 1937.
33	"'an organized attempt to falsify'": transcript, UIC, Oct. 8, 1937.
33	"The Japanese ambassador to Washington": transcript, UIC, Nov. 19, 1937.
33,34	"'anti-Japanism. . .China is such an abnormal country'": transcript, UIC, 1938.
34	"'irrefutable evidence. . .with complete implacability'": transcript, UIC, Nov. 8, 1937.
34	"Clifton Utley remained one of": Jackson, p 19.
34	"Utley also pioneered the Council's use": Jackson, p 19.
35	"'I've always thought of the Council'": transcript, UIC, Feb. 19, 1963.
35	"'the Council was young Stevenson's training'": Martin, p 97-98.
35	"'The Council made him a public'": Porter McKeever, *Adlai Stevenson: His Life and Legacy*, 1989, p 65.
35, 36	"'Under Stevenson, the Council changed'": Martin, p 125-126.
36	"'polishing them like a jeweler'": Edward McDougal in an oral interview with Dennis Allred, July 19, 1976.
36	"'the speaking style which during the 1952 presidential campaign'": Martin, p 126-127.
36	"'He would practice and practice and practice'": Utley to Rielly, Nov. 21, 1977.
36	"'Adlai had a driving ambition'": McDougal to Allred, July 19, 1976.

36	"'overflow luncheons…the attraction for many'": McKeever, p 64.
37	"'I wish I could squander'": Walter Johnson, p 326.
37	"'We have become an institution'" and "'Like the armament industry'" and "'Catastrophe, not culture'": Walter Johnson, p 302; 325-326; 361.
37	"'inasmuch as it is my conviction'" and "'asking you the following three questions'": Newton Jenkins in a letter to Adlai Stevenson, UIC, Oct. 5, 1935; Stevenson in a letter to Jenkins, UIC, Oct. 10, 1935.
37	"'for the first time in many years,'": Walter Johnson, p 308.
38	"'which provided for non-interference'": transcript, UIC, Feb. 15, 1936.
38	"'It was an exciting time'": Kenneth S. Davis, *The Politics of Honor: A Biography of Adlai E. Stevenson*, 1957, p 132-133.
38	"At one point, Colonel McCormick": from author interviews, undated.
38, 39	"'From Lake Forest and other outposts'": *Chicago Times*, Sept. 18, 1939.
39	"'has keen dark eyes,'": *Chicago Tribune*, Apr. 13, 1940.
39	"When one speaker talked about": *Chicago Daily News*, Jan. 11, 1941.
39	"'perhaps in time all of the Chicago newspapers'": Walter Johnson, p 333-334.
39	"'Why should you or your treasury committee'": Mary Welsh in a letter to Adlai Stevenson, UIC, Sept. 28, 1936.
39	"'by aspiring to the news pages'": Adlai Stevenson in a letter to Mary Welsh, UIC, Oct. 2, 1936.
39	"There is no record that Welsh replied": *Chicago Daily News*, Jan. 17, 1976.
40	"'there is unanimity on one point'": transcript, UIC, Nov. 4, 1938.
41	"'in a general European war'": transcript, UIC, Oct. 7, 1938.
41	"'Nazis decided that they would like'": transcript, UIC, Jan. 10, 1940.
41	"'is already on. It just depends'": transcript, UIC, Nov. 10, 1938.
41	"'says democracy is a failure'": transcript, UIC, Feb. 28, 1938.
41, 42	"'the final decision in this war'": transcript, UIC, Oct. 28, 1941.
42	"'extraordinary,'" and "'detestable,'" and "'mystic and dreamer'": transcript, UIC, Feb. 4, 1938.
42	"'If what we did at Munich'": transcript, UIC, Jan. 29, 1939.
42	"'It does not matter two pins'": transcript, UIC, Dec. 10, 1938.
43	"'It is my belief that the Western Democracies'": transcript, UIC, Feb. 1, 1939.
43	"'What is going on in Germany'" and "'insane people'" and "'and the only thing we want'": transcript, UIC, Jan. 3, 1939.
43	"Ross launched into an anti-Jewish tirade": Jackson, p 21.

44	"'If the law stands as it is now read'": transcript, UIC, Sept. 23, 1939.
44	"'It would help one set of belligerents'": transcript, UIC, Sept. 23, 1939.
44	"'Isolationism is a prelude to destruction'": transcript, UIC, Oct. 21, 1940.
44	"'A German victory'" and "'an abandonment of neutrality'" and "'The answer…is as simple'": transcript, UIC, May 21, 1940.
45	"'keep out of war'": *Milwaukee Journal*, Dec. 10, 1940.
45	"'are ready to dig in'": transcript, UIC, Mar. 4, 1941.
45	"'unless the United States feels strongly'": transcript, UIC, Mar. 4, 1941.
46	"'a passing insanity'" and "McCormick never joined America First": Smith, p 325, 407.
46	"To complicate matters, internationalists could be": Schneider, p 151.
47	"'the unhappiest period of my life'": Welling to Dell, July 7, 1976.
47	"In the spring of 1940": Mark Steven Wilburn, *Midwestern Interventionism and the European Crisis, 1935-1941*, unpublished dissertation, 1987, p 143-148.
47	"'public relations counsel'" and "'And then I went over'": Utley to Rielly, Nov. 21, 1977.
48	"It was a shrewd choice.": Wilburn, p 143-148.
48	"The White Committee was opposed": Schneider, p 139-141; Wilburn, p 155-157.
48	"A *Tribune* story quoted unnamed 'indignant members'": *Chicago Tribune*, Feb. 9, 1941.
49	"'You cannot destroy an ideology'" and "'the summit of mud-slinging'" and "'perfectly fantastic'": transcript, UIC, Oct. 4, 1940.
49	"'What are all those people doing'": *Christian Science Monitor*, Jan. 15, 1941.
49	"'mere paltry little European conflict'": Menzies, UIC, May 15, 1941.
49	"'Japan has no territorial ambitions'": transcript, UIC, Sept. 26, 1941.
50	"'I know of no plan'": transcript, UIC, Oct. 24, 1941; *Chicago Tribune*, Oct. 25, 1941.
50	"'an increased apathy and feeling'": Council speakers committee meeting minutes, UIC, Dec. 5, 1941.
50	"On December 12, the Board": Council Board meeting minutes, UIC, Dec. 12, 1941.
50	"'Whatever individual views'" and "'to promote discussion'" and "'and the Council on Foreign Relations'": *Foreign Notes*, Jan. 17, 1942.

Chapter 3: War and Post-war

51, 52   "'This is truly the first global or planetary'" and "'I seem to see'" and "'The fall of Singapore'": transcript, UIC, Dec. 16, 1941.

52, 53   "'Not only can we lose this war'" and "'Not in our present frame'": Martin, p 201.

53, 54   "'great ideal for tomorrow'" and "'twenty months ago'" and "'and after twenty years'" and "'The first step is to organize'" and "'The key, of course, is Russia'": transcript, UIC, Oct. 8, 1943.

54   "A Dutch diplomat who described": transcript, UIC, May 13, 1942.

54   "spoke on Irish neutrality": transcript, UIC, Oct. 5, 1942.

54   "'Sea power has saved us from defeat'": transcript, UIC, Oct. 17, 1942.

54   "'Major Alexander P. de Seversky also addressed'": Jackson, p 25.

54   "talked about psychological warfare": transcript, UIC, Feb. 8, 1943.

54   "praised short wave radio": transcript, UIC, Mar. 23, 1943.

54   "'The men now controlling Japan'" and "'feudal military spirit'": transcript, UIC, Nov. 14, 1942.

54   "'by execution or maltreatment'": transcript, UIC, May 10, 1943.

55   "'are not an aggressive-minded people'" and "'You can't build a fence'": transcript, UIC, Jan. 16, 1943.

55   "'the Russians need peace'" and "'in order to have peace'" and "'the Russians are going into the border'": transcript, UIC, Feb. 17, 1945.

56   "'to be a democratic republic'" and "'he wants to respect Poland's independence'": transcript, UIC, June 23, 1944.

56   "'The Germans are not democratically minded'": *Chicago Tribune*, Sept. 25, 1943.

56   "'as deep faith that they are different'" and "'If we can convince them'": transcript, UIC, January 4, 1944.

56, 57   "'dismembered into several states'" and "'Place an embargo on Germany'": transcript, UIC, Oct. 18, 1944.

57   "'On the sixth of June'" and "'a welterweight among heavyweights'" and "'the organs of the McCormick-Patterson Axis press'" and "'It is not that they do not wish'": transcript, UIC, June 19, 1944.

58   "'The respect and the maintenance'": transcript, UIC, May 22, 1943.

58   "'China in fact has made'": transcript, UIC, Apr. 24, 1944.

58   "'Once the Chinese people get started'": transcript, UIC, Mar. 17, 1944.

59   "'there is no dispute between the oil industry'": transcript, UIC, Dec. 8, 1944.

59   "'Our business in this period of building'": transcript, UIC, Dec. 1, 1944.

59   "'Let us think of the boys'": transcript, UIC, Dec. 5, 1943.

60	"'Maintain the present war-community of the United Nations'": transcript, UIC, May 22, 1943.
60	"'Let us make no mistake'": transcript, UIC, June 19, 1944.
60, 61	"'participation in a system of collective security'" and "'is the only secure path'" and "'I am not unmindful, whenever I speak'": transcript, UIC, Feb. 2, 1945.
61	"'The walls of isolation'" and "'a continuing organization of the United Nations'": transcript, UIC, Mar. 31, 1943.
61, 62	"'The so-called isolationists'" and "'You have a great newspaper'" and "'the power to act'" and "'One of the arguments which we hear'": transcript, UIC, Sept. 28, 1944.
62	"'take action by air, naval, and land'": transcript, UIC, Dec. 13, 1944.
62	"'No organization of peace'" and "'The states other than the Big Five'": transcript, UIC, Jan. 26, 1945.
63	"'the removal of the political, economic, and social'" and "'the expansion of private trade'" and "'Without it, the world will be able'" and "'Political isolationism and economic nationalism'": transcript, UIC, Apr. 4, 1945.
64	"'the charming wife of Professor Quincy Wright'": *Daily News*, June, 1942.
64	"a former history professor . . . Woodrow Wilson Foundation": *Foreign Notes*, June 20, 1942.
64	"Both membership and revenue suffered": Council Board meeting minutes, UIC, 1946-47.
64	"Wright quickly moved the Council's offices": Jackson, p 24-25, 32; Council Board meeting minutes, UIC, June 22, 1942, and Sept. 16, 1948.
65	"Wright made the Council busier than ever": Jackson, p 26; Council Board meeting minutes, UIC, Feb. 5, 1948.
65, 66	"The Speakers Bureau had been founded" and "If membership mostly held up": Jackson, p 26.
66	"For the first time, the Council sought": Council Board meeting minutes, UIC, May 12, 1947; *Chicago Tribune*, Dec. 17, 1948.
66	"The Council had been formed": Jackson, p 30.
66, 67	"In 1947, the Council began a series": Jackson, p 31.
67	"Melvin Brorby, one of Chicago's leading advertising men": Jackson, p 30.
67	"'Mel is a world citizen'": *World Events*, Winter, 1985.
68	"Only when the Young Men's Group succeeded": Jackson, p 30.
68	"'Our luncheons are educational'": *Chicago Sun-Times*, Mar. 9, 1959.
68	"'so successful it is embarrassing'" and "'We have sold about 1,100 tickets'": memo from Louise Leonard Wright to Sydney Stein, Jr., UIC, Apr. 8, 1948.

69	"'That beauty which came from a unity'": Louise Leonard Wright, transcript, UIC, May 25, 1945.
69	"'Mrs. Quincy Wright's new Paris hat'": *Chicago Daily News,* June 2, 1945.
69	"'with the understanding that you would get it'": Louise Leonard Wright in a letter to Quincy Wright, Louise L. Wright Papers, Schlesinger Library, Radcliffe College, Nov. 4, 1945.
71	"'two major adjustments'" and "'If we cannot ward off bombs'" and "'helicopter buses driven by tangential jets'": transcript, UIC, Sept. 27, 1945.
71, 72	"'the concept of the collective guilt'" and "'a jerrybuilt architectural monstrosity'" and "'We did not make the gigantic sacrifices'": transcript, Oct. 11, 1943.
72	"'I do not think we can retire'": transcript, UIC, Oct. 26, 1945.
72	"'We have such a tremendous responsibility'": transcript, UIC, Oct. 23, 1946.
72, 73	"'In the interest of world peace'": transcript, UIC, Nov. 13, 1945.
73	"'dual economy, a modern economy'" and "'The only way to solve the conflict'": transcript, UIC, May 13, 1946.
73, 74	"'The idea that one can or should pastoralize'" and "'I think . . . we can safely take for granted'" and "'The Germans do not seem disposed'": transcript, UIC, Feb. 21, 1946.
74, 75	"'The baby was tough'" and "'It is safe to say that each of these'" and "'maudlin optimism'" and "'Russian bloc'" and "'Considering their background, their education'" and "'we are witnessing the twilight'" and "'There have always been competing ideologies'": transcript, UIC, Mar. 22, 1946.
75	"'a world legislature'" and "'is between federation and annihilation'": transcript, UIC, Apr. 10, 1946.
75, 76	"'The United Nations, as now constituted'" and "'We need a single political management'": transcript, UIC, Dec. 6, 1946.
76	"'We, whether we like it or not'" and "'It is our responsibility'" and "'People, I believe, have the right'": transcript, UIC, Mar. 3, 1947.
76	"assured the Council that Russia's influence": transcript, UIC, Mar. 9, 1946.
76, 77	"'progressive democratic front'" and "'but the imposition by force'": transcript, UIC, July 2, 1946.
77	"'divergence of purpose'" and "'It seems evident that, as regards European recovery'": transcript, UIC, Nov. 18, 1947; *Chicago Sun,* Nov. 19, 1947.
78	"'That conference was a turning point'": transcript, UIC, Nov. 23, 1948.
78	"'There is going on today a war'": transcript, UIC, Nov. 29, 1948.
78	"'the exact import of which is very obscure'" and "'the bankruptcy of the Truman Doctrine'": transcript, UIC, Oct. 3, 1947.

78	"'Every believer in Americanism'": Sean Joseph Labat, *Creating Consensus: Chicago and United States Foreign Relations During the Early Cold War, 1945-1950,* unpublished dissertation, 2002, p 60.
79	"'an integral part of the western world'" and "'The struggle is not one between capitalism'": transcript, UIC, Jan. 30, 1948.
79	"'a revolt against democracy'": transcript, UIC, May 22, 1943.
79	"'By these methods, the Soviet Union'": transcript, UIC, Mar. 29, 1948.
80	"'double revolution'" and "'The masses in China, Japan, India'" and "'I don't think secular democracy'": transcript, UIC, Apr. 22, 1949; *Christian Science Monitor,* Apr. 28, 1949.
81	"'was not a rational or logical act'" and "'monstrous episode'" and "'Surely there is an international interest'": transcript, UIC, Feb. 25, 1949.
81	"The speech sold out its 1,200 tickets": transcript, UIC, Oct. 20, 1949; *Chicago Daily News,* Oct. 24, 1949.
81, 82	"'I have little doubt'" and "'The fundamental problem, so far as Asia'": transcript, UIC, Oct. 26, 1949.

Chapter 4: Cold War

83	"'The Russians mean to fight us'" and "'You have to be very patient'": transcript, UIC, Apr. 22, 1949.
84	"'We are in fact on the way'": Jackson, p 38.
84, 85	"But if the future was set" and "'the beginning of the end of the idea'": transcript, UIC, Feb. 22, 1950.
85	"'We seek to advance the best interests'": transcript, UIC, Feb. 10, 1950.
85	"'The world will find it more difficult'": Jackson, p 34.
86	"'the fact of resurgent nationalism'" and "'the Muslims who form the majority'" and "'sorely tried our patience'": transcript, UIC, May 11, 1950.
86, 87	"'panic and hysteria'" and "'Our nerves are shaken'" "In an atmosphere of lies'" and "'want America's help and friendship'" and "'a common fear of Russian aggression'" and "'the system of private enterprise'" and "'would-be builders of an American coolie empire'": transcript, UIC, Oct. 2, 1950.
87	"'the effete members of the Chicago Council'": *Chicago Tribune,* Oct. 5, 1950.
87, 88	"'is the greatest individualist I have ever seen'": transcript, UIC, Oct. 19, 1948.
88, 89	"'It is very important'" and "'We have not convinced the man of Asia'" and "'but they divine in us'" and "'we have done nothing to lighten the burden'" and "'fighting a certain man because he was communist'": transcript, UIC, Apr. 5, 1951.

89	"'what would be to them the most important freedom'" and "'the very things that we believe'" and "'When we fight this battle for freedom'": transcript, UIC, Sept. 9, 1952.
90	"'our equals'": transcript, UIC, Apr. 5, 1951.
90	"'such as it is understood'" and "'because she wants to find her own way'" and "'in Asia, nationalism is taking the shape'": transcript, UIC, May 23, 1952.
90, 91	"'oughtn't to be looking for somebody'" and "'What has happened in Korea'": *Chicago Tribune*, Dec. 9, 1950.
92	"'Communism controls the life'" and "'the totality of the effective agents'" and "'a total state'" and "'Peaceful coexistence is a pious hope'" and "'create those stubborn and irreducible facts'" and "'will bless the names of Marx and Lenin'": transcript, UIC, Dec. 14, 1950.
92	"'a dictatorship of the highest degree'" and "'some 97 percent'": transcript, UIC, Apr. 1, 1952.
93	"'We should activate the strains'" and "'I'm absolutely convinced that a policy'": transcript, UIC, Oct. 8, 1952.
93, 94	"'that the debate between the isolationists'" and "'public and dramatic recognition'" and "'to perform any kind of miracle'": transcript, UIC, Nov. 26, 1952.
94	"'Any nation that is fortunate enough'": transcript, UIC, Apr. 22, 1952.
94	"if the Council had to consider": *Gary Post-Tribune*, Jan. 4, 1952.
94, 95	"'doubly unwise'" and "'ascertain for itself how extensively'" and "'In a time of great international crisis'": Kenneth Colegrove in a letter to Walter Lichtenstein, UIC, Apr. 3, 1951.
95	"'as far as Schuman is concerned'": Melvin Brorby in a letter to Kenneth Colegrove, UIC, June 15, 1954.
95	"Colegrove wasn't the only one looking for Reds": Bud Schultz, *The Price of Dissent: Testimonies to Political Repression in America*, 2001, p 415; Frank Kusch, *Battleground Chicago: The Police and the 1968 Democratic National Convention*, 2004, p 128.
96	"'ultra-liberal, 99 percent'": Long-Range Planning Committee meeting minutes, UIC, Nov. 3, 1970.
96	"'where I was received'" and "'as a communist front'": Council Board meeting minutes, UIC, Dec. 2, 1970.
96	"'would lend a partisan appearance'": Council Board meeting minutes, UIC, June 16, 1971.
96	"'Khrushchev was in many ways'": Jackson, p 39.
96	"The Council itself began courting": *Chicago Daily News*, Aug. 16, 1955.
97	"The picketers were not so peaceful": *Chicago Tribune*, Nov. 15, 1958.
97	"'I see no hope of a federated Europe'": Jackson, p 39.

97	"'We have no fear of political risks'" and "'would prohibit the German people'" and "'third force'" and "'opportunities for American capital'" and "'Europe and the United States'": transcript, UIC, Mar. 10, 1958.
98	"'If it were like Pearl Harbor'": *Chicago Tribune*, Nov. 21, 1957.
98	"Abba Eban, by now the Israeli ambassador": *Chicago Daily News*, June 29, 1957.
98	"Henry Cabot Lodge, the US ambassador": *Chicago Tribune*, Apr. 25, 1959.
98	"'My political functions will cease'": *Chicago Sun-Times*, Dec. 17, 1957.
98	"'The State Department was terribly upset'": Richard Templeton in an oral interview with David Mellon, July 21, 1976.
99	"'the most nearly perfect international organization'": Jackson, p 38.
99	"'false liberty'": *Chicago Daily News*, Apr. 28, 1959.
99	"One big fish got away": *Chicago Daily News*, Apr. 15, 1959.
99	"'too identified with certain political convictions'": Council Board meeting minutes, UIC, Sept. 12, 1951.
99	"'The country is swinging away'": letter from Kenneth Colegrove to Daggett Harvey, UIC, Sept. 18, 1951.
100	"'It was agreed that there is no objection'": Council Board meeting minutes, UIC, Sept. 12, 1951.
100	"'the size of a pebble'": *New York Times*, June 12, 1952.
100	"McKeever moved his family": Jackson, p 36; McKeever in a letter to Melvin Brorby, UIC, Aug. 19, 1952; memo from Melvin Brorby to Council Board, UIC, Aug. 19, 1952.
100	"police beat at the *Chicago Sun-Times*": Maurice F.X. Donohue in a letter to Daggett Harvey, UIC, July 30, 1953; Carter Davidson in a letter to Daggett Harvey, UIC, July 14, 1953.
100	"'He was more interested in his own career'": Welling to Dell, July 7, 1976.
100, 101	"'was good in some things'": Brorby to Rielly, May 18-19, 1976.
101	"'The common conclusion of these self-studies'": Jackson, p 37.
102	"The Council stayed in the Lake View Building": Jackson, p 39.
102	"Most important, the Council began looking": Jackson, p 40.
103	"In 1959, the Council made": Jackson, p 40; *Chicago American*, Feb. 16 and 24, 1959; *Sunday Tribune*, Feb. 23, 1959; *Chicago Daily News*, Dec. 9, 1957.
103	"'the foyer was so chilly'": *Chicago American*, Feb. 24. 1959.
103	"For a decade, a new-fangled broadcasting medium": Jackson, p 42; "Future Plans," Council brochure, UIC, 1959.
104	"'benefits were not the Council's best means'": Jackson, p 41.

104	**"But Davidson spent so much of his time"**: from author interview, undated.
104	**"'Financing the Council is no different'"**: *World Events*, July 1955.
104	**"'Carter should have let a couple of people'"** and **"'My successor [Bane] almost put us'"**: Brorby to Rielly, May 18-19, 1976.
105	**"'a nightmare period'"** and **"'[Bane] would not even call'"**: Richard Templeton in an oral interview with Nora Dell, July 21, 1976.
105, 106	**"'undertook a substantial retrenchment'"** and **"'establish a surplus'"** and **"'It has therefore become clear'"**: "Future Plans," Council brochure, UIC, 1959.
106	**"But when he left in 1960'"**: Templeton to Dell, July 21, 1976.
106, 107	**"'The Council is a membership'"** and **"'The Council is not now successfully competing'"** and **"'the busy businessman'"**: Council program committee meeting minutes, UIC, Feb. 28, 1957.
107	**"'The Council was forced from the very beginning'"**: Briscoe, p 82.

Chapter 5: The Travel Club

109	**"He retired at age fifty-eight"**: memo, UIC, 1960.
109	**"'I looked across the table'"**: Templeton to Dell, July 21, 1976.
110	**"tripled the Council's membership"**: minutes from Council advisory committee meeting, UIC, Apr. 7, 1966.
110	**"total membership was 20,000"**: *Notes on World Events*, UIC, Feb. 1969.
110	**"The CAB forbade commercial airlines"**: author interview with John Rielly, Oct. 19, 2017.
110	**"'first-class catering, a complimentary bar'"** and **"The Council also arranged more elaborate"**: *Notes on World Events*, UIC, 1963.
111	**"'There has been some question'"**: Council Board meeting minutes, UIC, Sept. 29, 1964.
111	**"'are geared to appeal largely'"** and **"'be more selective, stressing experiences'"** and **"'prefer to make a general survey'"**: Council Board meeting minutes, UIC, Nov. 23, 1965.
111, 112	**"'charter flights took over the Council'"** and **"'once asked me'"**: author interview with John Rielly, Oct. 19, 2017.
113	**"'How did we ever get into the position'"**: *Notes on World Events*, UIC, Nov. 1965.
113, 114	**"'that freedom is indivisible'"** and **"'This seemed to be obviously'"** and **"'I am not an isolationist'"** and **"'badly overextended'"**: transcript, UIC, Dec. 9, 1969.
114	**"'One of the main consequences'"**: transcript, UIC, Dec. 10, 1968.
114	**"'people to look forward to us'"**: transcript, UIC, Jan. 10, 1961.
114	**"'going to be one of the great issues'"**: transcript, UIC, Jan. 10, 1961.

114	"'Russia no longer exerts completely'" and "'There's been a shake-up'": transcript, UIC, Jan. 10, 1961.
115	"'open civil war in Cuba'": transcript, UIC, Jan. 10, 1961.
115	"'remarkable for its youth'": transcript, Jan. 10, 1961.
115	"'produced a moral revulsion'" and "'is half modern and half rural'" and "'add up to evidence'" and "'A Soviet Union in a more nationalistic frame'": transcript, UIC, Jan. 8, 1963.
116	"'The UN is not the whole answer'": transcript, UIC, Feb. 19, 1963.
116, 117	"'about the most conservative country'" and "'By 'conservative,' I mean a country'": *Notes on World Events*, UIC, Oct.–Nov., 1964.
117	"Fromm's speech excited angry protests": *Notes on World Events*, UIC, Dec. 1964.
117	"'partisan points of view'" and "'frustrated and disappointed'": Council Board meeting minutes, UIC, Dec. 1, 1964.
117, 118	"'and spoke to Mauldin'" and "'I said to Bill'": Welling to Dell, July 7, 1976.
118	"'responsibilities of a great power'" and "'The United States today'" and "'must be willing to commit'" and "'responsibility in the conduct of foreign affairs'": transcription, UIC, Sept. 18, 1964.
118, 119	"'mass frustration, misery, despair'" and "'I wish that some of our statesmen'": *Notes on World Events*, UIC, Feb. 1965.
119	"'doesn't necessarily mean that it can'": *Notes on World Events*, UIC, Mar. 1965.
119	"'new men'" and "'The young men who have either gone abroad'" and "'not [find] any possible way'": *Notes on World Events*, UIC, May 1965.
120	"'Some Council speakers saw the future clearly'": *Chicago Tribune*, Apr. 7, 1967.
120	"'converge with Chicago'": *Notes on World Affairs*, 1965.
120	"'This is a dirty war'" and "'Laos is just about the end'": *Chicago Tribune*, May 17, 1962.
120	"From 1964 to 1973, American planes": Ben Rhodes, *The World As It Is: A Memoir of the Obama White House*, 2018, p 334-335.
121	"'give an emerging country'" and "'We reluctantly introduced American ground forces'" and "'We clearly have the initiative'": *Notes on World Events*, UIC, 1965.
121	"'The most important development'" and "'blunted or neutralized the Viet Cong'" and "'They think they can keep fighting'" and "'NATO is the kind of thing'": *Notes on World Events*, UIC, Nov. 1965.
121, 122	"'his fundamental urge to keep France'" and "'it handicaps all his efforts'": *Notes on World Events,* UIC, May 1966.
122	"'in the light of Asian history'" and "'the endless proliferation of violence'": *Notes on World Events,* UIC, May 1966.

122	"'maintain our defense perimeter'" and "'turned the tide of battle'" and "'we're going to have to commit'" and "'we could with virtual impunity'" and "'Should Southeast Asia fall to China'": *Notes on World Events*, UIC, 1966.
123	"'Without our engagement, without our involvement'" and "'It is a complete distortion'" and "'a lack of discrimination'" and "'we are forced to oppose revolutions'" and "'The fact that we have made a commitment'" and "'If West Germany should become communist'": transcript, UIC, Nov. 30, 1965.
123, 124	"'Not even the harshest critics'": *Notes on World Events*, UIC, 1966.
124	"'The present crisis paves the way'": transcript, UIC, June 9, 1966.
124	"'nothing to do with liberation'" and "'Aggression is no less aggression'": *Notes on World Events*, UIC, May 1966; *Chicago American*, Apr. 16, 1966.
124	"'demonstrated the limitations of force'" and "'In fact, many evidences'" and "'We have adopted the rationalizations'": transcript, UIC, Oct. 31, 1966.
124	"'The use of compulsion is repugnant'" and "The Chicago debate was a milestone": *Notes on World Events*, UIC, Feb. 1967; *Chicago Daily News*, Dec. 2, 1966; Binyamin Applebaum, *The Economists Hour: False Prophets, Free Markets, and the Fracture of Society*, 2019, p 33-43.
125	"'We will emerge from the current debate'": *New World Weekly*, May 19, 1967.
125	"'It will not get us out'": *Chicago Sun-Times*, Feb. 2, 1968.
125	"Robert W. Barnett, a deputy assistant": *Notes on World Events*, UIC, Dec. 1967.
125	"'There is a price'": *Chicago Sun-Times*, Oct. 15, 1969.
125, 126	"'is a showcase of bankruptcy'" and "'neurotic sense of insecurity'" and "'that we abstain hereafter'": *Notes on World Events*, UIC, Mar. 1969.
126	"'I never imagined a meeting'": transcript, UIC, June 25, 1969; author interview with David Rosso, Jan. 10, 2018.
126, 127	"'illegal, immoral, un-American, un-winnable'" and "'Interventionism is the most extreme form'" and "'That rape of Czechoslovakia'" and "'I have seen beginning in the '30s'" and "'Totally incoherent. Maybe I ought'" and "'There is a China'": transcript, UIC, Oct. 15, 1968.
127, 128	"'unfettered review of Chinese-American relations'" and "'There is both progress'" and "'In all my recent travels'": *Notes on World Events*, UIC, Nov. 1965.
128	"'to get rid of US bases'": Charles Taylor, *Notes on World Events*, UIC, Jan. 1967.
128	"'would go to war'" and "'as long as we maintain'": *Notes on World Events*, UIC, May 1967.

128	**"These analyses seemed to be sinking in"**: *Notes on World Events*, UIC, May 1966.
128, 129	**"'We expect Japan to look at things'" and "'reached the logical—from their point of view'"**: *Notes on World Events*, UIC, Feb. 1966.
129	**"'accoutrements'" and "'is not out front'" and "'is obliged to be paternal'" and "'the world's most deftly guided'"**: transcript, UIC, Mar. 14, 1969.
129	**"'a fear of being swamped'" and "'the slightest hope of winning'"**: *Notes on World Events*, UIC, Jan. 1968.
129, 130	**"'this small, shining, beautiful'" and "'and if we bitch them up'"**: transcript, UIC, Dec. 2, 1969.
130	**"One potentially exotic speaker"**: *Chicago American*, Jan. 23, 1966.
130, 131	**"'a stain on the face'" and "'accomplices'" and "'insulted me and my wife'" and "'discourteous and disrespectful'"**: *Chicago Tribune*, Mar. 1 and 2, 1970; *Le Monde*, Mar. 3, 1970; *L'Aurore*, Mar. 3, 1970, *New York Times*, Mar. 3, 1970.
131	**"'Foreign affairs...did not play'" and "'Wherever there was a threat'" and "'This is what history presented us'" and "'tribute to the people'" and "'I'm quite convinced'"**: transcript, UIC, Jan. 7, 1969.
132	**"'I tried to bring those people'"**: Brorby to Rielly, May 18-19, 1976.
132	**"'The idea was that the Council'" and "'This was its image'"**: Edward McDougal in an oral interview with Dennis Allred, July 19, 1976.
132	**"'had too much of an image'"**: Templeton to Dell, July 21, 1976.
132	**"'the critical issues of the day'"**: Council document, undated.
132	**"The first speaker was the secretary of state"**: Edward McDougal in an oral interview with Dennis Allred, July 19, 1976.
133	**"'It was set up for a purpose'"**: Richard Templeton in an oral interview with Nora Dell, July 21, 1976.
133	**"'The idea behind the Chicago Committee'"**: *Notes on World Events*, UIC, 1961.
133	**"'conceived of and sold to'"**: Alex Seith in an oral interview with David Mellon, undated.
134	**"'efforts in this direction'" and "'gave something of specific benefit'" and "'It is reasonable to conclude'"**: *Notes on World Events*, UIC, Aug. 1961.
134	**"'This is the most prestigious group'" and "'The group is conservatively oriented'"**: unattributed memo to William Colby, UIC, June 19, 1974.
135	**"'It never occurred to anybody'" and "'It never entered anybody's mind'"**: from author interviews, undated.
135	**"'Our range has thus far been limited'"**: Council Board meeting minutes, UIC, undated.
136	**"'Timely issues were discussed'"**: Council Board meeting minutes, UIC, May 10, 1966.

136	**"Various committees discussed ways"**: Council theme committee meeting minutes, UIC, Feb. 24, 1969.
136	**"'We are no longer a comfortable little Council'"** and **"'discussion, study, and specialization'"** and **"'an overall program which recognizes'"**: transcript, UIC, June 14, 1965.
137	**"Seith quickly took over the Council"**: *Notes on World Events*, UIC, Sept. 1969.
137	**"'disaster'"** and **"'heavy drinker'"**: from author interviews, undated.
137	**"'a complete mistake'"**: Brorby to Rielly, May 18-19, 1976.
137	**"'What he really was proposing'"** and **"'It was really demeaning'"** and **"'Alex never wanted me'"**: William Graham Cole in an oral interview with John Rielly, Aug. 13, 1976.
138	**"Under Eger and Seith"**: *Notes on World Events*, UIC, Sept. 1967.
138	**"'young enough to have energy'"**: Alex Seith in an oral interview with David Mellon, 1976.

Chapter 6: The Rielly Years

139, 140	**"'My goal at the start'"** and **"'Until the late 1970s'"**: author interview with John Rielly, Jan. 23, 2018.
140	**"'There's no comparison between the Council programs'"**: from author interviews, undated.
140, 141	**"'there's some possibility that I might not'"**: *Glencoe News*, Dec. 3, 1987.
141	**"A University of Chicago institution"**: author interviews with Rielly, Oct. 19, 2017, Jan. 23, 2018, Nov. 19, 2018, and Jan. 4, 2019.
141	**"'The Chicago Council sticks to'"** and **"'the presidential dark horse list'"** and **"'directly influence'"** and **"'turned into a nightmare'"**: *Chicago Tribune*, June 11, 1971.
141, 142	**"The conferences became an attempt"**: author interview with John Rielly, Jan. 23, 2018.
142	**"Rielly was a gifted talent scout"**: Council announcement, UIC, Apr. 5, 1988.
142	**"Later, in the 1980s"**: from author interviews, undated.
143	**"'There is little sentiment among the American public'"**: American public opinion and US Foreign Policy, 1975, UIC.
143, 144	**"Over the years, the Council had published"**: Council Board meeting minutes, UIC, Dec. 10, 1981.
144	**"'the Council was seen as a serious'"**: author interview with Rielly, Jan. 23, 2018.
144	**"'a fantastic tutorial, very sage advice'"**: author interview with Carol Byrne, Jan. 10, 2019.
145	**"In addition, he also recruited top"**: author interview with Rielly, Jan. 23, 2018.

146	**"The Chicago Committee already included":** *World Events,* UIC, 1976; Council development committee meeting minutes, UIC, Dec. 1973; author interview with Rielly, Jan. 23, 2018.
147	**"'It is increasingly important to strengthen'"** and **"'a significant alteration in the pattern'"** and **"'some selective cutting back'"** and **"'designed to reach those members'":** memo from John Rielly to Council Board, UIC, Nov. 17, 1971.
147	**"'the Council's mission is to educate'":** Council Board meeting minutes, UIC, Oct. 10, 1995.
147	**"The programs for teachers continued":** memo from Lawrence C. McQuade to Council president and Board, UIC, Apr. 18, 1973.
147	**"'We were glad to be rid of it'":** author interview with Rielly, Jan. 4, 2019.
148	**"'a limited number of projects'":** memo from Augustin S. Hart, Jr. to Council Board, UIC, Oct. 15, 1974.
148	**"Earlier, when Cole was executive director":** Council Board meeting minutes, UIC, Mar. 24, 1970; Council long-range planning committee meeting minutes, UIC, Apr. 2, 1970.
148	**"'There are many lessons to be learned'":** Council long-range planning committee meeting minutes, UIC, Apr. 2, 1970.
149, 150	**"'special relationship'"** and **"Both sides were in favor'"** and **"'intellectual partnership'"** and **"'affecting editorial content'":** letter from Rielly to Warren Manshel, UIC, Apr. 26, 1972; memo from Rielly to Council Board, UIC, June 2, 1972; unaddressed memo from Rielly, UIC, July 5, 1972; memo of understanding between Council and *Foreign Policy,* UIC, July 13, 1971; letter from Rielly to Richard Holbrooke, UIC, July 13, 1972; letter from Rielly to Warren Manshel, UIC, July 17, 1972; letter from Manshel to Rielly, UIC, July 27, 1972; letter from Rielly to Manshel, UIC, Aug. 14, 1972; memo from Rielly to Council Board, UIC, Sept. 22, 1972; memo of understanding between Council and *Foreign Policy,* UIC, Sept. 29, 1972.
150	**"'The Council has done much to help'":** *Chicago Tribune,* June 21, 1973.
151	**"'This does not mean that the United States'":** transcript, UIC, June 27, 1972.
152	**"'the proper relationship'"** and **"'Today, fifty years later'"** and **"'invoked as the justification":** transcript, UIC, Feb. 16, 1972.
152	**"'forget isolationism, new, old'"** and **"'Interdependence is no longer'":** *World Events,* Apr. 1973.
153	**"'To my mind, …neo-isolation would be":** *World Events,* Oct. 1970.
153, 154	**"'We are a wounded nation'":** *World Events,* 1973.
154	**"'The very climate of security'"** and **"'There will be no more need'"** and **"'Our European allies can and should'"** and **"'burden-sharing'":** transcript, UIC, Jan. 20, 1970; *New York Times,* Jan. 21, 1970, p 1.
154	**"'open up their society'":** *World Events,* 1977.

154	"'the decisive factor'" and "'psychological limit'" and "'It would not be a good thing'": transcript, UIC, Sept. 25, 1973.
154, 155	"Chicago politics nearly scuttled": author interview with Irene Hill, Oct. 19, 2018.
155	"'both economic and military parity'" and "'a new sense of vulnerability'" and "'great division and turmoil'": Notes on World Events, UIC, Jan. 14, 1971.
155	"'step back'": World Events, Apr. 1974.
155	"'Cold War nostalgia'": World Events, May 9, 1975.
155	"U Thant, the UN Secretary General": transcript, UIC, May 5, 1971.
155	"'the idea that peace'": transcript, UIC, Apr. 23, 1975.
155	"Representative Paul McCloskey": World Events, Nov. 12, 1971.
156	"'must devote more of its resources'" and "'the security and development'" and "'We cannot turn inward'": Peter G. Peterson, World Events, July 1971.
156	"'superpower rivalry'": World Events, Mar. 1975.
156	"'Balkanization of world politics'" and "'Our present condition resulted from'": transcript, UIC, June 2, 1975.
156	"'the biggest, strongest, most arrogant kid'": World Events, Oct. 3, 1975.
157	"Until 1976, Kissinger dominated": World Events, Apr. 6, 1976.
157	"'The time has come to build'": World Events, Aug.–Sept. 1976.
157, 158	"'All industrial societies are facing'": transcript, UIC, Jan. 13, 1978; World Events, 1978.
158	"'confusion about American foreign policy'": World Events, Mar. 1976.
158	"'Here and here alone, the taboo'": World Events, Oct. 3, 1972.
158	"'If they mean Palestine in addition to Israel'": World Events, Nov. 1974.
158, 159	"'For the people of Israel'" and "'maintaining double standards'" and "'is only transitory'": transcript, UIC, Mar. 25, 1971.
159	"'A vital element in this'": World Events, May 1972.
159	"'huge and rapidly growing'": transcript, UIC, Oct. 24, 1973.
160	"'are in fact subsidizing'" and "'Oil prices in the Middle East'": World Events, Oct. 2, 1974; Chicago Tribune, Oct. 11, 1974.
160	"'peace through strength'": transcript, UIC, Mar. 12, 1976.
160	"The Council had to wait thirty-six years": author interview with Alesha Black, Feb. 4, 2019.
161	"'Our secretary of state'": transcript, UIC, Mar. 15, 1976.
161	"'If Henry Kissinger can fly'": transcript, UIC, Oct. 12, 1971.
161	"'legend'" and "'helped to unify the Cuban people'": World Events, Nov. 9, 1971.

161	**"Nuclear policy dominated many programs"**: *Los Angeles Times*, Sept. 8, 1974; *World Events*, Oct. 1974.
161, 162	**"The Cold War's leading attempt"**: *World Events*, Dec. 1978; *World Events*, Oct. 1978.
162	**"The war began on Saturday"**: Emma Penick in a letter to Nora Dell, UIC, Nov. 6, 1973; Mrs. Charles Wyman in a letter to Nora Dell, UIC, Nov. 6, 1973; Dorothy Attermeyer in a letter to Nora Dell, UIC, Nov. 6, 1973; *Chicago Tribune*, Oct. 23, 1973; Chester Myszkowski, unidentified newspaper clipping, UIC, undated.
162, 163	**"'By Sunday noon, the spacious lobby'"**: Penick to Dell, UIC, Nov. 6, 1973.
163	**"'was a revolution for us'"**: author interview with John Rielly, November 19, 2018.
163, 164	**"Other foundations set up shop"**: minutes from Council Executive Committee meeting, December 10, 1981.
164	**"But the single biggest gift grew out"**: minutes from Council Executive Committee meeting, UIC Special Collections, December 14, 1987; *Chicago Sun-Times*, April 7, 1988; John Rielly in an email to the author, April 14, 2019.
164	**"Rielly, although admittedly parsimonious"**: Council accounting figures, UIC, 1985.
164, 165	**"By 1980, the long erosion"**: *World Events*, 1980.
165	**"'are exceedingly hard-working people'"**: *World Events*, Dec. 1981.
165	**"'It is an action which requires sacrifice'"**: transcript, UIC, Mar. 3, 1980; *New York Times*, Mar. 4, 1980.
166	**"'We are opposed to the dismemberment'"**: *Chicago Tribune*, Oct. 21, 1980; *World Events*, 1980.
166	**"Two years later, another secretary"**: *Wall Street Journal*, May 27, 1982; *Chicago Tribune*, May 27, 1982; *Chicago Sun-Times*, May 27, 1982.
166	**"'constituency for peace'"**: transcript, UIC, Apr. 11, 1983.
166	**"A churchman of a different order"**: *News Voice*, Sept. 29, 1983.
166	**"'Change in the effectiveness'"**: *World Events*, Winter, 1985.
167	**"'inert population only marginally stirred'" and "'There is no storm brewing'"**: *World Events*, 1980.
167	**"'inherently inefficient'" and "'there is little reason to think'"**: *World Events*, 1982.
167	**"'No sane American would change'" and "'The Soviets are stretched'"**: *World Events*, Apr. 1981.
167	**"'One cannot entirely blame the Japanese'" and "'The Japanese seem to feel'"**: *Chicago Sun-Times*, Mar. 1, 1982.
167, 168	**"Lee Morgan, chairman of Caterpillar"**: *Chicago Sun-Times*, May 23, 1983; *Chicago Sun-Times*, May 18, 1987.
168	**"'We should upgrade the issue'"**: *World Events*, 1988.
168	**"'is intolerable to the Palestinian population'"**: *World Events*, 1989.

168	"'dedicated to truth'" and "'that they must abandon their hostility'": *News Voice*, Apr. 13, 1989.
168, 169	"'balance of power politics'" and "'policies that strengthen dictators'": Jimmy Carter, 1976.
169	"'grand strategy'": transcript, UIC, Mar. 17, 1980.
169	"'bluff, bluster, and political symbolism'": *World Events*, Mar. 14, 1980.
169	"'nothing less than a potential disaster'": *Chicago Sun-Times*, Nov. 10, 1982.
169	"'encouraging'": *The Herald*, May 11, 1982.
169	"'three words: reciprocity, reliability'": WBBM-TV, March 16, 1984.
169	"Joseph Biden said that Carter stressed détente": *World Events*, 1984.
169, 170	"'Just as it would be blind'": *World Events*, Fall, 1988; *Chicago Tribune*, Sept. 14, 1988; *New York Times*, Sept. 14, 1988.
170	"'No illusions should be harbored'" and "'They're not going to converge'" and "'The Soviets will not disappear'" and "'We must rid ourselves'": audio recording, Council files, 1985.
170	"'bleak outlook'" and "'is coming to a dead end'": transcript, UIC, Nov. 14, 1977.
171	"'a new man who seems to be'" and "'to invent a new way of simulating'": audio recording, Council files, 1985.
171	"'a party man: reliable, obedient'" and "'young, ruthless, and not likely'": *World Events*, 1985.
171	"'an important milestone'" and "'General Secretary Gorbachev is a leader'": transcript, UIC, Oct. 23, 1986.
172	"'Gorbachev's current policy'": Zbigniew Brzezinski, *World Events*, Nov. 13, 1987.
172	"'The next president's greatest crisis'": *World Events*, Sept. 1988.
172	"'For Yeltsin, America is a holiday'": William Taubman, *Gorbachev: His Life and Times*, Norton, 2017, p 457-459.
172	"Yeltsin's reputation preceded him": author interview with Rielly, Jan. 23, 2018.
173	"'I do support Mr. Gorbachev'" and "'I particularly support him strategically'" and "'we find ourselves in a total crisis'": *World Events*, Sept. 12, 1989.
173, 174	"'the political system doesn't really work'" and "'because there is a vested interest'" and "'an inherently corrupt system'" and "'The problem of attaining peace'" and "'With the decline of communist ideology'" and "'There is an unusual period'" and "'Define for ourselves a set of relationships'": *World Events*, Sept. 20, 1989.

Chapter 7: New World Disorder

177	"'to educate the leadership'" and "'The number of people with discretionary time'": Council Board meeting minutes, UIC, Oct. 10, 1995.
177, 178	"'Gorbachev's period in office'" and "'a great challenge for many nations'" and "'Islamic fundamentalism may become'" and "'If the European community'": *Council Chronicle*, Apr. 16, 1990.
178	"'a new chill, a great leap'" and "'will produce within a few years'": *Council Chronicle*, 1990.
178	"'Two successive administrations'": transcript, UIC, May 21, 1991.
178	"'The effort to save the earth's environment'": *Council Chronicle*, May 1992.
178	"Margaret Thatcher was barely six months out": John Rielly in an email to the author, Nov. 30, 2018.
179	"'tone down'" and "'Any policy or program'": transcript, UIC, June 17, 1991; *The Guardian*, June 18, 1991.
179	"'firm opposition to a federal Europe'": *Chicago Tribune*, June 19, 1991.
180	"'repeat the mistake of 1946'" and "'spiritual and moral healing'": transcript, UIC, May 6, 1992.
180	"'No one should assume'": audio recording, Council files, Sept. 14, 1992.
180, 181	"'I'll never forget President Gorbachev'" and "'We Americans stand undisputed'" and "'a remarkable degree of consensus'" and "'emphasize the importance'" and "'Saddam Hussein is an annoying pain'": audio recording, Council files, Nov. 9, 1992.
181, 182	"'One of the most serious problems'" and "'when our economy is in its essence'" and "'It is possible to change'" and "'So, it is very difficult to expect'": transcript, UIC, Mar. 2, 1993.
182	"'One of our highest foreign policy priorities'" and "'The stakes are monumental'": transcript, UIC, Mar. 22, 1993.
182	"'Let no one be in doubt'" and "'the experiences and lessons'" and "'While there is no lack of German support'": transcript, UIC, May 26, 1993.
183, 184	"'the new world order'" and "'global turmoil'" and "'has not created an enhanced stability'" and "'Islamic crescent'" and "'neither a democracy nor a free-market'" and "'as the only global superpower'" and "'the victorious West is not projecting'" and "'Increasingly, much of the world perceives'" and "'must be actively engaged'" and "'I do not think that our present leadership'" and "'But I do think it is minimalist'": transcript, UIC, Mar. 12, 1994.
183, 184, 185	"'values'" and "'the use of the US military'" and "'to go in there and sort it out'" and "'a huge, huge difference'" and "'CNN effect'" and "'You see the people'" and "'You see the ethnic cleansing'" and "'But

	the United States of America has values'" and "'what does it say about the ones'": audio recording, Council files, May 15, 1995.
185, 186	"'The principal responsibility for the changed world'" and "'Faxes, cellular phones, satellites'": audio recording, Council files, Oct. 5, 1995.
186	"'The most urgent task'" and "'Russia must feel it belongs'" and "'a special security partnership'" and "'Russia's links with the Western world'": transcript, UIC, Apr. 19, 1995.
186, 187	"'Gorbachev recognized the Soviet Union'" and "'Everything he did was in his interpretation'" and "'Much of the power'": audio recording, Council files, June 12, 1996.
187	"'NATO can do for Europe's East'": audio recording, Council files, May 24, 1996.
187	"'What we are being asked to do'" and "'It will impose new demands'": transcript, UIC, Sept. 16, 1997.
187, 188	"'The desire to be a part of NATO'" and "'If we cannot provide'" and "'I believe every time'": audio recording, Council files, Feb. 19, 1998.
188	"'The major problem of the world'" and "'the one power that is really aware'": transcript, UIC, Nov. 25, 1996.
189	"'Even Helmut Kohl, the German Chancellor'": transcript, June 19, 1997; *Chicago Tribune*, June 20, 1997.
189, 190	"'We were wrong, terribly wrong'" and "'eleven major causes for our disaster'" and "'we don't have the God-given right'" and "'there may be problems'" and "'Now that this bloody century'" and "'The Cold War has ended'": Robert McNamara, audio recording, Council files, Apr. 24, 1995.
190, 191	"'We are seeing a new global architecture'" and "'We've gone from a world of superpowers'" and "'Whoever doesn't get it right'" and "'So they are shrinking their social safety nets'": audio recording, Council files, Apr. 28, 1996.
191, 192	"'very explosive situation'" and "'the very real possibility'" and "'a new kind of semi-private terrorism'" and "'out of a sense of weakness'": audio recording, Council files, Dec. 5, 2000.
192	"'more pragmatic than democratic'" and "'that Russia cannot prosper'" and "'the Empire struck out'" and "'it encourages China to play'" and "'I expect. . . that the new administration'": transcript, UIC, Jan. 17, 2000.
192	"'central question in our work'" and "'increasing unilateralism'" and "'the indispensable nation'" and "'openly confrontational stance with China'": transcript, June 12, 2001.
192, 193	"'one of the nation's largest and more prestigious'": *Chicago Sun-Times*, Apr. 1997.
193	"'For seventy-five years, the Chicago Council'" and "'We're proud as punch'" and "'there's something about telling daddy'": *Chicago Tribune*, April 28, 1997.

194	"'The end of the Cold War'": Council Board meeting minutes, UIC, Oct. 4, 1994.
194	"'Changes in corporate America'": Council Board meeting minutes, UIC, Oct. 7, 1997.
194	"'The number of large companies'": Chairman's report to Board, UIC, Apr. 14, 1998.
194	"'more attention to immigration'": Council Board meeting minutes, UIC, Oct. 10, 1995.
195	"'have 98 percent of the same constituencies'" and "'These are two organizations competing'": Council Board meeting minutes, UIC, May 24, 1983.
196	"According to Rielly, several members" and "In the end, Burnham seemed to be right": memos from Rielly to Duane Burnham, UIC, Nov. 25, 1997 and April 8, 1998; Council Board meeting minutes, UIC, May 13, 1997 and Dec. 17, 1998.
196	"'Anything that contributes to a further proliferation'": Executive Committee meeting minutes, December 17, 1998.
196	"The Asia society had bigger ambitions": memo from Rielly to Duane Burnham, UIC, Apr. 8, 1998.
196	"Marshall Bouton, who later succeeded Rielly": author interview with Marshall Bouton, Nov. 30, 2018.
198, 199	"'islands rather than an archipelago'" and "'one of the oldest and strongest'" and "'stands at the center'" and "'a key player in a broadly based effort'" and "'older, relatively well-to-do'" and "'elite'" and "'stuffy'": Richard C. Longworth, *Global Chicago: Two Reports on Chicago's Assets and Opportunities as a Global City*, 1998, p 9-11.

Chapter 8: Millennium

201	"'We've taken the Chicago Council'" and "'We put the Council on the map'": author interview with Marshall Bouton, Feb. 14, 2018.
202	"'transformed the Chicago Council's identity'": Andrew Selee, *What Should Think Tanks Do?*, 2013, p 17.
202	"Bouton, a native New Yorker" and "First, Bouton got a call" and "'Asia had risen'" and "'Chicago needed to contribute'": author interviews with Marshall Bouton, Feb. 14, 2018 and Nov. 20, 2018.
203	"'enabled me to hook my aspirations'": author interview, Feb. 14, 2018.
203	"'The Council's role is the same'": personal archives of Marshall Bouton, undated.
203, 204	"'to what has happened and its impact'": Marshall Bouton in a memo to John Madigan, Bouton archives, Sept. 27, 2001; Marshall Bouton in a memo to Council Board, Oct, 8, 2001.
204	"Board members of the two organizations": from author interviews; *Events This Month*, Council files, June 2002; memo from Marshall Bou-

205	ton to John Madigan, Bouton archives, Dec. 31, 2001; agreement between Council and Mid-America Committee, Council files, 2001.
205	**"An early task force"**: "Muslim/Non-Muslim Dialogue" Bouton archives, Aug. 6, 2004; memo from Marshall Bouton to Council Board, Bouton archives, Oct. 4, 2001; draft proposal to MacArthur Foundation, Bouton archives, Jan. 15, 2003.
205	**"The Global Chicago Center"**: author notes, undated.
205	**"The Center also published a 2004 book"**: Charles Madigan, ed., *Global Chicago*, University of Illinois Press, 2004.
206	**"'I misunderstood Chicago's thirst'"**: author interview with Bouton, Feb. 14, 2018.
206	**"Bouton's timing could not have been better"**: interview with Bouton, Feb. 14, 2018; *Chicago Tribune*, Sept. 17, 2003.
206	**"Not all these initiatives"**: author notes, undated.
206, 207	**"'Chicago is our primary constituency'"** and **"'must become a significant producer'"** and **"'the Council will operate'"**: CCFR, statement to the Board, Bouton archives, 2004.
207	**"'At present, the Midwest lacks'"**: "The Chicago Council and the Midwest," draft statement to the Board, Bouton archives, Aug. 9, 2004.
208	**"Despite this uneven progress"**: "The Development of the Council 2003-2010," Council files, Aug. 2010, p 7.
208	**"Bouton, well connected in China"**: Daley agenda in Shanghai, Bouton archives, Oct. 2004.
208, 209	**"Partially, the Council changed"** and **"Another reason for the name change"**: author interview with Bouton, Feb. 14, 2019; press release, UIC, Sept. 1, 2006; *Chicago Tribune*, Sept. 1, 2006; *Financial Times*, 2006.
209	**"'foreign'"** and **"'historic shift in the fundamental dynamics'"**: press release, UIC, Sept. 1, 2006.
209	**"The 2010 strategic plan also emphasized"**: "Draft Strategic Plan 2005-2010," Bouton archives, Apr. 7, 2005.
210	**"'has helped produce policies'"**: John Mearsheimer and Stephen Walt, *The Israel Lobby*, Sept. 11, 2007, p 279.
210, 211	**"Then the storm began"** through **"Years later, both Mearsheimer and Walt"**: from author interviews; John Mearsheimer and Stephen Walt in a letter to the Council, Aug. 5, 2007; *New York Times*, Aug. 16, 2007.
210, 211	**"'said he felt 'extremely uncomfortable'"** and **"'surely not the way'"**: Mearsheimer and Walt, Aug. 5, 2007.
211	**"'gritty, determined, measured'"** and **"'blind hatred of modernism'"**: transcript, UIC, Sept. 21, 2001.
212	**"'Pakistan is against terrorism'"** and **"'We are part of the international coalition'"**: transcript, UIC, Sept. 10, 2002.
212	**"'on the run'"** and **"'guessed'"**: *Chicago Tribune*, Sept. 11, 2002; author notes, undated.

212, 213, 214	"'Weapons of mass destruction,'" and "'a prime example of a regime'" and "could not possibly be from Chicago.": audio recording, Council files, Oct. 15, 2002.
212, 213	"'In every household there are two or three'" and "'a crazy argument'" and "'If you are for taking Saddam Hussein down'": audio recording, Council files, Sept. 23, 2002.
213	"'We didn't need [international support]'": audio recording, Council files, Sept. 25, 2003.
214	"'Right up until the end'": *Chicago Tribune*, Oct. 8, 2003.
214	"'a free, democratic, and successful Iraq'" and "'will require a commitment of many years'" and "'Americans must be prepared'" and "'Even after a government is formed'": audio recording, Council files, Apr. 19, 2006.
214	"'clearly is a booming success'" and "'the rise of democracy'" and "'If I read the media'": author notes, undated.
215	"'It is possible to have democracy'" and "'It is possible to have institutional reform'": audio recording, Council files, June 10, 2004.
215, 216	"Dick Prall was a rock guitarist" through "Two weeks later, *Revolution*": author interview with Dick Prall, Jan. 21, 2019; press release, *Revolution*, Revolutionary Communist Party, Dec. 13, 2005; *Daily Kos*, Dec. 14, 2014.
217	"'I don't know, but if you want to guess'": audio recording, Council files, Oct. 1, 2003.
217	"'disintegrate into chaos'" and "'in the name of a misguided sense'": transcript, UIC, July 12, 2004.
217	"'phased redeployment of US troops'" and "'We can't afford to be a country'": audio recording, Council files, Nov. 20, 2006.
217	"'the American moment is here'" and "'America cannot meet the threats'": transcript, UIC, Apr. 23, 2007.
218	"'Iraq, though measurably improved'" and "'Afghanistan is proving to be'": transcript, UIC, Apr. 22, 2009.
218	"'As we have found out'" and "'clear and impending danger'": audio recording, Council files, June 14, 2007.
218	"'[Iran's] economic lifeline is found'": audio recording, Council files, June 14, 2007.
218, 219	"'The European Union is about overcoming'" and "'Russia clearly has shown'" and "'Russia has again chosen'" and "'but piecemeal, below the radar'": audio recording, Council files, Sept. 8, 2008.
219	"'The last eight years'" and "'was not able to restructure itself'" and "'stuck in this gap'": audio recording, Council files, Dec. 10, 2008.
220	"'This will be our blueprint'": author interviews, undated.
220	"'to work alongside you'": Barack Obama, inaugural address, Jan. 20, 2009.
221	"In the meantime, GADI became": author interviews, undated.

221	"'positioned the Chicago Council'" and "'excellent regional reputations'" and "'burnish its national reputation'": Selee, p 18, 79.
222	"'this became an issue'": author interview with Bouton, undated.
222, 223	"'Do you not feel better?'" and "'It just shows how large a gap'" and "'there is not enough aggregate demand'" and "'a lot of routine jobs'" and "'generates a politics of anger'": audio recording, Council files, Oct. 7, 2010.
223	"'the American dream will continue'": audio recording, Council files, Apr. 18, 2013.
223	"'six drivers of global change'": Al Gore, quoted on Council website, Feb. 8, 2013.
223	"'We've lost confidence in our institutions'" and "'global instability, because everything flows'": Chuck Hagel, taped text, October 13, 2011.
223	"'left scars that may be permanent'": Peter Orszag, quoted on Council website, Nov. 13, 2012.
224	"'There's a more rigorous vetting system'" and "'I mean, Donald Trump'": audio recording, Council files, Apr. 28, 2011.
224	"'a crying shame and a crying waste'" and "'the US will have to talk'": audio recording, Council files, May 8, 2011.
224	"'I blame the Americans'" and "'paralysis in Washington'" and "'the Taliban are refusing'": Ahmed Rashid, quoted on Council website, Sept. 9, 2013.
224, 225	"'large-scale centralization'" and "'the creeping but constantly expanding'" and "'For someone like me'": audio recording, Council files, Apr. 27, 2012.
225	"'Russia... is threatened by countries'": Anne Applebaum, quoted on Council websites, Dec. 5, 2012.
225	"'is about as not-ready'" and "'bellicose statements'" and "'they were really harming the fabric'" and "'We're not going to be able'": Chris Hill, quoted on Council website, Apr. 10, 2013.
225, 226	"'the great convergence'" and "'If you need optimism'": Kishore Mahbubani, quoted on Council website, Mar. 7, 2013.
226	"'a card-carrying member'" and "'overreaching'" and "'There's no alternative to a world'" and "'We can only shape that world'" and "'The Middle East has become'" and "'inconceivable'" and "'the lion's share'" and "'But that's what we did'": Richard Haass, quoted on Council website, May 24, 2013.
226, 227	"'We're situated to maintain'" and "'Yes, America will decline'" and "'This is the Era'": Robert Kagan, quoted on Council website, Jan. 23, 2013.
229	"Apart from these gifts": internal Council data; author interviews, 2019.

229, 230	"The Council had a choice": author notes; Gregory Holyk in an email to the author, June 10, 2011; Rachel Bronson in an email to the author, June 9, 2011.
231	"'We arrived here from Europe'" and "'It was May, about seventy degrees'" and "'we spent an extra twenty-four hours'": author interview with Ivo Daalder, July 30, 2018.
231	"The first Obama Administration was ending": from author interviews, undated.

Chapter 9: All Over Again

233	"At 10 a.m. on the morning of November 9": author notes, undated.
233, 234	"'The basic contours of the international order'": Daalder in a memo to Council Board, Council files, Dec. 13, 2016.
234	"'We are nonpartisan but not neutral'": "An Open Letter to the Midwest," Daalder, Council files, undated.
235	"'to make Chicago the go-to place'": *Chicago Magazine*, Sept. 10, 2013.
235, 236	"'to adapt to these changes'" and "'one of the premier global affairs organizations'" and "'centers of excellence'" and "'with a small in-house research'": Daalder in a memo to Council Board, Council files, undated.
237	"When he arrived in Chicago": author interview with Daalder, July 30, 2018.
237	"Other major gifts came in": Daalder in a memo to Council Board, Council files, undated.
237	"Notably, the family of Lester Crown": Council announcements, Council files, June 11, 2015 and Aug. 10, 2018.
237	"'think tank to watch'": James G. McGann, "2015 Global Go To Think Tank Index Report," Feb. 9, 2016.
238, 239	"'paradox of American power'" and "'are increasingly important actors'" and "'We need to remain'" and "'I am concerned by a tendency'" and "'For a superpower like the United States'" and "'global reach'": transcript, Council files, Sept. 16, 2013.
239	"'a massive deindustrialization'" and "'appalling mess'" and "'a colossal transformation'" and "'People feel cheated'" and "'People feel despair and anger'": transcript, Council files, Oct. 22, 2013.
239, 240	"'getting to Denmark'" and "'political decay'" and "'vetocracy. . . A rule by veto'": transcript, Council files, Oct. 28, 2014.
240	"'the revolt of the bosses'" and "'We're two Americas now'": transcript, Council files, Jan. 9, 2014.
240	"'alpha-geeks'" and "'required a whole set'" and "'plutocrats'" and "'staying in the same hotels'" and "'getting to the tipping point'": transcript, Council files, Jan. 22, 2014.

240	"'I draw your attention to the resilience'" and "'What we are doing is very bold'": transcript, Council files, Apr. 23, 2014.
241	"'Europe's basic flaw'" and "'economically powerful and geopolitically fragile'" and "'a massive de-legitimation of main-stream parties'" and "'rise of hatred'" and "'a massive, intelligent, and embittered class'" and "'this isn't temporary'": transcript, Council files, Feb. 3, 2015.
241	"'deliberative to a fault'" and "'seems steadfast in his resistance'": transcript, Council files, Nov. 13, 2014.
242	"'There's been no action'" and "'There's little sense that the government'" and "'Such a disappointment'" and "'My basic attitude is a deep'": transcript, Council files, Jan. 23, 2014.
242	"'able to do a set of things'" and "'give us the prospect'": transcript, Council files, May 28, 2014.
242	"'China's development is a good thing'" and "'are sticking to pro-market policies'" and "'is a labor fallacy'": transcript, Council files, Feb. 18, 2014.
242, 243	"'High-paying jobs…have mostly not'" and "'not because high wage jobs'" and "'Wages are probably several percent'": audio recording, Council files, Jan. 31, 2015.
243	"'The China I encountered'" and "'What do I want?'" and "'Chinese dream'" and "'a greater control over their lives'": transcript, Council files, May 20, 2014.
243	"'Now…the once successful growth model'" and "'China's banking system'" and "'misallocation of resources'": transcript, Council files, Nov. 4, 2013.
243, 244	"Zhang Weiying, a professor of economics": transcript, Council files, Jan. 27, 2015.
244	"'sanctity of contracts, transparency'" and "'are beginning to take their toll'" and "'We accept the rules'" and "'We have neither the ability'": transcript, Council files, Dec.17, 2014.
244	"'The best way to survive'" and "'Can China grow peacefully?'": transcript, Council files, Apr. 8, 2014.
245	"'very much in control'" and "'sooner or later'": transcript, Council files, Feb. 24, 2015.
245	"'The major issues facing this country'" and "'the media's sound-bite mentality'": transcript, Council files, Mar. 19, 2015.
245	"'private frustration, anger, and disgust'" and "'Every day, I was at war'" and "'inquisitional, uncivil, incompetent, micromanaging'" and "'put reelection before the national interest'" and "'Television cameras have the same effect'": transcript, Council files, Jan. 28, 2014.
245, 246	"'a war without end'" and "'exemplifies something about us'" and "'at worst, we will do more harm'": transcript, Council files, Apr. 1, 2014.

246	"'is behind the resurgence'" and "'we have to look straight at'": transcript, Council files, Apr. 14, 2014.
246	"'take away the crutches'" and "'The US has to get out'": transcript, Council files, May 12, 2014.
246	"'a perversion of Zionism'" and "'had a serious belief'" and "'in complete disarray'" and "'a factory for violent extremism'" and "'Making peace can still be done'" and "'Work very hard, sweep away'": transcript, Council files, Jan. 15, 2015.
247	"'was barely on life support'" and "'the alternative to a two-state'" an"'There has to be a separation'": transcript, Council files, Mar. 17, 2015.
247	"'We are a country of whispers'" and "'Nobody speaks out loud'": transcript, Council files, June 12, 2014.
247	"'I am my own man'" and "'made mistakes in Iraq'" and "'inconsistent and indecisive'" and "'America does not have the luxury'" and "'Our security, our prosperity'": transcript, Council files, Feb. 28, 2015.
248	"'orders of magnitude more difficult'" and "'Westernizers'" and "'Slavophiles'" and "'have a grip on the lever'": transcript, Council files, Mar. 11, 2015.
248	"'Foreign military elements'" and "'That's formally known as an invasion'" and "'are the better tool'" and "'through a series of miscalculations'": transcript, Council files, Mar. 19, 2015.
248, 249	"'long gone. In its place'" and "'hundreds of thousands were killed'" and "'Yes, my political generation'": transcript, Council files, Sept. 22, 2016.
249	"'Whatever happens in the next two weeks'" and "'who said that to remain safe'" and "'As I enter my final three months'": transcript, Council files, Oct. 27, 2016.
250	"'for the first time really'" and "'but what happens in Washington'" and "'look back and say'": transcript, Council files, Sept. 8, 2016.
251	"'the good luck or the sheer genius'" and "'Was about a recognition'": transcript, November 29, 2016.
251	"'We no longer have to worry'" and "'We are in a dangerous new era'": transcript, Council files, Dec. 14, 2016.
252	"'the economic and cultural importance'" and "'but our national politics'": transcript, Council files, June 7, 2017.
252	"'the growing tribalism in the nation'" and "'we have not succeeded in persuading'" and "'rise up and say'" and "'take the argument to their countries'": transcript, Council files, June 7, 2017.
252	"'a feeling that the political system'": transcript, Council files, Apr. 11, 2017.
253	"'The glue of democracies'": transcript, Council files, Apr. 20, 2018.
253	"'certain trends that are worrisome'" and "'an identification with a tribalist nationalist group'": transcript, Council files, Apr. 20, 2018.

253	**"'the first anti-democratic president'"**: Madeleine Albright, *Fascism: A Warning*, Apr. 10, 2018, p 246.
253	**"'People are wondering who we are'"** and **"'Why we're not talking'"**: transcript, Council files, Apr. 20, 2018.
253	**"'specific grievances of specific groups'"**: transcript, Council files, Oct. 10, 2018.
254	**"'came to the presidency'"** and **"'the good news is'"** and **"'recommit to the fundamentals'"**: Daalder and James M. Lindsay, transcript, Council files, Oct. 25, 2018.
258	**"'We will. . . make sure that the issues'"**: statement by Daalder to Council staff, Council files, June 2, 2020.
259	**"'We are part of the independent, fact-based'"** and **"'It is not our role'"** and **"'We can be angry and sad'"**: statement by Daalder to Council staff, Council files, Nov. 2020.

Index

A

Aaron, David, 161
Acheson, Dean, 69
Addams, Jane, 21
Agresti, Olivia Rossetti, 22
Albright, Madeleine, 192, 213, 253, 254
Aldis, Graham, 18, 30, 34, 60
Ali Khan, Liaquat, 86
Allen, Jay, 33
America First Committee, 46–50
"American Policies Abroad" books, 25
Angell, Norman, 21
Applebaum, Anne, 225
Arbatov, Georgy, 143–144
Asia Society, 195–196, 199, 202, 204
Aspin, Les, 184–185
Atlantic Conferences, 140–143, 164, 204

B

Bailey, Thomas, 11–12
Baker, James, 185–186
Ball, George W., 12, 36, 118, 152, 167
Ball, Joseph H., 61
Balz, Dan, 251
Bane, Charles, 104–105
Bar-Ner, Uri, 168
Barnes, Harry, 22
Barnett, Robert W., 125
Bayar, Mahmut Celâl, 99
Becker, Gary, 223
Bell, Laird, 64
Beneš, Edvard, 58, 60, 64, 79
Benning, Alice, 30
Bere, James F., 167
Bernardin, Cardinal Joseph, 166
Bertini, Catherine, 219–220
Bess, Demaree, 34
Beyrle, John, 248
Biden, Joseph, 142, 156, 187–188, 258
Binder, Carroll, 60

Black, Alesha, 220
Blair, Tony, 217–218, 248
Blair, William McCormick Jr., 67
Bohlen, Charles E., 131
Borchard, Edwin M., 44
Bouton, Marshall
    as Council leader, 196, 199, 201–210, 235, 237
    retirement of, 201, 227, 231
Brandon, Henry, 158
Brandt, Karl, 71–72, 73
Brandt, Willy, 154
Brexit, 241, 249–250, 252
Brorby, Melvin, 95, 100–102, 104, 132, 137
Bryan, John, 178, 194
Brzezinski, Zbigniew, 122–123, 155, 172, 182–184
Buck, Pearl, 88–90
Bullitt, William C. Jr., 44
Bundy, McGeorge, 141, 143
Bundy, William, 126
Burnham, Duane, 194, 196
Bush, George H. W. and administration of, 169, 172, 175, 176, 180–181, 185
Bush, George W. and administration of, 192, 212, 224, 225, 238, 241–242
Bush, Jeb, 247
Byrne, Carol, 144
Byrnes, Robert F., 114

C

Carter, Jimmy and administration of, 160, 161, 165, 168–169
Cassel, Douglass, 216
Casten, Sean, 228
Castle, William R., 37–38
Castro, Fidel, 99
Cecil, Lord Robert, 20
Cheney, Dick, 180
Chicago Committee, 132–135, 145–146, 195, 204

Chicago Council on Global Affairs
 founded to combat isolationism and nationalism, 1–8, 260
 governing structure of, 145
 locations, 64–65, 102, 233, 235–236
 as nonpartisan and educational, but not neutral, 2–5, 7, 234, 260
 at 100 years, 259–260
 2006 name and mission statement changes, 5, 23, 203, 208–210
 see also specific eras, programs, and publications
Chicago Council Survey, 143–144, 149, 209, 229, 236–237, 256–257
Chicago Tribune. See McCormick, Robert R.
Christopher, Warren, 182
Church, Frank, 125–126, 142
Churchill, Winston, 144, 180
Chute, Oscar, 137
Clemenceau, Georges, 18–20
Cleveland, Harlan, 115
Clinton, Bill and administration of, 176, 181–182, 187, 191, 192
Clinton, Hillary, 220–221, 250
Close, Upton, 41
Coats, Dan, 251
Cohen, Roger, 229, 236, 246
Colby, William, 134
Cold War. *See* 1950s
Cole, William Graham, 96, 135, 137, 141, 145, 146, 148–149
Colegrove, Kenneth, 16, 94–95, 99
Collier, Mary Louise "Polly" Root, 14, 26, 259
Connally, John, 154
Corporate Service Program, 145–146, 195, 203
Coulter, Harris, 172
Coulter, Thomas, 112
Council on Foreign Relations (CFR), 13, 14, 23, 131, 136, 156, 195–196, 204, 209, 226
Cousin, Ertharin, 257
Covid-19 pandemic, 3, 236, 237, 254–257, 260
Cox, Henry, 138
Crane, Burton, 33
Cross, Ernest, 85
Cross, Samuel H., 72–73

Crown, Lester, 204, 227, 231, 237
Cudahy, John, 49–50
Culver, John, 161
Currie, Austin, 166

D

Daalder, Ivo, 230–231, 248, 253–254
 as Council leader, 233–238, 255, 258, 260
Daley, Richard J., 153, 207
Daley, Richard M., 6, 208
Dam, Kenneth, 202
Darmstadter, Joel, 159
Davidson, Carter, 100–102, 103, 104, 106, 110, 120
Dawes, Rufus, 20
De Seversky, Alexander P., 54
Deuel, Wallace, 32, 41
Diamond, Larry, 251
Dickinson, Jacob, 24
Ditchley Foundation conferences, 144–145
Dodd, William E., 41
Donovan, William J., 78
Douglas, Emily Taft, 65
Douglas, Paul H., 22, 24, 47
Doxiadis, Constantinos, 120
Doynel de Saint-Quentin, René, 39
Du Bois, W.E.B., 21
Dukakis, Michael, 169–170
Dulles, John Foster, 92–93, 97–98
Dushkin, Alexander, 26

E

Eban, Abba, 80–81, 98, 158
Eger, Edmond I., 109–111, 137, 138, 139, 145, 146
Eisenhower, Dwight and administration of, 70, 93–94, 97, 98
Emanuel, Rahm, 254
Evans, Gareth, 211–212

F

Fadiman, Clifton, 75
Field, Kay, 117–118
Fischer, Joschka, 219
Fisher, Irving, 23
Fisher, Walter, 36
FitzGerald, Frances, 159–160

Floyd, George, 257
Ford, Gerald, 143, 160
Foreign Notes, 25, 29, 30, 68
Frankel, Max, 157, 167
Franks, Oliver, 78
Freedman, Max, 127
Freehling, Stanley, 106
Freeland, Chrystia, 240
Friedman, George, 240
Friedman, Milton, 124, 165
Friedman, Thomas, 190–191, 212–213
Fromm, Erich, 116–117
Fukuyama, Francis, 224, 239–240, 253

G

Gaidar, Yegor, 181–182
Galbraith, John Kenneth, 120, 165
Gall, Carlotta, 246
Garten, Jeffrey, 251
Gates, Robert, 245
Gaulle, Charles de, 121–122
Gayn, Mark, 127–128
Gebhardt, Richard, 178
Geithner, Timothy, 242
Gelb, Leslie, 196
Gerasimov, Gennadi, 155
Ghali, Paul, 121–122
Gideonse, Harry D., 44
Glenn, John, 169
Glickman, Dan, 220
Global Chicago Center, 149, 199, 204–205, 227, 236
Global Chicago report, 198, 205
Global Cities Forum, 149, 236–237, 252, 255
Golan, Dr. Galia, 168
Goldberg, Arthur, 125
Gorbachev, Mikhail, 155, 169–175, 180, 186, 195, 196
Gore, Al, 178, 223
Gorshel, Alec, 129
Gratz, Gustave, 21
Gray, Hanna, 133
Greenspan, Alan, 147
Grew, Joseph C., 54, 62, 64
Gunther, John, 33, 42
Gutman, Rick, 95

H

Haass, Richard, 226
Hagel, Chuck, 223
Haig, Alexander M. Jr., 166
Halberstam, David, 168
Hale, William Browne, 4, 13, 15–16, 18, 22–23, 24, 25, 48
Halifax, Lord, 54–55, 64
Halloran, Richard, 129
Haqqani, Husain, 246
Harkabi, Yehoshafat, 158–159
Harman, Jane, 248
Harper, Paul V., 66
Harper, Samuel Northrup, 24
Harrison, Gilbert, 117
Harrison, Marguerite E., 14, 20
Hart, Augustin S. Jr. ("Gus"), 148–149, 227
Hart, Gary, 169
Harvey, Daggett, 91
Hauser, Philip, 118–119
Hearst, William Randolph Jr., 96
Hershey, Lewis, 124
Herzog, Chaim, 188
Hibbard, Susan Follansbee, 13–14, 20, 24, 259
Hill, Chris, 225, 244–245
Hill, Irene, 154–155
Hillman, Sidney, 20–21
Hills, Carla, 202
Hilsman, Roger, 125
Hindus, Maurice, 31, 76
Hiss, Alger, 66
Ho Chi Minh, 89
Hodge, John R., 87–88
Hoefs, Richard A., 138
Holbrooke, Richard, 149
Hoover, Herbert, 43, 160
Hottelet, Richard, 114–115
Hull, Cordell, 37–38
Humphrey, Hubert, 96, 138, 140
Hunter, Robert, 187
Huntington, Samuel, 149
Hussein, Saddam, 181, 212–214, 218

I

Ickes, Harold L., 37, 59
Iklé, Fred C., 161
Indyk, Martin, 246–247

J

Jackson, Jesse, 135
Jameson, Sam, 128–129
Jandrey, Frederick W., 97
Jenkins, Newton, 37
Johnson, D. Gale, 119
Johnson, U. Alexis, 124
Judson, Clay, 46

K

Kagan, Robert, 226–227
Kahin, George McTurnan, 125
Kalischer, Peter, 114
Karzai, Hamid, 215
Kasai, Juiji George, 49
Kendrick, Alexander, 114
Kennedy, David M., 132
Kennedy, Edward, 124, 161–162
Kennedy, John F., 114, 115, 117–118
Kerensky, Alexander, 21
Kerry, John, 249
Keynes, John Maynard, 31
Khalidi, Rashid, 168
King, Niamh, 222
Kinkel, Klaus, 186
Kirk, Alan G., 92
Kirkpatrick, Helen, 54, 72
Kissinger, Henry, 143, 150–151, 156–158, 173–174
Klaus, Václav, 224–225
Knerr, Hugh, 54
Kohl, Helmut, 142, 164, 171, 189, 192
Kohn, Hans, 56, 79
Koldyke, Patricia, 227
Krishnamoorthi, Raja, 228
Krugman, Paul, 216–217, 242–243

L

La Guardia, Fiorella, 72
Lake, Anthony, 187, 191–192
Lange, Oskar, 55–56
Lasswell, Harold, 24
Lattimore, Owen, 86–87, 94
Lazear, Edward, 224
League of Nations. *See* 1920s; 1930s
Lemmon, Walter S., 54
Levy, Phil, 228, 236, 254
Lichtenstein, Walter, 17, 32, 64

Lie, Trygve, 85
Lindbergh, Charles, 46, 48, 49
Lindsay, James M., 253–254
Lippmann, Walter, 84–85, 93
Livingston, Arthur, 22
Lodge, Henry Cabot, 98
Lord, Winston, 178
Luce, Edward, 252–253
Ludwig, Emil, 33
Lugar, Richard, 220
Luttwak, Edward, 161

M

MacArthur, John, 163
MacLeish, Archibald, 54
Madigan, John, 212
Mahbubani, Kishore, 225–226
Makarios, Archbishop, 98
Malik, Charles, 92
Malott, Robert H., 167–168
Manly, Chesly, 91
Manshel, Warren, 149
Marshall, George C., 77–78, 175
Martin, John Bartlow, 35, 36
Masaryk, Jan, 42, 59–60, 79
Matlock, Jack, 186–187
Matskevich, Vladimir V., 96
Mauldin, Bill, 117–118
Mboya, Tom, 99
McCarthy, Joseph and McCarthyism, 84, 86, 87, 94
McCloskey, Paul, 155
McCloy, John J., 73–74
McCormick, Robert R., 29–30, 38, 60–61
  as isolationist, 12, 18, 45–46, 70, 78, 90–91, 132, 150
McDougal, Edward D. Jr., 12–13, 36, 117, 132
McGovern, George, 161
McKeever, Porter, 35, 100, 102
McLaughlin, Isabella, 26
McNally, Tom, 164–165
McNamara, Robert S., 170, 189–190
McNaughton, Frank, 153–154
Mearsheimer, John, 210–211, 244
Mellon, David, 138, 193
Menshikov, Mikhail, 97
Menzies, Robert, 49
Mercouri, Melina, 130

Michalopoulos, Andre, 56–57
Mid-America Committee (MAC), 180, 195, 204, 207
Miliband, David, 245–246
Miller, Douglas, 41–42
Miner, Thomas, 102, 195, 204
Mondale, Walter, 169
Montgomery, Harle, 172
Montgomery, Kenneth, 172
Moon, Lisa, 221
Morgan, Lee, 167–168
Morgenthau, Hans, 122–123
Morse, Wayne, 124
Moskow, Michael, 202, 207
Mounk, Yascha, 251, 252
Mowrer, Edgar Ansel, 32, 51–52, 57–58, 60, 65–68, 75–76
Mowrer, Paul Scott, 33
Murrow, Edward R., 40, 102, 114–115
Musharraf, Pervez, 212
Muskie, Edmund S., 156, 165–166

N

Nathan, Robert R., 73
Nehru, Jawaharlal, 81–82, 86, 111
Netanyahu, Benjamin, 246–247
Niebuhr, Reinhold, 59
1920s, and aftermath of World War I, 1–26
 Council leadership, 6, 13–17, 26
 Council's independence and, 23–24
 education and nonpartisanship, 15–18
 isolationism and, 1–8, 9–13, 17–18, 112
 speakers, 12–13, 14, 18–25, 26
1930s, and lead-up to World War II, 27–50
 Council finances, 29, 37
 Council leadership, 29–31, 34–37
 isolation, interventionism, and neutrality issues, 27–29, 44–50, 112–113
 plight of German Jews and, 32, 39–41, 43, 46
 speakers, 31–34, 37–43
1940s, World War II and aftermath, 51–82
 Council finances, 66–67
 Council leadership, 63–69
 Council programs and cooperative studies, 65–68
 isolation and interventionism issues, 7, 52, 60–63, 70–71, 78
 speakers after war, 71–82
 speakers during war, 54–59, 64

United Nations, atomic era, and world government, 59–63, 70–71, 74, 76, 84, 175
1950s, and Cold War, 63, 70, 75, 77, 78, 83–104
 Council finances, 102–107
 Council leadership, 91, 94–96, 99–101, 104–105, 132
 nonpartisanship and, 91, 95–96, 99
 radio and, 103
 speakers, 83–90, 92–99
 television and, 103, 104
1960s, Vietnam and social issues, 109–138
 business community and Chicago Committee, 131–134, 146
 Council finances, 109, 139
 Council leadership, 109–112, 135–138
 nonpartisanship and, 117
 population issues, 118–120
 race relations and, 134–136
 speakers, 114–131, 135,
 television and, 136
 travel programs, 103, 109–111
1970s, 1980s and end of Cold War, 139–174
 Council finances, 141–143, 150, 163–164
 Council leadership, 139–150
 Council's 50th anniversary, 150–151
 Reilly and national foreign policy emphasis, 141–154
 speakers, 150–162, 164–174
 travel programs, 140, 162–163, 164
1990s and changing world order, 175–199
 changes in city of Chicago and, 197–199
 Council leadership, 176–177, 192, 194–196
 Council's 75th anniversary, 192–193
 speakers, 177–192
Nitze, Paul, 161
Nixon, Richard and administration of, 105, 124, 130–132, 137, 141, 143, 151, 154–156
Nkrumah, Kwame, 98
Notes on World Events, 133–134, 153

O

Obama, Barack and administration of, 160, 217, 220–222, 230–231, 238, 241–242
Obama, Barack Sr., 99

Ogburn, William F., 71
Orszag, Peter, 223–224
O'Ryan, John F., 23
Osborne, George, 248–249
Osnos, Evan, 243

P
Page, Benjamin, 143
Paisley, Reverend Ian, 166
Palyi, Melchior, 33
Panetta, Leon, 245
Peabody, Marietta, 144
Pearson, Lester, 62
Pencek, Emma, 162–163
Perlmutter, Amos, 168
Peterson, Peter G., 156
Phillips, William, 38
Pickering, Thomas, 218, 242
Polk, William, 119
Pompidou, Georges, 130–131
Posen, Adam, 242
Powell, Colin, 180–181
Prall, Dick, 215–216
Pritzker, Penny, 244

Q
Querrey, Kimberly, 228

R
Rashid, Ahmed, 224
Rasmussen, Anders Fogh, 239
Reagan, Ronald, 160, 169
Reich, Robert, 222–223
Riahni, Ameen, 26
Rice, Condoleezza, 213–214
Richardson, Elliot, 154
Rielly, John E., 111–112, 136, 196
    background, 96, 138, 140–141
    Council finances and, 141–143, 150, 163–164, 176–177, 228
    Council leadership and national foreign policy emphasis, 139–140, 141–154, 162, 194, 201, 237
    retirement of, 150, 192, 199
Robertson, Lord George, 142, 199
Robinson, Renault, 135
Roosevelt, Eleanor, 76, 89
Roosevelt, Franklin D. and administration of, 37, 45, 63, 91, 249
Roselli, Bruno, 22
Rosenthal, Lessing, 26
Ross, Colin, 43
Ross, Dennis, 218
Rosso, David, 126
Rothkopf, David, 240
Rumsfeld, Donald, 124, 214
Rusk, Dean, 125, 132
Russell, Lord Bertrand, 42
Ryan, Shirley, 228

S
Safire, William, 172
Said, Edward, 168
Saito, Hiroshi, 33
Sakharov, Vladimir, 171
Salisbury, Harrison, 156
Salvemini, Gaetano, 22
Sánchez, Yoani, 247
Schevill, Ferdinand, 22, 24
Schmidt, Helmut, 177–178
Schmitt, Bernadotte E., 22, 24, 56
Schoenbrun, David, 114, 126–127
Scholl Fellowship, 227, 243
Scholl, Pamela, 227
Schönemann, Friedrich, 32
Schorr, Daniel, 114
Schultz, Sigrid, 45
Schuman, Frederick L., 32, 78, 84, 94–95
Scott, John, 79
Scott, Samuel C. III, 257, 259
Searl, Milton, 159
Seith, Alex, 133, 136–138, 145, 146
Sen, Binay Ranjan, 90
September 11, 2001 attacks, 175–176, 199, 241–242
Sevareid, Eric, 113–114, 131
Shah, Rajiv, 219–220
Shamir, Yitzhak, 168
Shriver, R. Sargent, 46Shulman, Marshall, 67, 166
Sikorski, Radosław, 218–219
Silk, Leonard, 171
Simes, Dimitri, 171
Simmons, Adele, 198
Siniora, Hanna, 168
Smedley, Agnes, 58

Smeltz, Dina, 230
Smith, Hedrick, 240
Smith, Herman "Dutch," 138, 198
Snow, Edgar, 128
Stassen, Harold, 61
Steele, John, 123–124
Stettinius, Edward R. Jr., 63
Stevens, Edmund, 55
Stevens, Ernest, 20
Stevenson, Adlai E. II, 10, 52–54, 64, 133
   as Council leader, 29, 34–39, 47–48, 141
   presidential bid in 1952, 36, 70, 100
   United Nations and, 74–75, 115–116, 144
Stevenson, Adlai E. III, 152
Stoneman, William, 33, 45, 121
Stowe, Leland, 32, 55, 64
Strauss, Mrs. Harold, 111
Straw, Jack, 212
Strong, Maurice F., 159
Strong, Walter A., 22
Sullivan, Thomas, 242
Susman, Louis, 231

T

Taft, Robert, 7
Tagge, George, 141
Takaishi, Shingoro, 33–34
Taylor, Charles, 128
Taylor, Maxwell D., 120–121
Templeton, Richard H., 98, 104, 105, 106, 109, 132, 133
Tett, Gillian, 252
Thatcher, Margaret, 165, 178, 196
Thomas, Norman, 45
Thompson, Dorothy, 31
Thompson, Robert, 220
Thompson, William "Big Bill," 12, 208
Thurow, Roger, 221
Tilton, Glenn, 237
Toon, Malcolm, 166–167
Tower, John, 122
Toynbee, Arnold, 80, 83, 97
Tree, Ronald, 144
Trichet, Jean-Claude, 240
Truman, Harry S. and administration of, 7, 69–70, 72, 77–78, 84, 92–93, 152, 176
Trump, Donald J. and administration of, 221, 233–234, 238, 249–254, 258–259
Tsiang, T. F., 58
Turner, Stansfield, 170
2000s, 2010s, and Council's policy influence, 3, 201–231, 233–260
   after 9/11 attacks, 203–204
   Council finances, 227, 228–229, 235, 255–256
   Council leadership, 201–210, 211, 216, 219–220, 227, 230–231, 233–238, 258, 260
   Covid-19 pandemic and digital programs, 3, 236, 237, 254–257, 260
   endowed fellowships, 227–228
   food and agriculture programs, 219–222
   isolationism, populism, and 2016 election, 233–234, 238, 249–254, 258–259
   racial issues and, 257–258
   speakers, 210–219, 222–227, 238–254
   television and, 205
   think tank role, 205–208
   travel programs, 204

U

U Thant, 155
Utley, Clifton, 36, 38
   as Council leader, 8, 29–31, 113, 141
   radio and, 34, 45–46, 63, 66, 101
   World War II issues, 31–32, 40–41, 44–45, 47–48, 50
Utley, David, 38
Utley, Garrick, 8, 113, 121, 151, 259

V

Vance, Cyrus, 165
Vandenberg, Arthur, 70, 78
Vietnam War. *See* 1960s
Viner, Jacob, 24
Von Coudenhove-Kalergi, Count Richard, 21
Von Kühlmann, Richard, 31
Vu Van Thai, 124

W

Waldheim, Kurt, 155
Walt, Stephen, 210–211
Wang Yang, 244
Ward, Barbara, 94, 122, 129–130
Weiying, Zhang, 243–244
Weizsäcker, Richard von, 182
Welling, Harriet, 14, 34–35, 46–47, 100, 117-118
Welsh, Mary, 39
White, Leigh, 76–77
White, William Allen, 47
White Committee, 47–48
Wickersham, George, 16, 24
Wieczorowski, Robert E., 136
Wilson, Woodrow, 10, 15–16
Wolf, Martin, 239, 252
Wood, Robert E., 48
Woodward, Frederick, 66
World Spotlight program, 103, 104
World Understanding Award, 31, 102, 151
World War I issues. *See* 1920s
World War II issues. *See* 1930s; 1940s
Wright, Louise Leonard, 14, 63–69, 95, 99
Wright, Quincy, 21, 24, 29, 47, 64, 69
Wyman, Mrs. Charles W., 163

Y

Yeltsin, Boris, 172–173, 182, 186–187
Yoo, John, 215–216
Young, George, 21
Yu Yongding, 243

Z

Zakaria, Fareed, 250
Zell, Leah Joy, 228